Contemporary Psychology Series: 2

Families:
A Context for Development

David White and Anne Woollett

The Falmer Press

(A Member of the Taylor & Francis Group)
London • New York • Philadelphia

UK   The Falmer Press, 4 John Street, London WC1N 2ET

USA   The Falmer Press, Taylor & Francis Inc., 1900 Frost Road, Suite 101, Bristol, PA 19007

First published 1992

A catalogue record for this book is available from the British Library

Library of Congress Cataloging-in-Publication Data are available on request

Jacket design by Benedict Evans

Typeset in 10/11.5pt Garamond
by Graphicraft Typesetters Ltd., Hong Kong.

Printed in Great Britain by Burgess Science Press, Basingstoke on paper which has a specified pH value on final paper manufacture of not less than 7.5 and is therefore 'acid free'.

Contents

We would like to dedicate this book to Owen Hawkes,
and to Hugh and Annis White.

Series Editor's Preface

For most people the family is by far the most significant social institution in terms of the impact it has on the quality of their daily life and experience. The family is also the foremost influence on the developmental processes that form the adult personality and the adult's orientation to interpersonal relationships. Whether we grow up as anxious or confident, trusting or suspicious, ambitious or contented, sociable or shy is determined very largely by our early experiences of family life.

The family is also a remarkably pervasive institution across time and place — so much so that it is the only social institution for which it is possible to claim a biological basis. Of course there are cultural variations in family size and structure and in the definitions of the rights and duties of the various members of the family. Similarly, the family has undergone changes within each culture as the bases of economic relations change and as value change follows on from these. However, nearly all societies have found it necessary to institutionalize sexual relationships and child rearing in a way that a person from a different culture would still recognize as the family.

In current Western European culture the procreating couple are placed at the centre of each family's social universe and satellites (children, grandparents, etc.) revolve around them in varying numbers and orbits. These systems have overlapping spheres and at any one time a person may be both a child in one family and a parent in another, but we expect the strongest bonds to be between parents and dependent children even if this causes strains on other types of family relationships such as the relationship between adult children and their parents, or the relationship between siblings.

Clearly other focal points for family organization are possible and, indeed, exist in Oriental cultures presently, and have existed previously in Europe. Experimental variations in family forms have also been tried from time to time (for example, pooling child care and rearing roles) but have never taken hold as a major competitor to more traditional forms. This is not to say that changes in family relations are not possible, but the motivation of parents to have the major influence over the development of their 'own' children, and to receive love and affection of unique intensity from them, is very strong and resistant to change.

White and Woollett systematically dissect the structure of contemporary family relationships and show how each family member influences the development of the others — not only how parents influence their children, but also vice versa. They also look at the way in which the intense emotional bonds can become distorted, hurtful and damaging. Just as family relationships potentially provide for some of the most positive and satisfying interactions we ever experience, so they have the potential to deal us devastingly negative outcomes — disloyalty, degradation and abandonment. Over the past few years one other aspect of family relationships — the abuse of children — has been thrown howling into the spotlight. Gone are the days when the cosy fiction that the only dangers to the innocence of children came from perverted strangers lurking in parks or alleyways. Ninety per cent of children who are abused physically or sexually suffer their abuse at the hands of their parents or siblings within the four walls of the family home.

Families: A Context for Development is the second in a new series oriented to the beginning, but committed student of psychology and related disciplines. Each book in the series assumes no prior acquaintance with its topic and no familiarity with psychological theory and method. However, each volume takes the reader a long way beyond a superficial tour of the quasi-scientific ideas and myths that contaminate pop psychology. The student who takes the trouble to use these books fully will find themselves acquiring a scientific approach to understanding relationships and other key concepts while being guided gently through the major theoretical approaches and the massive corpus of empirically derived data of which contemporary psychology exists.

Raymond Cochrane
Birmingham
March 1991

Foreword

This book came into being for a number of reasons. In part it reflects our interests and research on children and their development in family settings and on the adjustments women and men make as they become (or do not become) parents and bring up children. We would like to take this opportunity to express our gratitude to all the families who have let us into their homes to observe them and who spent time talking to us about parenting and childrearing. They taught us about the myriad ways in which families operate and raise children.

The ideas generated by our research have permeated our teaching. We find ourselves drawn increasingly to examining the context families provide for young children as they grow and develop and the impact children have on their families. We are often asked to suggest a book for students about children and families. We have always found it difficult to recommend any single book because those developmental textbooks which mention families tend to do so at a great gallop before getting back to describing laboratory-based studies of such things as language development or the 'strange situation', that are often considered to be proper study of child development. Additionally the research they use is almost exclusively drawn from the United States of America, with little consideration of the appropriateness of findings for other societies, including the UK. We were therefore very pleased when Ray Cochrane gave us the opportunity to write a book which puts families centre stage and reflects research and theoretical developments in the UK as well as the USA.

Fortunately, the paradigms and theoretical approaches within social and developmental psychology are changing. These changes have helped to bring into the mainstream many of the ideas and approaches to children and families we discuss. This is the case especially for our emphasis on development in adult life as well as childhood and on the need to consider seriously the experiences and accounts of mothers, fathers and children. When we first tried to incorporate families into our lectures it seemed to be an unconventional thing to do. We owe thanks to many past and current colleagues in the Psychology Department at the Polytechnic of East London (some of whom knew it as North East London Polytechnic) and elsewhere. They include

Harriette Marshall, Ann Phoenix, Paula Nicolson, Denis Gahagan, Averil Clegg, Maire Messenger-Davies, Neelam Dosanjh-Matwala, Jan Hadlow, Louise Lyon, Naomi Pfeffer, Nancy Worcester, Mariamne Whatley, Eva Lloyd, and Jackie McGuire. They supported us in our belief that a more family-centred approach to developmental psychology was not only relevant to students in their future lives as parents as well as psychologists but that such an approach was theoretically and academically acceptable. However, any mistakes, misrepresentations and misinterpretations we acknowledge as our own.

Our students also deserve our thanks. They encouraged us in our questioning of current psychological orthodoxies and our recognition that children and their families had lives outside the psychology experiment. Many also experienced difficulties with psychological theories which assumed that all children live in white, middle-class, nuclear, 'happy ever after' families. They tolerated, more or less enthusiastically, having ideas tried out on them as we rethought our courses.

We would also like to thank our families who provided us with useful (if at times painful) experiences and insights into the operation of different aspects of family life, including our parents, Margaret and Bryn Lewis, Marjorie White and happy memories of Geoffrey White. Especial thanks go to those members of our families who put up with our neglect and rearranged much of their lives to give us the time to write this book; Glennys, Hugh and Annis White, Paul Hodge, Helen, Owen and Alan Hawkes.

Chapter 1

Families as a Context for Development

Psychological Approaches to Families

Families are a fact of life for most children. They provide the context in which children grow up and the most permanent and consistent of their relationships. In their families children first learn social and cognitive skills, how to relate to and care for others, how to cope with disappointments and losses. In their relations with their parents and siblings, children first learn about themselves and others, about their own individuality and preferences and how to influence other people. Families continue to play an important part in people's lives even once they have become independent and left home. It comes as no surprise therefore that the family is considered by some psychologists to have a special significance, as the following quotations indicate:

> Psychologists have long been interested in family relationships. For many decades, that involved a particular focus on the mother's relationship with the child, which was seen as the crucial context for growth, and studies of the mother-child dyad have been the hardiest perennial in the developmental field. (Minuchin, in Hinde and Stevenson-Hinde, 1988: 7)

> Development, it has been argued, can only be understood if it is seen as a joint enterprise involving parent as well as child; the role of *both* needs to be specified. The failure to take an interactionist view is probably the single most important reason why we do not as yet have an adequate socialisation theory.... (Schaffer, 1986: 766)

In contrast, much psychological research seems to be based on assumptions that children's development can be considered without reference to their families. As a result, studies are conducted in the laboratory rather than in the home and may, therefore, tell us relatively little about how children behave in real situations, as Dunn (1988) indicates:

> Children have rarely been studied in the world in which ... developments take place, or in a context in which we can be sensitive to the subtleties of their social understanding. Psychology has developed as an experimental science, with all the strengths ... that this implies, but also with the consequence that the developments within the complex emotional world of the family have been neglected. (Dunn, 1988: 5)

When the family is recognized, it is often as a marginal or peripheral interest to which lip service needs to be paid. As a result it is treated as a factor external to children while influencing their behaviour and development. 'The child' and 'the family' remain two distinct units rather than being seen as interconnected and interrelated (Ingleby, 1986).

In this book we put the family centre stage. This requires a reassessment of much that is generally considered as the subject matter of and the approach to child development. Most textbooks start at the child's conception and progress through infancy and childhood and sometimes consider adolescence. We follow a similar chronology but instead of focusing exclusively on children with references occasionally to mothers and even more occasionally to fathers, we take 'the child in the family' as our unit of analysis. We do this by drawing upon ideas and material from developmental and social psychology, lifespan development and the ecology of human development and from a variety of other disciplines and approaches to families and family functioning, including sociology, anthropology, systems theory, and feminism.

Learning and Development in a Family Setting

Children grow up in networks of social relationships and much of what they learn is about their social world. They learn about people and how to anticipate their behaviour, about how people's behaviour varies according to their mood, their personality or whether others are present. They learn about themselves, what kind of people they are, how others respond to them, what it means in this society to be a girl or a boy, to be black or white, to be handicapped or sick. Children's families and social networks are both the world which they inhabit and the world they are learning about.

Family relations are intense and emotionally highly charged. Love and affection, longing and despair, anger, hatred and aggression all find expression. Children love their parents but are often angry and struggle hard to resist their control. Mothers and fathers may feel passionately for their children but can also feel frustration, anger and despair as they see their children acquire habits of which they disapprove and see themselves submerged in the work of childcare. In the familiar and emotional exchanges between family members, especially those in which their own interests are at stake, children gain a practical grasp of some of the causes of distress, anger, and happiness in other family members, and of the demands and rules that operate in their families and the wider world. Studies conducted in families suggest that the intense feelings experienced and expressed in families intensify children's desires to learn and to use their skills to best effect and intensify too parents' desires to support their children's understandings (Dunn, 1988).

By making the child in the family the unit of study, we are taking a broader approach than is generally employed. We consider the development of children within the social networks of their families and the impact families have on children's development. But we also examine the experience of other family members and the significance for women and men of becoming parents and bringing up children. Families vary considerably. The experiences of parents and children and how they feel about themselves are influenced by the kinds of family in which they live, such as whether families are headed by one parent or two, whether families are poor and live in difficult circumstances, and whether mothers and fathers work outside the home. Families, like individuals, do not exist in a vacuum but, as Lerner and Spanier indicate, are positioned in wider historical, cultural and ideological contexts:

> Children are invariably born into a social network, typically a family. The family, too, is embedded in a social system. The family, the primary institution responsible for transforming societal maintenance and perpetuation goals into directives for the new individual, is thus at the core of socialization. Hence the family is society's adaptational unit. (Lerner and Spanier, 1978: 1)

A consideration of families as the context of development raises a number of issues. These are outlined here and will be drawn upon throughout the book.

1. Individuals Develop through their Relations with Others

This idea is assumed and taken as given by many psychologists and has been the subject of much psychological research. Yet the processes by which individuals influence one another and are instrumental in one another's development are difficult to isolate, as Schaffer makes clear:

> That parents do have an effect on children may seem obvious, yet in practice it has often proved extraordinarily difficult to demonstrate such an effect. It is ironic that despite the enormous amount of research in this area we still face the challenge of specifying as to what really goes on between parent and child that has such an impact on the child's development. It may be argued that much of the past research has been simplistic in its expectation of one-to-one relationships between environmental input and child outcome. (Schaffer, 1986: 769)

One reason why it is difficult to relate family variables to development is that family relations and the ways in which people influence one another are extremely complicated. Mothers, fathers and siblings influence children's development directly through their relationships with them, the pressures they exert for mature behaviour and the models and support they provide. But interactions take place within a framework of other interactions and relationships. For example, mothers' discussions with young children may be interspersed with discussions with fathers, telephone conversations with grandmothers, chats with neighbours or arguments with older children. Indeed, the amount of language addressed directly to young children may be small compared with the amount of language young children hear addressed to people around them.

Children's development may be influenced in a number of less direct ways. One form of indirect influence comes through the presence of a third party. Mothers, fathers and siblings all behave differently towards young children when they are alone with them than when someone else is present. They talk, for example, more to young children when they are on their own with them than when another person is present (Clarke-Stewart, 1978; Corter *et al.*, 1983; Golinkoff and Ames, 1979). Family members set one another examples of how to interact with children and of the demands they can make of them. In this way, parents' behaviour and their expectations of their children come to be more alike (Beail and McGuire, 1982; Santrock *et al.*, 1982). Families may also influence one another indirectly by the family atmosphere they help to create. In happy and harmonious families children may feel secure and parents may be more attentive. Conversely when there is tension and relations are strained, parents may feel themselves undermined and unable to look after their children as well as they would wish. Depression and unemployment may create strain as children find their parents less responsive or no longer able to give them the treats and outings they have come to expect. A positive change in family circumstances may improve the family atmosphere (Lamb, 1982). Other kinds of indirect or second order effects concern changes in family size and composition. The birth of a second child, for example, means readjusting the interaction patterns amongst mothers and older children (Dunn and Kendrick, 1982; see Chapter 6). Divorce and family breakdown also influence the nature of the relationships with other family members (Hetherington *et al.*, 1982; see Chapter 7).

It is usually assumed that influence is unidirectional, from parent to child, but children also influence parents and siblings may influence one another. Parents' behaviour is modified by the characteristics and behaviour of children and influences in families are often circular and mutual (Bronfenbrenner, 1979). From an early age children modify parents' expectations, their feelings about their children and their behaviour. Children's sex, their health, temperament and personality, their social and communicative skills have an impact on the feelings and behaviours of those around them (Beail and McGuire, 1982; Belsky *et al.*, 1984; Hargreaves and Colley, 1986). In this way children mould the behaviour of others and hence, to some extent, the experiences they encounter (see Chapter 5).

2. Families as Systems of Interlocking Relationships

A systems approach has been employed in the study of families. One benefit of this approach is to make clear the variety of groupings or subsystems within families. The mother-child relationship is the subsystem which has been given greatest consideration and mothers' interactions with their children form the greatest body of research on family relations (see Chapter 4; Hinde and Stevenson-Hinde, 1988). This is because mothers are seen as the most critical influences on children's development and because mothers and young children are more readily available to researchers than other subjects. Since the 1970s the father-child subsystem has also been explored (see Chapter 5). This has opened up the field of family psychology in important ways. Fathers relate to their children in many ways which are similar to mothers but there are also differences: fathers are usually considered to be less sensitive and less predictable in their interactions with young children than are mothers. The parent-child subsystem is concerned predominantly with the nurturance and protection of children and with the development of children's competence and their gaining of autonomy. Mothers and fathers fulfil their functions in somewhat different ways (see Chapter 5). We need to be cautious, therefore, about the use of the non-gendered term 'parent' which equates mothers' and fathers' relationships with and their activities around children (Busfield, 1987; New and David, 1985; and see Chapters 2 and 5).

The variety of relationships is further emphasized when other subsystems are examined: for example the relations between siblings (brothers and sisters) and grandparents add further to the diversity of relationships (see Chapter 6). In these, children encounter different kinds of relationships and demands. In the sibling subsystem, children deal more with reciprocal relations, cooperation and competition, and coping with jealousy, and are prepared for relations with peers and activities outside the family (Vetere and Gale, 1987).

An important family subsystem, but one which has been less extensively studied in developmental psychology, is the relationship between father and mother. The nature and quality of parents' relationships have an impact on their satisfaction with one another as partners and as parents (see Chapters 2 and 5). But this subsystem is also significant for children. A good relationship between parents provides a secure base for children. When the parental relationship breaks down there are often long-term and negative consequences for children (see Chapter 7). The parental subsystem also acts as a model for children providing them with information about marital relations. Adults who were abused as children tend to replicate in their own adult relationships the abuse they witnessed or were subjected to as children (see Chapter 8).

The different subsystems are interconnected and events and relationships in one subsystem influence those in another. The interconnections between subsystems can be seen in the following example. A positive parental relationship, in which fathers show respect for and praise mothers' caretaking skills and mothers feel well supported and confident, affects the mother-child subsystem. In this situation mothers may feel more positive towards their children and express more warmth and affection (Belsky *et al.*, 1984b). These connections between subsystems can inhibit as well as facilitate interactions and relations between people. For example, a mother may find it hard to form a good relationship with a difficult child and her problems may overflow into the parental subsystem and put pressure on the relationship between mother and father (Hinde and Stevenson-Hinde, 1988).

Relations within families often involve more than two people (especially for children living in extended families). Children may interact with mothers AND fathers and may play with siblings AND mothers at the same time. The models of social interaction commonly employed in developmental psychology tend to be applicable only to interaction between two people. Current approaches to mother-child interaction, for example, stress the value of maternal responsiveness (see Chapter 4). But when other people are present mothers are less sensitive and take less account of the child's perspective or understanding and a great deal of the activity and the talk that goes on in families is directed to adults or older siblings (Woollett, 1986). Young children are less able to get involved until they have learned how to operate in larger group settings. To participate successfully in family conversations for example, children need to be able to tune in to conversations which are not directed to them nor necessarily focused upon their interests or needs, and they need to make relevant interventions and to add new information (Dunn, 1988). This kind of experience in larger family groupings may help prepare children to acquire the social skills necessary for participation in peer groups and other relationships outside the family (Rubin, 1980) (see Chapter 6).

Most research has focused on the family as a number of two or three person units, but families can be considered as units in their own right with their own qualities and characteristics and rules of organization (Vetere and Gale, 1987).

3. Families are about Parents as well as Children

Psychological research on families is interested predominantly in children and only rarely in the development of parents and others. Mothers and sometimes fathers are used in studies but their focus is on aspects of parents' behaviour which have developmental significance for children. It is usually assumed that there is a correspondence between children's needs and parents' (and especially mothers') needs. As a result models of good mothering are extrapolated from ideas about children's needs and propensities. But mothers' and children's needs are not necessarily identical and there are often major contradictions for women between expectations that they relate sensitively to their children and their own needs for self-expression (Nicolson, 1986; Phoenix *et al.*, in press; Urwin, 1985).

Nor is there consideration of how mothers or fathers feel about their children's behaviour and why parents behave as they do. An understanding of parents' feelings and behaviour may help to explain the links found between mothers' and fathers' behaviour and children's development. Mothers may behave similarly but their reasons for doing so may differ. For example, one mother may ignore a child's request for assistance because she believes the child needs to be encouraged to work independently while another may ignore her child because she is tired and depressed. The differences in parents' moods and motivations for their behaviour may provide better information about their children's development than the similarities in their behaviour.

To understand why parents behave as they do and what parenthood means to them we need to know how parenting relates to other activities and other relationships in their lives. Development is a lifelong process. The family provides a context for adult as well as child development. Motherhood is a major source of status, identity and fulfilment for women although at times many women experience motherhood as unsatisfying and find it incompatible with their other identities and activities (Boulton, 1983; Phoenix *et al.*, in press) (see Chapter 2). Parenting is physically exhausting work requiring patience, endurance and commitment. To cope well with young children, it is necessary to see the world in the child's terms and to recognize the child's needs and developmental limitations (Belsky *et al.*, 1984b). Although parenting can be fulfilling for men and can give their life meaning and structure, men's identity as fathers is less central than motherhood is for women. Fathering often allows men to express emotions and engage in activities not otherwise encouraged. For many men relations with their young children allow them legitimately to show affection. The developmental significance of these are rarely mentioned or examined.

Parenting does not take place in a vacuum. It involves substantial changes in all aspects of people's lives and relationships. Becoming a parent influences women's and men's relations with their own parents. They may re-establish or reaffirm their relations with their own or their partner's family but parenting can increase conflict as grandchildren become a means whereby old quarrels are reawakened. Parenting also influences fathers' and mothers' participation in the labour market. Mothers often cease to be employed outside the home with the birth of a first child, although many return later to the world of work (see Chapter 5). There has been considerable interest in how mothers combine work and parenting. Usually research concentrates on the problems women experience, reinforcing views about the difficulties of being a working mother and the risks for children's development (Scarr and Dunn, 1987). But there is little evidence about how parenting relates to men's work identity. Men often work longer hours because parenting increases their financial commitments. There has been less interest in how men keep their family commitments separate from their work and the psychological costs of splitting these two aspects of their identities (Bronfenbrenner, 1986). Parenting also structures people's friendships. Women tend to get to know and become friends with other women with children (Urwin, 1985).

Conflicts of Interest

Models of motherhood imply that families have coherent goals and this view of family life is reinforced in the 'happy families' approach which characterizes much of the childcare advice (Phoenix *et al.*, in press). This presents a view of family life in which women find fulfilment and are able to set aside their own feelings to be sensitive to their children, and fathers are involved in childcare and successful in their careers. Children growing up in this idealized environment are considered to develop into intellectually alert, emotionally stable and socially skilled children and young people. In such a context parent-child relations are defined in terms of companionship and equity, with parents being 'friends' with children (Newson and Newson, 1976). Parents are still expected to control children, not explicitly through their superior power or force but by ensuring their children's compliance through the use of rational explanation. Negative feelings are usually denied and relations are assumed to be free of conflict, thereby suggesting that conflict is an indication of pathological family functioning or poor child management (Urwin, 1985; Walkerdine and Lucey, 1989).

However, once we begin to recognize that families are the context for parental as well as children's development questions are raised about the compatibility of the needs of different people in the family and how resources are allocated (Hinde and Stevenson-Hinde, 1988). There is considerable potential for conflict as the needs and demands of mothers, fathers and children push and pull in different and sometimes incompatible directions (Vetere and Gale, 1987). Accommodations are often possible and in most families a compromise is arrived at which is generally acceptable. These arrangements are subject to renegotiation as individuals develop and family structures change (Rapoport *et al.*, 1977). In spite of the fact that good mothers are supposed to control their children through good management and explanation, conflicts and clashes are commonly reported in families and many mothers resort to punishment including physical punishment (see Chapters 4 and 8) (Dunn, 1988; Newson and Newson, 1968). Children are not always prepared to be managed but resort to aggression, screams, shouts and temper tantrums to get their own way. By doing so they expose the power relations and the basically undemocratic nature of adult-child relations. Mothers may get angry and upset at children's resistance because it exposes the ineffectiveness or inadequacy of mothers who are not able to control their children (Walkerdine and Lucey, 1989).

In many families there are insufficient resources, including financial resources, time, energy, space, love, affection and attention. When resources are scarce there are likely to be conflicts as, for example, fathers and children struggle for mothers' attention or mothers and fathers try to find time for themselves (Moss *et al.*, 1986). These clashes may rarely surface publicly, but studies of the impact of stress and divorce suggest that conflicts within families may be as damaging for children as the eventual breakup of the marriage itself (Furstenberg and Seltzer, 1986) (see Chapter 7). Feminist analysis stresses the importance of considering the power differentials within families. These vary from family to family but generally men exercise greater power than women and adults greater power than children. These power differentials help to explain why the experience of marriage and family life is different for women than it is for men (Morgan, 1985). Research on domestic violence and child abuse points to the ways in which some family members get their needs met regardless of the costs to others (see Chapter 8).

4. Variability and Changes in Family Form

Ideas about 'proper' or 'normal' family forms underlie much of what is written about families. Conventional families are headed by a heterosexual couple. It used to be assumed that this meant husband and wife but in recent times the reality of cohabitation is acknowledged in the use of terms such as partner and common-law wife. Children in conventional families are born to mothers who are young but not too young; mothers under 20 and over 35 are beyond the normal limit (Phoenix *et al.*, in press). Families should be small, preferably with two or three children who have genetic, biological and social links with their parents. The status of families in which children are adopted, are stepchildren or who are born as a result of using reproductive technologies is more marginal. Conventional families live together in a household unit, in a nuclear rather than extended family. It is also assumed that fathers are breadwinners and mothers are full-time caretakers. This construction of the family, often portrayed in media images, is used to define normal families and distinguish them from those labelled as unconventional or deviant. Many families, however, are not of this form. That such a construction of conventional families exists even though it does not reflect the reality of family life for many people indicates the power of the construction as a model to which people aspire and as a standard against which they make judgments about themselves and others. Those who do not conform are seen not merely as different but as deviant or inadequate.

Families differ in a variety of ways. Some children live in nuclear families with parents and others in larger or extended family units with grandparents, lodgers or nannies (see Chapter 6). Not all families are headed by two parents. Some women have children on their own. Especially when they are young, single mothers tend to be poor and live in worse housing than mothers with partners who are employed. But mothers bringing up children on their own are not necessarily poor and may be supported by their own families (Phoenix, 1991). Mothers are increasingly in paid employment outside the home. This influences how families operate and their arrangements for childcare, with mothers who are employed using paid care such as nannies or childminders as well as their extended families. Other children live in what could be considered one-parent families because parents (usually fathers) are in prison, work away from home or have jobs which involve considerable travel. Not all children are brought up by their parents. When parents are dead or unable to care for them, children are brought up in institutions or foster homes. While it is assumed that families are based on biological relationships between parents and children, remarriage, adoption and the use of some reproductive technologies mean that relations between parents and children may be entirely social relationships.

Even when families conform to normative patterns, they often do so only for a relatively short period because families change all the time. Some changes are culturally bound and tied up with the age of children and parents whereas others are non-normative and often unplanned and unwanted. Research tends to be most interested in transitions in family life when there is a dramatic switch from one state or family form to another. These transitional points create pressure for change and adjustment for the entire family (Parke, 1988). A major change is the birth of a first child, as men and women become parents. Studies have concentrated on this initial stage of family building when it is assumed that the greatest changes take place. Studies of adoption and the use of reproductive technologies point to the variety of ways in which families are created (see Chapter 3). As children get older, they go to school, make friends outside the family and eventually leave home. Issues around dependency and separation, control and aggression vary with children's age and parents have to change their techniques of childcare (see Chapter 6). Insofar as it is considered, it is usually assumed that mothers will experience the increasing independence of their children (often termed the 'empty nest') as problematic. However, what evidence there is suggests that many mothers (and fathers) cope well and enjoy being able to spend more time developing interests which are not so closely linked to their children's activities (Llewelyn and Osborne, 1990).

But families change in ways which are less expected and less wanted. They change as a result of sickness of handicap of parents and children (see Chapter 9). Increasingly parents divorce and children are brought up in families headed by one parent (usually the mother). Marital breakdown and divorce bring about major changes. Parents have less energy for children and are less responsive to their needs. Parents often remarry and step-parents and stepbrothers and sisters are brought into the family. Remarriage may bring a new stability but one which requires adjustments for parents as well as children (see Chapter 7).

Changes and adjustments continue over the life course (Vetere and Gale, 1987). Families do not cease to exist when children grow up and leave home. Close affectional relations may continue and family members may continue to be dependent on one another emotionally and in other ways. This may be seen especially at times of transition. When children are born, grandparents often become more involved with their children, for example, buying baby equipment and baby-sitting. When parents divorce, grandparents may again be able to support their children and grandchildren. And parents maintain contact with their own parents, spending time with grandparents and taking care of them as they get old and frail.

These different forms of families are discussed throughout the book. However, we have more information about some kinds of families than others. Most of the research on 'normal' family development is done on conventional middle-class families, with black, single-parent and working-class families studied more when the focus is on problems (see Chapter 11) (Phoenix *et al.*, in press). As a result we have less information about normal interaction patterns in unconventional families and problems in normal families, so we do not have a good basis for assessing the relative advantages and disadvantages of different family forms. Although there is not a great deal of evidence, the pattern of results is fairly unanimous. Psychologically healthy personalities can develop in many different social groupings and departures from the conventional norm of family structure are not necessarily harmful to children. All family forms have strengths and weaknesses and no one form has the monopoly on how best to meet children's needs at all times (Scarr and Dunn, 1987; Schaffer, 1986).

5. Families Operate in Historical, Cultural and Ideological Contexts

The ecological approach to development stresses that development takes place in a variety of contexts, of which the family is one. Others include school and day care, friendship networks and employment. Technological developments have transformed some aspects of family life. The availability of contraception means that people can more easily control their family size. Decreased infant mortality rates and longer life expectancy are changing family composition with fewer children and more elderly relatives. Economic changes and unemployment force some couples to be more flexible about gender and family roles (Belsky *et al.*, 1984b; Bronfenbrenner, 1986). These all influence parents' lives, their feelings about and relationships with children.

Children and parents are also embedded in a network of cultural beliefs and practices. One of the most controversial of these sets of beliefs relates to motherhood. Current social practices and orthodoxies define women's roles as mothers, encouraging them to stay at home when children are young, to put childcare above other aspects of their identities, to behave sensitively to their children and to see themselves as the most important influence in their children's lives. These beliefs affect how mothers operate on a day to day basis and discourage their engagement in other activities. They also influence the decisions of policy makers who decide whether facilities such as day care are made available, making it harder or easier for women to pursue other interests or engage in paid employment (Brannen and Moss, 1988; Phoenix *et al.*, in press; Urwin, 1985). These beliefs and prescriptions for practice are not constant but vary over time, situation and culture (LeVine, 1980; Newson and Newson, 1968; Schaffer, 1986) (see Chapter 11).

As they move beyond the family, children move into different spheres and cultural settings including the school. They have greater contact with other families and the wider society through television which draws them into the market economy and creates motives for consumption (Kessel and Siegel, 1981). The wider context also provides children with a framework in which to construct models of parental behaviour and to compare their models with those of other children. Parents are often made aware of such comparisons, by comments such as 'Jason's parents let him stay out that late' or 'Parminder's parents let her have more pocket money' (Schaffer, 1986).

The cultural context does more than provide a framework in which parents formulate their own childcare beliefs and practices. Some elements of these practices are compulsory. Parents have to take reasonable physical care of their children, they have to send them to school, they are not supposed to abuse them or to allow them to be employed under age. So while the family is often seen as being within the private sphere, there is also public management and surveillance of family relations (New and David, 1985; Phoenix *et al.*, in press). Surveillance takes a number of forms. Parental practice is monitored by people such as health visitors, social workers and teachers and, even though it is often asserted that children need their mothers, children can be taken away from them. Surveillance can also be seen in terms of the legislation and rules around adoption and access to reproductive technologies which ensure that only people who conform to society's ideas of good parents are allowed to employ these ways of creating families (see Chapter 3). The beliefs current in a society also define normal development and good parenting. Cultural values are often articulated as if they are established facts of nature (and hence natural). In this way cultural expectations about parental and family behaviour permeate the ways in which families operate and children are brought up (see Chapter 11). Psychology has been involved in producing and has given credence to concepts such as 'maternal deprivation', 'sensitive mothering' and 'bonding' and mothers being the critical influence on children's development (Ingleby, 1986; Morgan, 1985; Phoenix *et al.*, in press; Urwin, 1985).

6. Psychologists Studying the Family

Like families, psychologists are products of their time and their culture. As Brannen and Moss (1988) point out, this colours the ways in which they set about studying families:

> Research is neither neutral nor objective. It is conducted by individual researchers, who bring to their work perspectives and beliefs shaped by class, gender and race as well as by personal circumstances and experience. These perspectives and beliefs influence how researchers define the issues to be studied, how they interpret their data and the conclusions they draw from it. (Brannen and Moss, 1988: 9)

The experience of being part of a family and perhaps of bringing up their own children influences the questions psychologists ask. If they have struggled with the contradictions of family life in our society, for instance as mothers trying to work or as women whose careers it is assumed will be broken by motherhood, they may have become more interested in the issue of working mothers.

However, direct personal experiences are not the only influence. The theoretical perspective of researchers also guides their activities. For example, when considering the questions to ask of children whose parents are divorcing, a psychologist with a strong psychoanalytic background is likely to want to know about (and generate hypotheses about) children's attachment and security and how children cope with the loss of one of their parents. A cognitive psychologist, in contrast, is likely to want to ask about how children understand divorce proceedings and conceptualize divorce and their new families (Kessel and Siegel, 1981). Only occasionally do psychologists ask children or parents to say which issues are of relevance to them. One exception is the longitudinal study of Newson and Newson who asked mothers to reflect on what they were doing as parents (Newson and Newson, 1968; 1976). In addition, psychologists and family researchers address the questions society considers to be important. For example, when women are needed in the labour force one might expect psychologists to be asked to investigate questions about the kinds of day care which are best for the children of working mothers. But when women are not needed, we would expect the questions to change and to focus instead on issues such as the possible harm that can come to young children when their mothers are in paid employment.

Like other members of the community, psychologists are subject to media portrayals of family life and to the prevailing values of society. Psychologists tend to be white, male and middle-class and to have their homes in the more affluent areas. Their position in society exposes them to some values and ideas more than others and as a consequence some seem more reasonable or 'natural' than others. Their value systems and their constructions of parenting and childrearing are rarely challenged because they are shared by others who help to shape social policy and legislation and deal with children from a professional point of view. For example most psychologists do not question middle-class assumptions about the desirability in children of sociability, compliance to authority, and success educationally, and the undesirability of aggressiveness and insensitivity to others. Consequently parenting styles which result in compliant, sociable and intellectually curious children are held up as the ideal. 'Good' parents do not punish their children physically, instead they explain why rules are set and why they need to be followed. This may be good preparation for those children who experience consistency in their lives but may be inadequate preparation for children who face a world in which rules are poorly defined or ignored by the adults around them. For a child growing up in a poor inner-city area or preparing for life in the commodity markets, aggressiveness, deviousness and unconcern for the welfare of others may be signs of successful adaptation rather than signs of psychopathology (see Chapter 11). We do not explicitly comment on these values throughout the book, but the reader should remain alert to them.

Further Reading

BELSKY, J., ROBINS, E. and GAMBLE, W. (1984b) 'The determinants of parental competence', in LEWIS, M. (Ed.) *Beyond the Dyad*, New York, Plenum Press.

Factors associated with parental competence (that is parents' provision of an environment which enables children to acquire the capacities required for dealing effectively with others) are examined. The authors argue that to be competent parents need to be sensitive and involved with their children. Three main determinants of parental sensitivity are patience (allowing them to hold their feelings back), endurance (to cope with the hard work of parenting) and commitment (which enables parents to invest energy and patience in their children). They also consider child factors which may make the tasks of parenting more or less difficult.

BRONFENBRENNER, U. (1986) 'Ecology of the family as a context for human development: research perspectives', *Developmental Psychology*, **22**, pp. 723–42.

Brings together a wide range of studies which examine factors which influence how families function as a setting for children's development. The variety of contexts within which families operate and create linkages between children's family lives and the wider community are considered. These include other settings into which children move such as day care and school and the wider worlds in which parents spend time, such as fathers' and mothers' employment experience and parental support networks.

SCHAFFER, H.R. (1986) 'Child psychology: the future', *Journal of Child Psychology and Psychiatry*, **27**, pp. 761–79.

An interesting review of issues in developmental psychology. Schaffer argues for the need to consider the context in which children develop and to recognize the variety of family forms, including those created through reproductive technologies. It points to some of the methodological problems involved in linking social and family factors with children's development.

VETERE, A. and GALE, A. (1987) *Ecological Studies of Family Life*, Chichester, Wiley.

This book takes the family, rather than individuals, dyads or triads within families, as its unit. It discusses theories of family functioning and ways of characterizing how families operate, how their members relate to one another and their shared meanings and understandings. This provides a wider setting in which to consider mother-child or father-child relations. Family functioning is considered over time as family concerns and meanings change, for example as children grow older and leave home or as parents get divorced.

Chapter 2

Family Formation: Adjustments to Parenthood

Most people become parents and parenthood is a major source of identity for men and women. Parenting brings about changes in what people do on a day to day basis, in their major concerns and interests, in how they relate to other people and feel about themselves and others. Adjustments are made as men and women become parents with the birth of a first or a second or subsequent child. However, it is generally assumed that the changes in identity and in adjustments are greatest with the birth of a first child and hence it is this transition which is most studied. In this chapter we discuss the birth of a first child; the birth of later children is considered in Chapter 6.

The changes and adjustments parenthood bring are different for women and men. Women carry and give birth to children and their lives are changed substantially by motherhood. They tend to give up employment outside the home, if only temporarily, during their first pregnancies. This means that they may lose the social contacts employment brings and may feel isolated if they have few alternative social networks. Pregnancy and birth are medical as well as personal and social events: women's pregnancies and births are medically supervised and this may influence how women experience the transition to parenthood. There are other factors which may influence women's adjustments to parenthood. These include whether or not the pregnancy was planned, the physical symptoms and discomforts of pregnancy, women's support networks and especially whether they have a partner or are a single parent, their age, and what becoming a mother and having a baby means to them.

Motherhood is a powerful part of women's identity. It is seen as a means by which women achieve full adult status and demonstrate their adult feminine identity. For many women motherhood is the most important means by which adult status is achieved and hence a powerful means of self-validation. Employment infrequently provides women with a valid alternative identity, as it can do for men. Because motherhood is seen as a central aspect of women's lives and identity and as a normative life event, it is assumed that all women should want to become mothers. In this context, the questions asked about motherhood tend to be about women who appear to reject motherhood or about those who become mothers in unusual or non-normative circumstances. These include very young mothers, older mothers, women having children without a male partner, women who adopt children or those who give birth as a result of some of the more dramatic forms of reproductive technology. Studies of these mothers give us information about their experiences but they also throw light on what are considered to be the normative or conventional ways of becoming parents and 'proper' adjustments to parenthood in our society.

In contrast, men's lives are usually changed less by parenthood. They are less involved in childcare and usually maintain more social contacts and activities outside the home, largely provided through the world of work. Compared to mothers, there are less clear cut assumptions and expectations about men's reactions to becoming a parent and their involvement in parenting. Expectations about what is appropriate for men are changing, and media presentations of men committed to children have become more frequent. There is considerable debate about the extent to which the media presentation is reflected in the behaviour of most men. Certainly, changes in expectations have made it easier for some men to become involved and have prompted psychologists and others to examine men's involvement. The level of men's involvement in childcare and their interest in parenthood varies considerably and psychologists have looked especially at the reasons for such variation and the implications of fathers' involvement for their children's development (see Chapter 5).

Decisions and Motivations around Parenthood

Having children and becoming parents is seen as beneficial and satisfying for men and women, but also costly. Parenthood and parenting can provide people with close and enduring relationships by strengthening old ties or providing the opportunity for the formation of new ones. Children are often seen as a physical manifestation of the parents' relationship and as bringing parents closer together. Parenthood can enhance the quality of couples' relationships with one another and also lead to closer ties with other family members, especially with their own parents. Children help to create new social networks; other families are encountered through attending antenatal classes, playgroups and schools, children make friends and introduce their parents to one another, thereby helping parents to form new friendships. Children can also provide new interests, activities and sources of pride for parents as they help their children grow and develop. They can add variety to parents' lives and increase their prestige when their children achieve new levels of attainment. Children validate parents' status as adults and ensure parents' acceptance within their families and as responsible members of their community. At the same time children are viewed as costly. They can be draining financially, socially and emotionally. They are costly financially because they require special equipment, furniture, clothes and toys, and their hobbies too can be expensive. They also place restrictions on parents' activities and their time together. Because children are demanding of their parents' time and attention they allow parents less leisure time and less time to be alone together or to pursue other interests. Furthermore, children restrict mothers' opportunities for employment and thus the pleasures that can be derived from work and contact with workmates. Children can be a cause for anxiety, with parents worrying about their children's health, safety and well-being, and their behaviour and development, especially when they behave badly (Michaels and Goldberg, 1988; Newson and Newson, 1976; Phoenix *et al.*, in press).

Assumptions about the value of parenthood, especially for women, provide the ideological context in which men and women make decisions about parenthood. Whatever else they do with their lives, women are supposed to become mothers. Childlessness, whether chosen or not, is seen negatively, as an indication of social or personal inadequacy (Phoenix *et al.*, in press). From an early age, girls and young women see motherhood as part of their future lives, even when they are critical of their own mothers' lives and know the disadvantages and problems motherhood can bring (Lees, 1986). Many mothers work outside the home, but they are encouraged to see their employment as secondary to motherhood. Indeed this is assumed by employers who are, as a result, less likely to consider seriously the employment of *all* women, whether they are mothers or not (Phoenix *et al.*, in press; Sharpe, 1984).

In contrast parenting is only one role among many in men's adult lives. Men are encouraged to become parents but it is not normally expected to impinge on their working lives. Employment is usually seen as more central to men's identity than parenting. Men who ask for time off work to help with their children may be viewed as less reliable employees. As a result, childcare is seen as the responsibility of women and the provision of creches or parental leave are considered (if they are considered at all) when employing women but not when employing men. In families in which mothers as well as fathers are employed outside the home, with few exceptions, women do more childcare than men and take responsibility for organizing childminders or other alternative childcare (Brannen and Moss, 1988; New and David, 1985).

Women's and men's strategies and decisions about becoming parents and their reactions to pregnancy vary widely. Some men and women make conscious decisions about becoming parents. They try to plan their pregnancies and to ensure that their children are well spaced. Although men may participate in the decision making most see their partner as the principal instigator of decisions about the timing and size of families. Other people however have less clear cut plans. Many intend becoming parents one day but conceive sooner than they wanted or intended to. For others conception is unexpected and unwanted and they have to decide how to proceed. Some women decide to have their babies and bring them up even though they are not in a stable relationship and cannot count on the support of a male partner. Yet others feel that they cannot do so and seek a termination of their pregnancy (Broome, 1984; Phoenix, 1991).

Changes and Adjustments during Pregnancy

Women's and men's initial reactions to the pregnancy vary considerably. Some recognize that they are pregnant immediately and they and their partners begin from the start to make plans and introduce changes into their lives. Others come to accept the pregnancy more slowly; they may view their pregnancy as real only once they feel the baby move inside them (quickening) or when they see the baby on the ultrasound screen (Birksted-Breen, 1986; Farrant, 1985). Because men do not experience pregnancy directly, they may be less aware of the day to day changes pregnancy brings. They also experience less pressure to make decisions about giving up work, attending antenatal clinics and going for tests, or reading up about pregnancy and making preparations for the birth. Lewis found in a study of first-time fathers that once their partners were pregnant nearly three-quarters of the men said they were happy at the prospect of becoming fathers (Lewis *et al.*, 1982). Most men thought the pregnancy brought them closer to their partners and they saw themselves as supportive. But other fathers reacted differently. Some said their initial reaction was resentment of the interruption a child would bring to their plans for their careers and social life. And still others reported panic and surprise when they heard; some had not envisaged a child as an outcome of their relationship and worried about the extra responsibilities involved in supporting their partner and the child. These negative reactions were more frequent amongst men who were not married.

Women's adjustments during pregnancy vary considerably from woman to woman and for the same woman at different points in the pregnancy. This is not surprising given the contradictory images of pregnancy in our society. On the one hand, pregnant women are seen as powerful, attractive and feminine but simultaneously, on the other, as vulnerable, frail, at the mercy of their hormones, over-emotional, fat and sexually unappealing (Antonis, 1981). Women see motherhood as fulfilment and a major source of achievement. But at the same time they are fearful of the pain and the risks of childbirth to themselves and to their baby and view negatively the work and the drudgery involved in childcare (Gordon, 1990). Although about half of first-time mothers are pleased to be pregnant many have mixed feelings and a few are unhappy at the pregnancy. Mixed feelings are often related to whether women want to be pregnant at the time and their initial physical reactions. Women report a variety of unpleasant or distressing symptoms in the early months, some more serious than others. These include tiredness, indigestion, vomiting and nausea, depression and anxiety. These symptoms tend to decrease as the pregnancy progresses and other factors such as their size and their difficulty in getting about and their anxieties about what their births will be like influence women's reactions (Oakley, 1981; Wolkind and Zajicek, 1981).

Because of the ways in which pregnancy and childbirth are managed in many western societies, pregnancy involves considerable contact with medical professionals who monitor the pregnancy, advise women about childbirth and define what are normal and abnormal adjustments. Prenatal screening and testing using ultrasound scans and amniocentesis are becoming increasingly routine. Although they can provide reassurance for parents about their babies' well-being, screening can lead to a short-term increase in parents' anxieties, drawing to their attention the possibility of health problems in their unborn child or raising worries about how the baby is progressing. In this way screening may influence how women come to think about their pregnancies and their unborn children, for some making the child seem more real, but for others making them reluctant to become emotionally involved with the unborn child until they feel confident of their baby's condition (Farrant, 1985; Stanworth, 1987). Medical approaches to pregnancy and antenatal care emphasize the potential for problems and encourage women to be passive and to adopt a sick role. Only rarely is consideration given to the support women need as they cope with different and sometimes conflicting feelings (Antonis, 1981; Oakley, 1981).

Pregnancy brings changes in women's social relationships and these may influence how women adjust to becoming a mother. Most women stop working outside the home shortly before the birth of their first child. Giving up work involves the loss of their income and the social contacts with people at work. Women with close family or friends may take this in their stride. But other women can become isolated and consequently may need more support and companionship from their partners. If this is not provided the relationship may be weakened and the mother feel more uncertain about the pregnancy. But for many couples, pregnancy is a time of closeness; each becomes more attentive, supportive and affectionate to the other. This may be especially so when men show their interest in their partner's pregnancy by attending antenatal clinics and classes and helping with housework (Oakley, 1981; Wolkind and Zajicek, 1981).

There is also evidence of intrapersonal change and development, as women acquire new identities and are treated differently by other people. These changes are sometimes seen as inherently problematic but there is little evidence of higher rates of psychological or psychiatric problems during pregnancy. Women's adjustments to pregnancy reflect their personalities, their general coping strategies and their adjustments to other life events. Women's adjustments are also associated with what motherhood means to them in terms of their relationships with the baby and their partners. Women with a history of depression and anxiety are more likely to be depressed and anxious in pregnancy and after the baby is born. The transition to parenthood may trigger unresolved issues related to being dependent on other people. Women may be anxious about how they and their partner will cope with the demands of a small baby. For some women a central issue is the loss of control over their body during pregnancy and childbirth and a more general loss of control over their lives which looking after a small child entails. Some women deal with such issues more effectively than others. Those with a positive attitude to new experiences may enjoy the challenge offered by babycare and others look forward to having the opportunity to view life through a child's eye. Women whose self-esteem is low are somewhat more likely to experience problems during pregnancy and postnatally than those whose self-esteem is higher. Women with good social support can call on this to cope with any stresses they encounter. Difficulties in adjustments during pregnancy are not necessarily linked to problems later. Physical symptoms in pregnancy, feeling isolated at home, and dealing with their increased dependency on their partners may raise issues which women deal with in positive ways (Beail and McGuire, 1982; Birksted-Breen, 1986; Gerson *et al.*, 1984; Michaels and Goldberg, 1988; Wolkind and Zajicek, 1981).

It is assumed that pregnancy requires more difficult adjustments for women who are single, and those who are younger than 20 or over 35 years. The pregnancies of young and single women are considered problematic because they are assumed to be unplanned and unwanted. Many young and single women do feel unable to cope with their pregnancies, as the high termination rates indicate. But for many young women the negative stereotypes associated with being young, single and pregnant are unwarranted. Many are pleased to be pregnant, they adjust well and are supported by their partners and families (Broome, 1984; Phoenix, 1991). Older women are seen as problematic in medical terms. However, any greater difficulties older women experience because of their age tend to be compensated for by the stability of their relations, and their positive attitudes to their pregnancies (Phoenix *et al.*, in press).

For men the changes and adjustments during pregnancy are generally more remote. For many the changes centre on an increased sensitivity and supportiveness of their partners. By becoming sensitized to how women are responding they can begin to share with them the joys and anxieties of the pregnancy: the excitement when the baby begins to move, concerns about the baby and about the results of tests and concern about their partner's tiredness and isolation. Men also make adjustments of their own, as they experience new demands made of them as expectant fathers. The pregnancy may change the way in which they view themselves, and many men perceive themselves as becoming more mature and more responsible and they see their lives as fuller and more meaningful. With the pregnancy many men believe that their responsibilities to their partner increase; this may cause panic in some, but most perceive themselves as shouldering responsibility successfully. Part of their perceived responsibility is to provide financially for the increased costs children introduce. Many men in pregnancy and early childhood seek overtime working or better paid jobs. Although they see themselves supporting their partner and preparing themselves for the arrival of their child most men do not actively seek to become informed: they rarely attend clinics and classes, or read books. Instead they look to the mother to provide them with any information they may need. Pregnancy can be a time when fathers worry more than usual. Their worries centre around their anxiety about their partner's health and well-being as well as that of the baby: they may worry about the impact of a baby on their relationship, and especially the extra costs and responsibilities parenting will bring; they may worry too about their ability to relate to the child once born. Such stress manifests itself sometimes in psychosomatic complaints such as toothache, backache or nausea. These changes are reflected in men's relationships with their partners. Fathers show greater concern and give more help with housework during pregnancy and report that relations are very close. Although sexual relations may change, with many couples reporting having intercourse less frequently especially in late pregnancy, marital satisfaction in pregnancy is generally good (Beail and McGuire, 1982; Condon, 1987; Moss *et al.*, 1987a; Scott-Heyes, 1983; Wolkind and Zajicek, 1981).

Childbirth

In industrial countries, almost all babies are now born in hospital and hence their births are medically supervised. Medical intervention is the norm rather than the exception, with some interventions having a major impact on women's experiences of childbirth. Labour is frequently induced and accelerated, painkillers are used routinely and many babies are delivered with forceps or by caesarean section (Moss *et al.*, 1987b; Wolkind and Zajicek, 1981). Mothers stay in hospital for some days after their babies are delivered. On the postnatal wards they may be given help with the tasks of childcare and especially with the establishment of breastfeeding. Women's reactions to the medical management of their births have been the focus of many studies. These indicate that for many women the benefit in terms of the reduced mortality rates of a highly interventionist approach has to be set against the psychological costs. The impact of an alien environment on women's anxiety and their ability to relax may result in a further need for intervention. Although some women submit fairly readily to the control of medical professionals, others feel helpless, angry and alienated from what they increasingly feel should be a pivotal emotional experience for themselves and their partners (Antonis, 1981; Birksted-Breen, 1986; Oakley, 1981; Wolkind and Zajicek, 1981; Woollett *et al.*, 1983). The birth experience may influence mothers' initial reactions to their newborns. Women who are disappointed with their birth experiences show less interest in their newborns (Booth and Meltzoff, 1984). When large amounts of drugs are used in labour and babies are delivered by forceps or caesarean section they are more likely to need special care and hence to be separated from mothers. This may have implications for mothers' relationships with their children.

Fathers' Presence at Delivery

During the 1970s it became common for fathers to be present during labour and at the birth of their babies. It is now a generally accepted part of the childbirth experience, and, indeed, fathers' commitment may now be questioned if they are not present (Woollett and Dosanjh-Matwala, 1990). Fathers' presence is considered valuable because of their support for mothers during labour and delivery and their involvement later with their children (Moss *et al.*, 1987b; Oakley, 1981; Parke, 1981). Fathers' support takes many forms, including rubbing mothers' backs, mopping brows, timing contractions and breathing along with mothers. They can act as mediators between mothers and the medical staff, relaying mothers' needs to staff when necessary, although how effectively they do this probably depends on their prior training and their general ability to be supportive and put their partners' needs first. They may also reduce the unfamiliarity of the setting. When fathers or a friend are present during labour, mothers relax more, experience less pain and hence need less medication, and have shorter labours. Fathers may also help to enhance the emotional experience for mothers by enabling or encouraging mothers to express their feelings and relate what is happening to their relationship with one another and with the wider family. Mothers may be pleased by their partner's excitement with the new baby and the birth becomes part of their shared history as a couple to be talked over later. Fathers may also help mothers to make links between the baby and the wider family, by pointing to family resemblances and by anticipating family reactions to the baby (Beail and McGuire, 1982; White and Woollett, 1987).

Many fathers report their pleasure and excitement at being present at birth. It can increase their feelings of self-esteem and self-worth. At the same time fathers find birth shocking and overwhelming emotionally. However fathers' feelings are not always positive. Some fathers feel unprepared and many feel lonely, confused, anxious and bored at times, as they see their partners in pain and are unable to assist, especially because there seems to be no clear role for them. Some are annoyed if they are asked to leave when they had planned to stay. Some fathers are enthralled and engrossed in their newborns: they hold their babies, look at them, and talk about them. Allowing or encouraging fathers to have contact with their newborns is often considered to increase their commitment. Some, but not all, studies find that fathers who are present at birth or have contact with their babies soon after birth are somewhat more likely than fathers without this experience to interact with babies, with more touching, holding and cuddling, and they are more involved in babycare (Palkovitz, 1985; White and Woollett, 1987). The high level of interest shown by some fathers points to the value of fathers' presence at birth and sets up expectations of what being at their babies' birth might mean for men.

Fathers' presence at birth has not been shown to have any longer-term impact. Fathers who are committed to being involved with their children may show their commitment in many ways, including finding out about childbirth and attending classes, being supportive of their partner during pregnancy, holding and interacting with their newborns, and taking an active part in day to day care. Fathers who want to be involved may therefore ensure that they are present for the delivery, and their presence reflects their level of commitment rather than being its cause. Studies generally consider only whether fathers are present or not rather than looking at their intentions or what they do when they are present. The value of looking at fathers' intentions can be seen in studies with fathers who had planned to be present but who were excluded for medical reasons. These fathers were later found to be as involved with their babies as fathers who were at the birth suggesting that fathers' intentions and attitudes may be better predictors of their later involvement than whether they were present or not (Palkovitz, 1985; White and Woollett, 1987).

What fathers do when they are present may also be an important variable. Fathers who take an active part, who are supportive of mothers and talk to mothers about the baby may be more involved than those who are present at the mothers' insistence or talk only about their own feelings. Fathers' commitment may also vary over time and may be influenced by a range of factors, only one of which is their presence at birth. Some fathers attend because it is expected of them but find themselves drawn in and their involvement with their child increasing as a result. But equally possible is that fathers demonstrate their commitment by their presence at birth but that this is not sustained into the early months because of work or other pressures or is not translated into day to day care. In addition, when fathers' presence at delivery does have positive outcomes, it may do so more indirectly through their relationship with mothers. Fathers' presence may be seen positively by the mother as an indicator of fathers' acceptance of and interest in the child and this may be built on in terms of parental closeness and joint interest in the child and fathers' sense of competence around the child (Nicholson *et al.*, 1983; Palkovitz, 1985).

Early Relations with the Baby

It is now common for mothers to be given their babies to hold soon after they are born and some mothers start to breastfeed in the delivery room. As a result this is now part of women's expectations around childbirth. Separation of mother and baby for long periods of time, unless the baby needs special care, is now much less common. The nature and the intensity of women's feelings after childbirth are related to their general attitudes rather than to their hormone levels. Mothers who consider that babies are interesting and childcare a satisfying career and who had sought contact with infants prior to delivery are more likely to engage with their newborns than women with less positive attitudes (Fleming *et al.*, 1987). Babies tend to stay with mothers on the postnatal wards where mothers take charge of their babies during their stay in hospital. Often this means that babies stay with mothers at night rather than being taken to a nursery. Women are not always enthusiastic about taking total charge of their babies' care postnatally, especially if they are recovering from a caesarean birth (Macfarlane, 1977; Moss *et al.*, 1987b; Woollett *et al.*, 1983).

These practices reflect, in part, current paediatric and psychological concern about the early establishment of mother-child relations. Klaus and Kennel (1982) argued that early contact was essential for the establishment of good mother-child relations. In their studies mothers who were given their babies to hold soon after birth showed more interest in them and had a closer relationship with them than did mothers whose babies were kept in nurseries away from them. During this initial contact mothers were found to spend a considerable time in looking at their newborns, touching and talking to them. Klaus and Kennel considered that this helped mothers to become attached to (or bond with) their babies. They also argued that this initial contact with newborns had long-term effects on mothers' relationships with their children and their children's development. However, their findings have been questioned (e.g. Bronfenbrenner, 1979; Svedja *et al.*, 1980) and few psychologists now believe that contact in the initial hours of life has the immediate or longer-term effects which Klaus and Kennel claimed. The establishment of a social relationship with a baby is a more complex, flexible and drawn out process, based on getting to know the baby and establishing a mutually satisfying pattern of interaction. Whether they have longer-term consequences or not, mothers' and fathers' initial contact with their newborns is a rich emotional experience which may help to promote concern for the child's well-being.

Early Adjustments in the Home

The first few weeks of a first-born's life mark a new phase for parents. The early weeks are hard work and make great demands on parents' physical and emotional resources. Parents feed and care for their babies, they get to know them and learn to understand their cries and noises, likes and dislikes. This involves the development of new skills and sensitivities. The work can seem endless and it has a relentless quality: no sooner is the baby fed, changed and bathed than it is time to start again. The care of babies disrupts established routines and reduces parents' opportunities to pursue their own interests and activities (Belsky *et al.*, 1984b; Michaels and Goldberg, 1988; Oakley, 1981).

Many mothers are anxious in the early weeks. This, with their tiredness and the restrictions on their independence, may trigger depression (Nicolson, 1986). New mothers often have little experience of childcare and if their expectations do not match the reality of mothering, women may feel undermined, angry or frustrated. Such feelings may be exacerbated if the child is ill or is difficult to soothe (Antonis, 1981; Birksted-Breen, 1986). Personality factors influence how women cope in the early weeks. Women who do not see themselves in traditional feminine terms find the work of childcare and the need to be totally child-centred in the early weeks more difficult than women who see themselves in more traditional terms. Their difficulties at this stage may also relate to the greater discrepancies for them between the day to day activities of childcare and their expectations of motherhood or their lives prior to becoming mothers (Belsky *et al.*, 1984b). Mothers' capacity for active and adaptive coping and their ability prenatally to visualize themselves as mothers are related to successful transition (Heinecke *et al.*, 1983). Women who are isolated or not well supported may have no one to talk to about their feelings. As a result they may attribute them to their own incompetence rather than recognizing them as normal reactions to a demanding and complex situation.

Fathers and families may be interested in the child and may therefore be less aware of the difficulties women are experiencing. During pregnancy, women are protected, but once they become mothers, women are expected to cope with the competing demands of their child, their partners, the tasks young children create and their own needs (Birksted-Breen, 1986).

But the early transition to parenthood is also a positive time. Parents are usually proud of their new baby and their achievement as parents and enjoy their mutual interest in the baby. They experience pleasure in getting to know the baby. The feelings the baby elicits have an intensity which parents may not be prepared for. This is frightening and rewarding at the same time. Looking after a baby may increase parents' sense of their own worth and competence as they develop parenting skills and bring together their image of their ideal child and themselves as ideal parents with the reality of caring for and loving their own child (Belsky, 1981; Michaels and Goldberg, 1988).

Changing Relationships

Early parenting brings about changes in mothers' and fathers' relationships with others. Often the birth of a child leads to closer relationships with women's own mothers as women develop common interests and call on their mothers' experiences. This may be particularly helpful for women having children on their own (Birns and Hay, 1988; Phoenix, 1991). Parents' own parents often provide financial support and become involved in the care of their grandchildren and parents are drawn back into the wider family network (Tinsley and Parke, 1984). But the relationship in which there are greatest changes is that between mother and father. The birth of a new baby brings a new person into the family, one who is very demanding and cannot wait patiently for food or comfort. Some parents find the insistence of the new baby more difficult to deal with than others, and some have problems sharing their partner's affections and attention with the baby (Michaels and Goldberg, 1988). Marital satisfaction influences the extent to which fathers are involved with their babies and their satisfaction with parenting. Close father-child relations are more likely when the marital relationship is good, although mothers seem better at ensuring that their relationships with their babies are not contaminated by poor marital relationships (Belsky, 1984; Hinde and Stevenson-Hinde, 1988).

A new baby also increases the amount of work to be done. There is a major potential for conflict as parents search for ways of finding extra time or energy and have to cut back on other activities (Busfield, 1987). The needs of parents for sleep or to pursue their own interests often have to be put aside and this may trigger a crisis in marital relationships (Belsky *et al.*, 1984b; Grossman *et al.*, 1980). Strain between couples in the postnatal period manifests itself in a number of areas, most frequently in dissatisfaction with the division of labour within the family. Many young people have a commitment to equality in terms of housework and childcare. During pregnancy, couples often share housework and when the baby first comes home fathers often take time off work. But after this initial period, more traditional roles are adopted, with mothers taking responsibility for and doing most of the childcare and related housework. Fathers' contribution to housework and childcare is reduced over the course of the first year. Initially this reduction in fathers' involvement is triggered by their return to work, leaving mothers with greater responsibility. As a result mothers become more competent and confident in their ability to care for the baby. This can leave fathers feeling somewhat excluded, and so reduce still further their attempts to learn and get involved. Mothers may then become critical of fathers' incompetence and be less supportive of fathers' future attempts to help (Moss *et al.*, 1987b; Oakley, 1981; Ruble *et al.*, 1988).

These changes may lead to conflict, with mothers experiencing overload and wanting more help and fathers seeing their role in more traditional terms. Mothers often say that because fathers are at work all day, they do not recognize the pressures mothers experience as full-time caretakers and the physically and emotionally draining nature of childcare (Moss *et al.*, 1987b). Fathers may respond to the new responsibilities of parenthood by working longer hours to earn more or to further their careers. This may mean that, whatever their initial intentions and expectations, help with childcare and housework is subordinated to activities outside the home. When this happens women report more negative feelings about their partners and about the effect of the child on their relationship with their partner (Ruble *et al.*, 1988).

A major complaint amongst parents of young babies is the lack of time they have to spend together. Moss *et al.* (1987a) found that the level of marital satisfaction amongst a group of first-time parents was generally high, but the area in which there was greatest dissatisfaction was in the amount of child-free time. This manifests itself in a reduction in affection, nurturance and support for one another, and in fewer shared activities, especially when relations during the postpartum period are compared with those during pregnancy (Belsky *et al.*, 1983; Scott-Heyes, 1983). The quality of the marital relationship and the lack of time together may also be important to mothers because of their increased dependence on fathers. Mothers need fathers to help with the extra work but they also need their reassurance and support. This is especially so for first-time mothers who have fewer outside sources of support and companionship. Most mothers with very young children are not in paid employment outside the home and so lack the support and contact with the outside world which employment brings. In the early weeks they may have little opportunity to develop close ties with other women in a similar situation and this may put a strain on the marital relationship (Brannen and Moss, 1988).

In spite of the pressures and the work overload in the early weeks, most parents adjust well. Moss *et al.* (1987a) found only a small percentage of parents for whom the initial transition to parenthood was difficult and whose marriages were weakened. These tended to be younger and less well-educated couples who had been married or cohabited for a comparatively short time. These couples may experience difficulties because they have had little time to adjust to their lives as a couple before having to make personal and financial adjustments as they become parents. Their difficulties may also be a reflection of a generally poor relationship before the woman became pregnant rather than being a result of having a child. Poor relationships are rarely improved by having children. This suggests that when considering how people make the transition to parenthood we need to take account of continuities in people's lives as well as changes. This means considering such things as how they cope generally with changes in their lives, what access they have to social supports, how they feel about children and childcare.

Single Mothers

In 1989 a quarter of births in the UK were to women who were not married, although half of these were to women who were cohabiting or in stable relationships, leaving about 12 per cent of mothers who are bringing up children on their own. A number of these women are also young (about a quarter of births to single women in the UK and a third in the USA are to women under 20). Many single women enjoy their pregnancies, and feel positive about being mothers and the companionship their children provide. But many single mothers are poor and often find it difficult to be the kind of mother they would like to be. Being a single mother does not in itself influence how women relate to their children, but mothers who are single AND living in poverty are usually less responsive and engage in less verbal interaction with their children than mothers in better circumstances. Some single mothers are well supported by their families who provide financial assistance and help to look after the child. Under these conditions, mothers usually feel positive about themselves and their children and children benefit from their relationships with grandparents, uncles and aunts (Phoenix, 1991). Many single mothers go on to marry or to establish long-term relationships and so single parenthood is often a relatively short-term experience (see also Chapter 7).

Role of the Child

The child also contributes to parents' adjustments in the early weeks, with some child characteristics making adjustments easier than others. Gender is one such characteristic. A number of studies have revealed a preference for sons, although this depends in part on the existing sex composition of the family. At birth fathers react differently to boys and girls, with boys being held longer and talked to more than girls. This preference can also be observed in the neonatal period, when fathers touch and talk to first-born sons more than first-born daughters. Mothers do not differentiate between boys and girls. On the basis of these early reactions, it might be predicted that fathers would be more involved in childcare when they have sons. Children's gender is also related to how parents feel about themselves as parents and to how they adjust to one another (see Chapter 5).

Children's health and their temperaments also play a part. The parents of a child who is ill, or one who cries a great deal or is less easy to soothe, may feel that they are inadequate parents. The temperament of a child refers to the relatively enduring characteristics they display such as their degree of sociability, their adaptability to change and the quality of their mood. Some children are temperamentally more difficult to deal with than others (Goldsmith *et al.*, 1987). If a child continues to be difficult, parents may begin to feel angry and in extreme cases even to abuse the child. However, parents' perceptions of their children are more powerful predictors of their reactions than their baby's behaviour. It may matter less whether a baby cries a great deal, for example, than how the mother makes sense of and feels about the baby's behaviour. One mother may consider her baby cries a great deal, whereas another mother, with a baby who cries just as much, may consider that her baby cries only occasionally and be less upset by the baby's crying. This suggests that while the characteristics of babies should not be dismissed, how parents perceive their behaviour and the extent to which there is a mismatch between their expectations and their baby's behaviour may be more crucial in predicting how parents adjust (Belsky, 1984; Belsky *et al.*, 1984b; Heinecke *et al.*, 1983).

In Conclusion

The transition to parenthood is a long and complex process, spanning pregnancy, childbirth and the period of bringing up a child. How men and women respond depends on a multitude of factors including their personalities and general strategies for coping, the context in which the transition takes place, including work relations, what the pregnancy means for the man and woman and the course the pregnancy takes. Adjustments are made by the woman and her partner, individually and as a couple, and by their families. The reactions and support of families are important for many women but they seem to be especially so for women having children without a male partner. Becoming a parent is significant individually and socially. But it is also a major medical event in people's lives as in many societies the transition is now medically managed and requires close contact with clinics and hospitals. How pregnancy and childbirth are perceived and managed by professionals can have a significant effect not merely on the health and well-being of mother and baby but on mothers' and fathers' experiences of the event. Health professionals have a major impact on what are defined as normal and abnormal adjustments during pregnancy and childbirth and these often influence men's and women's sense of how well they are doing as parents. This chapter has only considered the adjustments of parents into the early months of parenting. However, as children become older they make new demands of their parents and these demands have to be accommodated. Consequently, parenthood calls for constant adjustments and so remains a transitional state throughout children's lives.

Further Reading

BUSFIELD, J. (1987) 'Parenting and parenthood', in COHEN, G. (Ed.) *Social Change and the Life Course*, London, Tavistock.

An accessible review of the area which demonstrates the increased interest in the parental perspective and a recognition that what is considered best for children is not necessarily what is best for parents. Two studies of mothers' experiences of bringing up preschool children are summarized.

MICHAELS, G.Y. and GOLDBERG, W.A. (Eds) (1988) *Transition to Parenthood: Theory and Research*, Cambridge, Cambridge University Press.

A collection of reviews and reports of research on the transition to parenthood. Of particular relevance are chapters which discuss the motivations of men and women as they choose to become parents, the adjustments they make and personality and other factors (including the quality of the mother-father relationship) associated with the nature of their adjustments.

PALKOVITZ, R. (1985) 'Fathers' birth attendance, early contact, and extended contact with their newborns: a critical review', *Child Development*, 56, pp. 392–406.

WHITE, D.G. and WOOLLETT, A. (1987) 'The father's role in the neonatal period', in HARVEY, D. (Ed.) *Parent-Infant Relationships*, New York, Wiley. Reprinted in Woodhead, M., CARR, R. and LIGHT, P. (Eds) (1991) *Becoming a Person*, London: Routledge.

Both review research of fathers' birth attendance and early contact with newborns and indicate that there is little evidence to suggest that fathers' presence at birth and early contact with their newborns increases their later involvement with their children. Fathers' expectations and perceptions of the birth may be more important predictors of their relationships with their children than whether or not they are present at delivery.

PHOENIX, A. (1991) *Young Mothers?*, Cambridge, Polity Press.

Research on young mothers is reviewed to consider why young motherhood is viewed as problematic. From a British study of women who became mothers under the age of 20, Ann Phoenix argues that structural factors, such as women's occupational experience and the availability of housing and family support, are more predictive of how women cope than is their age.

RUBLE, D., FLEMING, A.S., HACKEL, L.S. and STANGOR, C. (1988) 'Changes in the marital relationship during the transition to first time motherhood: effects of violated expectations concerning the division of household labour', *Journal of Personality and Social Psychology*, 55, pp. 78–87.

A longitudinal study which indicates some of the changes and adjustments couples make as they become parents. Many women expressed greater dissatisfactions with their marital relationships after the birth of their first child, especially when they found they were doing more housework and childcare than they had expected. Other aspects of the marital relationship are not necessarily affected.

WOLKIND, S. and ZAJICEK, E. (1981) *Pregnancy: A Psychological and Social Study*, London, Academic Press.

A longitudinal study of East London women pregnant with their first babies. The reactions of many women varied during the course of their pregnancies and were associated with factors such as whether they had support from families and the nature of their pregnancy symptoms. The findings are used to evaluate ideas about 'normal' adjustments to pregnancy and the transition to motherhood. The authors argue that pregnancy is best viewed as a transitional period.

Chapter 3

Different Forms of Family Building: Reproductive Technology and Adoption

The account of the transition to parenthood in Chapter 2 considered those situations where a family is created through the conception and birth of children to mothers on their own and to two parents. But families are created in other ways. One way is as a result of remarriage (see Chapter 7). Families are also created through adoption and the use of reproductive technology. These forms of family building are used mainly by people who wish to become parents but have fertility problems. We consider the implications of these ways of family building for children and their parents. Looking at different family forms raises many issues about what are considered 'normal', 'natural' or desirable ways of having and bringing up children.

Reproductive Technology and Family Building

About one in seven couples who want to have children experience difficulties in conceiving and about one in five pregnancies are lost through miscarriage. Reproductive problems can be stressful because they prevent women and men from engaging in an important part of adult life. Infertility and miscarriage are stressful for people, too, because they involve loss. This includes loss of control over their lives and their bodily functioning, as people discover they cannot conceive or give birth to live, healthy children or are not able to do so when they wish. Once they have problems many people seek medical help and some are enabled to become parents through a variety of medical procedures, some of which are discussed here. Some of the procedures are medically complex and these have a low rate of success. They also raise complex questions, emotionally and ethically. We know comparatively little about the ways in which people cope with infertility investigations and, if investigations are successful, with the ensuing pregnancy and bringing up of children. Many people who miscarry or experience infertility go on to become parents and we might predict that how they parent may be influenced by their reproductive histories. Children born to parents who experienced reproductive problems might be viewed as special and brought up differently from those children whose conceptions and births are more straightforward. But it may be that once people become parents, reproductive difficulties fade into insignificance as they cope with the day to day activities of childcare (Pfeffer and Woollett, 1983).

Those who do not become parents have to come to terms with the losses involved. This process is similar in many respects to bereavement as people mourn the lost opportunity to form a close relationship with a child and the loss of an identity they had hoped to acquire through parenting. As part of their adjustment, childless men and women cope with the negative stereotype associated with childlessness in our society and their nonconformity to societal norms which value parenting as an essential part of normal adult development. A major task for those with reproductive problems is finding a positive identity for themselves in the face of negative stereotypes of childlessness (Phoenix *et al.*, in press).

Artificial Insemination by Donor (AID)

The oldest and one of the simplest reproductive technologies is artificial insemination by donor (AID). This is used when a man is infertile to enable his wife or partner to conceive. Any child then born to the parents has its mother's but not its father's genes. The woman carries and gives birth to the child which the couple care for and bring up. The major adjustment for parents whose children are conceived with AID is that the father is not genetically linked to the child. He is however the social father; he can be involved in the pregnancy and can be present at the child's birth as well as participating in the child's upbringing. The physical growth and development of children is not considered to be at risk because of the ways in which they were conceived (Haimes, 1989). However, the psychological significance for parents and children of conception as a result of AID has not been investigated. The major negative impact for children conceived through AID and for their parents may result from their recognition of the differences between them and children in conventional families, especially if they hear about their conception in stressful circumstances (Humphrey and Humphrey, 1988; Pfeffer and Woollett, 1983; Rowland, 1985; Stanworth, 1987).

In Vitro Fertilization (IVF)

In the last two decades, a number of other techniques have been developed which allow some infertile women to have children. The best known of these is 'in vitro fertilization' (IVF). The first IVF (or test-tube) baby was born in 1978. IVF was developed to bypass a woman's infertility resulting from blocked Fallopian tubes. The procedure for IVF is as follows. Ova or eggs are obtained from the woman. To do this the maturation of the ova is carefully monitored, using hormone assays, and when they are thought to be about to rupture from the ovaries (ovulation), they are removed surgically. The ova are then mixed with the sperm (conception) and if the eggs develop and begin to divide, a number are placed inside the woman's uterus (implantation). It is common to implant more than one fertilized egg in the hope of increasing the chances of establishing a pregnancy. Replacing a large number of eggs increases the effectiveness of IVF, but it also increases the likelihood of multiple pregnancies. Twins and other multiples are associated with higher mortality rates and other complications of pregnancy and birth and they present parents with considerable problems with childcare. Caring for two, three or more babies is a substantial drain on parents' energies and on family resources (Botting *et al.*, 1990). Because IVF is a difficult process, there is a high chance of failure at every stage, making it a stressful procedure psychologically as well as medically (Crowe, 1987; Stanworth, 1987). IVF enables a woman who could not do so otherwise to conceive and give birth to a baby which carries her own and her partner's genes. It is not clear what are the effects, if any, of the stress involved in the conception and subsequent pregnancy on parents' relationship with the child or their adjustments to being parents.

Surrogacy

More recently surrogacy has emerged as another 'alternative' form of family building. Here one woman contracts to carry and give birth to a child for another woman. The surrogate mother gives birth to the child who is then brought up by the receiving parents. In some respects surrogacy is similar to adoption except that the agreement between the surrogate and receiving mother is made prior to the child's conception rather than after the birth. Usually the child shares some of the receiving parents' genes but is carried by and borne to another woman. There are different versions of surrogacy: the surrogate mother may conceive using insemination with the receiving father's sperm or even have introduced an embryo fertilized in vitro from the receiving mother's egg and the receiving father's sperm (Stanworth, 1987).

Adoption

A common form of alternative family building is adoption, when children are brought up by people who did not conceive or give birth to them. Adoption is a way of creating families and of normalizing children and adults who do not fit neatly into conventional family patterns (Haimes and Timms, 1985). In the past especially, it was a way of overcoming infertility and providing illegitimate children with families. Adoption usually happened soon after children were born, but older children who would otherwise be brought up in care are now being adopted as well.

Psychological interest in adoption has concentrated largely on the development of adopted children and especially the ways in which their development provides information about the relative influence of genetic and environmental factors and the role of early experience. Because there are no genetic links between adoptive parents and their children, their development has been compared with that of children reared in conventional families where there are both environmental and genetic links between parents and children. In addition adopted children have little opportunity for establishing contacts with their mothers in the first hours or weeks of their lives. As a result, those who argue that such early relations are crucial for development consider that the capacity of adopted children (and especially those adopted after infancy) for close relationships may be compromised. Such approaches have tended to ignore other features of the adoption experience for children and parents which may have an impact on parents' relations with their adopted children and their children's development. In particular they fail to take account of the stressful events and disrupted relationships children may have experienced before they are adopted (Tizard, 1977).

Adoptive parents often decide to adopt because they are unable to have their 'own' children. They may be distinguished from children's biological parents in a number of ways: they tend to be older, are more likely to be middle-class and, because of the efforts they have made to have a family, they may have a greater commitment to parenting. But at the same time their confidence in their parenting skills may have been undermined by their infertility. Their anxieties about their parenting skills may have been increased by the stress of the adoption procedures which involve in-depth questioning about their lives and relationships. Parents may be concerned about the reactions of others to the adoption and whether grandparents and other family members will readily accept and love an adopted child. They may also have fears about the children's background and parentage and the impact this might have on their development.

Studies of adoptive parents and adopted children, such as that of Raynor (1980), suggest that adoption is frequently successful. Even when there are problems, conflicts and disappointments, parents' and children's feelings about the adoption tend to be positive. Satisfaction with the adoption is greater when parents and children feel there are similarities between them. These include whether they look alike, whether their temperaments are similar and whether or not they have shared interests. Such factors may be related to how well parents and children in conventional families get on together but comparisons of conventional families and those with adopted children do not examine this issue.

In general the long-term development of adopted children is satisfactory. This is especially true of children adopted before age 2 years, although boys are rated as giving more concern and experiencing more problems than girls. The intellectual development of children adopted early is similar to that of other children. Any problems children might experience at the time of the adoption, seem to be more than compensated for by the stability and the quality of the environment provided by their adoptive families. On measures of social development and emotional well-being, however, adopted children do less well than their contemporaries (Lambert and Streather, 1980). This suggests that emotional well-being may be more susceptible to the stresses of the adoption process.

Tizard (1977) has studied the longer-term development of two groups of older children who had spent time in institutions before being adopted later, the first group between the ages of 2 and 4 and the second between the ages of 4 and 7. Children in the first group were visited shortly after the adoption when they were 4½ years old, at age 8 and again at age 16. They were compared with children who had lived in the same institutions but were returned to their families. By age 8, children who were adopted between ages 2 and 4 had good relations with their adopted parents and performed better on intellectual tasks than the children who were restored to their families. As in the Lambert and Streather study, there was some concern about children's emotional well-being. At age 4½ there was little evidence of behaviour problems, although children seemed to be adult-centred rather than peer-centred and did not demonstrate the usual reticence about approaching strangers. At age 8 children had some problems at school; they tended to be fidgety and disobedient, found it difficult to settle and were less popular with other children than their classmates.

The fact that adopted children were doing better than children restored to their families probably reflects the greater commitment of the adoptive parents. It suggests that putting a child into a family may not be sufficient to ensure their emotional well-being and intellectual development and points to the value of commitment on the part of parents. However, Tizard's study suggests that even when parents are supportive and highly committed, adopted children may still experience difficulties in their relationships with adults outside the family and with children at school. These findings are similar to those reported in Sweden by Bohman and Sigvardsson (1985). To evaluate the full effects of adoption, adopted children need also to be compared with those who remain in institutional care or are brought up in foster homes.

The second group of children studied by Tizard (1977) were adopted later still, between the ages of 4 and 7 years. They were still doing well, but not as well as children adopted earlier. There was less evidence of the intellectual improvement noted in those adopted at a younger age (Hodges and Tizard, 1989a; 1989b). Hodges and Tizard (1989a) suggest that one explanation of this is that later adopted children had less opportunity for establishing close relationships with parents before they went to school. Some of the later adopted children may also have experienced greater problems because of the disruptions in their lives including the breaking of established ties with foster parents or staff in the institution when they were adopted. They may therefore have come to their adoptive families with some confusion and anxiety about themselves and their families of origin. Children who are adopted later may also have a different understanding of what is happening. When children are adopted as small babies their awareness of their adoption comes gradually and in the context of their adopted family. Children adopted at a later age have clearer understandings of what adoption entails and the complications it may bring. Another issue which has been examined is the way in which adopted children form a clear and positive sense of themselves, especially given the negative assumptions and expectations associated with adoption. As Haimes and Timms (1985) suggest, adoption is a marginal status. Adopted children are at the edge of certain social boundaries and may think of themselves and be treated by others as different or deviant. Finding out about their natural parents and how they came to be adopted may be one way in which they can build up their history or life story and create a sense of themselves which includes their early lives.

Overall, there is evidence to suggest that the adoption of children before they are 2 and possibly before they are 7 years can be very successful with children leading an emotionally and intellectually satisfactory life. It certainly suggests that, while all efforts should be made to find a home for children as soon as possible, that because a child comes into care late that it is not 'too late' for them to benefit from adoption. These findings also question assumptions about the critical nature of close mother-child relations in the early months of life.

Transracial Adoption

In the late 1960s a number of transracial adoption schemes were set up in which black and mixed race children were adopted by white parents. This was seen as a way of giving children a home at a time when black parents could not be found to adopt children. These adoptions were closely monitored to assess their success and the development of children's identity. In general terms the adoptions were successful. Children, siblings and parents said they got along together well, children could confide in their parents and they all enjoyed family life (Gill and Jackson, 1983). In terms of children's racial identity the position was less clear cut. Many children lived in white areas and had therefore little opportunity for contact with children from their own ethnic community. Few children had clear positive racial identities nor were they very interested in exploring such issues, although this was not seen as a problem by children or parents. However it has been suggested that as children grow up and look for jobs and accommodation and form close relationships outside their families, children adopted into white families may find themselves less prepared for the racism they encounter.

Because of such concerns adoption policy has changed and adoption agencies now make greater efforts to find adoptive homes which more closely match children's ethnic backgrounds. This may be especially important for children who are adopted after infancy and hence have a sense of their ethnic identity before they are adopted. Children adopted into families of similar ethnicity are more likely to meet children and young people from their own community in their schools and neigbourhood and to have access to information about their culture.

While transracial adoptions set up within the UK and the USA are now unusual, children are adopted from abroad. This practice has a long history in countries like Sweden where there have always been few babies for adoption and in the USA where mixed race US-Vietnamese babies were brought to the USA to be adopted at the end of the Vietnam war. Currently adoptive parents travel to countries like India or Columbia where war and poverty mean that some mothers will give up their babies for adoption. Children adopted from abroad are removed from their culture of origin and so later may have very little opportunity to find out about their natural parents. They may also have less opportunity to find out about their own culture compared with children adopted by white parents in the USA or the UK.

Issues Raised about Parenting

The numbers of families created by adoption and these 'medical' forms of family building are relatively small. In 1988 the number of children born in the UK was 780,000. This compares with about 1,000 babies and 4,000 older children who were adopted, about 1,200 born as a result of IVF and probably twice as many conceived through AID (Humphrey and Humphrey, 1988; OPCS, 1989). However, partly because they involve new and contentious issues, these forms of family building have generated considerable discussion and even legislation. They raise a multitude of ethical and moral questions about the control of reproduction and the process of family building. Parents' or would-be parents' attitudes to these different forms of family building vary as do those of people in a position to influence and control their use and availability, such as politicians, judges, bishops, doctors and social workers. When children are conceived, born and brought up in conventional families, parenting is seen largely as a private matter. However, alternative forms of family building bring private behaviour into the public arena and make it clear that parenting and having children is not just an issue for individuals but for the wider society as well. The opportunity to become a parent through adoption, AID or IVF is tightly controlled and is available only to those who fit society's ideas of what constitutes good parents (Haimes, 1989). This means heterosexual couples, married or in stable long-term relationships, who are not too old (sometimes this is defined as 35 or 40 for women, but often older for men). This scrutiny is then justified in terms of what society thinks is an appropriate context for the creation of families and the upbringing of children (Phoenix *et al.*, in press).

These forms of family building also raise for psychologists important issues about parenting and about children and their psychological development. They encourage discussion of beliefs and ideas which are often firmly held about what constitutes a 'proper' family and what children need for development. These are interesting and important questions, but it is possible only to guess at the impact of some ways of family building because society has been concerned with the legalities rather than their psychological implications for parents and children. As a result, there has been very little research and so we have little information. Some of the psychological issues are outlined here.

Parenting as Genetic Inheritance

With conventional families, children carry the genes of both parents. Genetic inheritance provides some parents with a sense of continuity and commitment to the future in their children. This continuity is sometimes expressed in terms of carrying on the family name and is hence related to some parents' preferences for at least one boy. One attraction of procedures such as IVF is that the children conceived are genetically related to their parents. With other forms of family building, the genetic link between parents and children may be partially or completely broken. With adoption, for example, there is not usually a genetic link between parents and children. Their relationship is built entirely on the caring and concern which adoptive parents have for their children and on their children's response to that caring.

With step-parenting, with AID, and often with surrogacy there are some genetic links between parents and children. Stepchildren are related genetically to one but not to both of the parents involved in their day to day care. Children conceived through AID have their mother's but not their father's genes and in surrogacy the usual position is for children to have the father's but not the mother's genes. Sometimes it is argued that this is a preferable arrangement than adoption because parents will be more committed to taking good care of a child who is partially 'theirs' than one with whom there is no genetic link. However, there is an imbalance between the two parents in their genetic closeness to the child and this is sometimes seen as an issue for parents (Humphrey and Humphrey, 1988; Schaffer, 1986).

Early Experience

A difference between adoption and AID and IVF is that the mother carries and gives birth to the child conceived by AID and IVF. For some mothers carrying and giving birth to a child are important aspects of their identity as mothers and their relationships with their children. They also allow parents to participate in some of the activities which characterize the transition to parenthood in our society. The significance of the mother-child relationship before and immediately after birth is reinforced by psychological and medical conceptualizations of 'bonding' and early attachment. Close physical contact between mother and child is often linked with, if not given as a precondition for, their psychological attachment and the development of social relationships with one another, in spite of the lack of evidence (Rutter, 1981; Svejda *et al.*, 1980).

Those who become parents without giving birth have to come to terms with their difference from conventional families. Parents who adopt older children have also to adjust to coming late into their children's lives. This may mean accepting that their children have had experiences and relationships which parents cannot share. Adopting a child later in life may seem more difficult because of current beliefs and ideas about the primacy of early experience. In conventional families it is not possible to isolate the effects of early and later experiences. There is therefore little evidence to support beliefs about the overwhelming significance of early as distinct from later experience but such ideas continue to be widely articulated (Clarke and Clarke, 1976). When such ideas are seen as important, parents who do not have the opportunity to get to know their children in the early months may be anxious about whether they can form close relationships with one another.

[handwritten note overlapping text: "idea of family split, no being able to have children or another mother etc... only daughters. or divorcing — impact on child. Some religions do not require divorce / marriage"]

... ns between parents, provid-
... nt and as a gift which one
... out children as a physical
... with one another (Phoenix
... building mean that parents
... their own or do not result
... another. IVF is the only
... woman clearly has 'their'
... perm are brought together
... -parenting the child more
... s child. On the other hand,
... believe that the process of
... procedures is evidence of
... which results from such
... ollett, 1983). Whether or
... is genetically linked to parents, parents share the bringing up and looking after of children. They are accepted as parents by other people and acquire a position within the community and their wider family, as they make parents into grandparents and sisters into aunts and so on.

Secrets in the Family

The stigma of infertility and illegitimacy has meant that parents whose families were built in these different ways often remained silent about their children's origins. Even though attitudes have relaxed somewhat, parents often fear the reactions and the curiosity of others and so prefer to remain silent about how their families have been formed (Pfeffer and Woollett, 1983). Sometimes the differences between families built by alternative means and those built in conventional ways are obvious and cannot be hidden, such as when parents adopt an older child or a child from a different ethnic community. But in other cases the differences are less obvious. With AID and IVF, for instance, children are born to their mothers and information about their conception is not generally public knowledge, so families can, if they wish, 'pass' as conventional families and the secret can remain hidden (Haimes, 1989).

Keeping secrets has both advantages and disadvantages. The advantages centre around maintaining the appearance of a conventional family. In this way parents feel that they are like others and that they can keep their heads up in respectable society. But maintaining secrets can be costly in psychological terms. Energy goes into hiding rather than dealing with issues and avoiding situations where the truth might be revealed. When secrecy is maintained people never have the opportunity to talk to other people and obtain support. But information may surface at difficult or stressful times to be thrown at children or parents. And it is rare for a secret to be really hidden. Anxieties expressed to neighbours about fertility problems may raise suspicions when a woman does become pregnant and the arrival of an adopted baby rarely goes unnoticed. When family or friends have some information, there is always the worry that they will disclose or raise children's suspicions about their origins (Haimes and Timms, 1985; Humphrey and Humphrey, 1988).

The advantages of secrecy have to be balanced against children's rights to know about their origins and the costs of their discovering such information under distressing circumstances. Partly to prevent this, with adoption it is current policy to be open with children about their origins and their biological parents and to encourage them to obtain any information they feel is important to them for their identity or sense of themselves. But with the reproductive technologies the advice given to parents is not to disclose such information and often parents have little information to give (Haimes, 1989; Rowland, 1985). Secrets are not, of course, just an issue for families built in unconventional ways. There are secrets in many families who work hard to keep them hidden. These can include children being conceived before marriage or extra-maritally, domestic violence or child abuse. With step-parenting, secrets may centre around the discord in the family prior to divorce, or relations with the non-custodial parent.

In Conclusion

We have indicated some of the unconventional or alternative ways in which families are created and the adjustments parents make. These alternative family forms are here to stay and as Schaffer (1986) argues need to be considered by psychologists studying children and their development. Some, such as IVF, will always remain a minority form, whereas being step-parented or being brought up in a family headed by a single parent are likely to become a more usual part of growing up. In addition, children may experience several family forms throughout their lifetime. The child conceived through IVF, for example, may go on to experience conventional family life but also divorce and step-parenting. Alternative family forms encourage psychologists and others to recognize the different aspects of parenting and family life which go together in conventional families but are becoming increasingly fragmented. In this way we can examine the relative influence of different aspects of parenting for parents and children.

Further Reading

BRODZINSKY, D.M. and SCHECHTER, M.D. (Eds) (1990) *Psychology of Adoption*, Oxford, Oxford University Press.

An up-to-date account of research predominantly from the USA which considers the adjustment and adoption experience of adoptive children and parents. Chapters consider issues such as identity, inter-racial adoptions and the experience of birth mothers.

HAIMES, E. and TIMMS, N. (1985) *Adoption, Identity and Social Policy: The Search for Distant Relatives*, Aldershot, Gower.

The experiences of adults adopted as children as they search for their families of origin are described. The questions such searching raises are discussed. These include people's attempts to construct their life history, their feelings of being different and their sense of themselves as adopted children. Searching means adoptees (and often their adopted and birth parents) acknowledging and coming to terms with the knowledge of the adoption, a status usually viewed as marginal and hence to be kept secret.

HERSOV, L. (1990) 'The seventh Jack Tizard Memorial Lecture: Aspects of adoption', *Journal of Child Psychology and Psychiatry*, **31**, pp. 493–510.

Changes in adoption practices over the last two decades and the outcomes of adoption are evaluated. Because older children and children with experiences of deprivation, abuse, neglect, and institutionalization are being adopted in larger numbers than was the case in the past, more adopted children are likely to be seen as having problems. This does not necessarily mean that adoption is not a good way of caring for children, but suggests that such issues need to be more fully considered.

STANWORTH, M. (Ed.) (1987) *Reproductive Technologies: Gender, Motherhood and Medicine*, Cambridge, Polity Press.

A series of essays in which different kinds of reproductive technologies (such as artificial insemination by donor, in vitro fertilization and surrogacy) are examined and their implications for women who experience such treatment and for ideas about motherhood are assessed.

TIZARD, B. (1977) *Adoption: A Second Chance*, London, Open Books.

The findings of a study of children adopted from institutions between the ages of 2 and 7 are presented and are used to evaluate psychological ideas about adoption and about the reversibility of effects of early experience.

Chapter 4

Mothers and Children

Infants are physically immature and vulnerable. For their survival they need to be cared for and protected. In our society the bulk of this caring is provided by mothers. The fact that babies and children are cared for primarily by mothers has implications for both children and mothers. Because they spend a considerable amount of their time together, mothers and children get to know one another very well and they develop close emotional ties. These ties, or attachment bonds, are a powerful source of personal gratification and identity for mothers. They provide an emotionally charged atmosphere in which children grow, develop and learn about the world.

Because psychological theories assume that mothers play the central role in their children's development, most research looks just at mothers. This research considers mothers' attitudes towards childcare as well as their behaviour and their relationships with their children. Studying mothers is popular on theoretical and practical grounds. Because mothers, rather than fathers or others, are at home with their children during the working day they make convenient research subjects. Restricting the number of people being studied to two minimizes the complexity of data collection and analysis. The cost of restricting research in this way is that it provides a limited view of the context in which mothers and children relate and in which children grow and develop. Research which takes a wider view and considers the child in the wider family context is discussed in Chapters 5 and 6.

Research has focused predominantly on younger children. Again this is a result of practical as well as theoretical considerations. Theoretically it is assumed that what happens in the early weeks and months of life is of key importance for later development, providing a foundation for later learning and development. Studies of adoption are amongst those which question assumptions about early experiences as determinants of later adjustments (see Chapter 3). Younger children are used in most studies. Once children go to school their interactions with mothers are less easy to study. Even though it is less frequently studied, the entry of children into the world beyond the family and children's establishment of relationships with people who are not part of their families may be important developmentally. Older children are discussed in Chapter 6.

In this chapter we look at work from a variety of theoretical approaches which uses different techniques to study mothers and children. Studies attempt to describe the nature and quality of mothers' relations with their children, often contrasting them with the relations mothers and children have with other people. Studies also consider individual differences in mothers' relations with children and try to relate them to individual differences in children's development. Individual differences in mothers' behaviour so identified are then used to define 'good' or 'good enough' mothering and mothering considered as non-optimal. The origins of such differences are sought in terms of child and maternal characteristics, and the circumstances in which mothers and children live, such as the involvement of fathers in childcare. However, mothering also takes place within a wider economic and cultural context, which defines expectations and values around motherhood and influences women's perceptions of themselves and their children (see Chapter 11). The society or culture in which women have and bring up children defines what is appropriate behaviour (Phoenix *et al.*, in press).

Attachment

Early accounts of mother-child relations, and in particular that of Bowlby (1969) stressed the intense emotional aspects of such relations and their developmental significance for young children. By the time they are 4 or 5 months old children know their caregivers and can distinguish them from others and by 7 or 8 months they show a strong preference for those they know and often protest when they are absent or when they depart. This happens because they have established close relationships or bonds. Attachment theory takes a monotropic approach, stressing the establishment of a bond with one figure, usually the mother, although there is evidence that young children do become attached to several people as the work with fathers and siblings makes clear (see Chapters 5 and 6). Schaffer and Emerson (1964), in a classic study, found that by 18 months almost all the children they examined were attached to at least one person other than their mothers and often to several. The most common alternative figures were fathers, with older children coming next. Even when it is recognized that children may be attached to several people, it is still often assumed that children's relationships with their mothers have special qualities which are not found in other relationships. Mothers are therefore seen as having a special responsibility for children's emotional development and mothers' absence from the home is seen as having very different consequences from fathers' absence (Scarr and Dunn, 1987).

The relationships between children and their attachment figures is built upon a developing repertoire of behaviours. These include, on the children's part, crying, smiling and babbling. These are signals which bring mothers (and other people) close, to which mothers respond and hence which ge[...] the interactive sequences between mothers and children. Wl[...] mothers smile back, expressing pleasure in their interactions[...]

the exchange. Smiling is a powerful signal resulting for mothers in a sense that they are good mothers and in warmth towards the child. In this way babies may elicit positive behaviour even when mothers are tired or their circumstances are difficult. Crying is equally effective as an elicitor of maternal behaviour. However, children who cry a great deal, while they capture their mothers' attention and get their needs met, may not reap the same benefits in terms of maternal warmth nor do they give mothers the same sense that they are doing well and are in tune with their children (Stern, 1977). As they get older, children maintain proximity in other ways including crawling after their mothers, following them and clinging to them, and later children's attachment can be expressed in other ways such as asking questions about where the mother is going or when she will return.

Attachments are built upon what children do and on the responses they receive from others. Ainsworth *et al.* (1974) argue that good relations and secure attachments result from mothers' sensitivity to children's signals and proximity-seeking behaviour. Mothers who respond quickly and appropriately to their babies' cries of hunger, discomfort and boredom have more satisfied and securely attached children. Mothers who are slow to respond or who do not read their babies' signals well tend to find it difficult to cooperate with the baby in routines around feeding, bathing etc. They seem awkward and out of step in the dance of social interaction (Stern, 1977). The children of such mothers seem to be less firmly attached. Ainsworth *et al.* (1974) suggest that about 65 per cent of middle-class US children are firmly attached to their mothers, with secure attachment being somewhat less common amongst children whose mothers are young or bringing up children on their own.

Secure attachments are considered to be important because they provide a safe base from which children can explore and learn about the world and in which they learn how to control their anxiety and stress. Attachment is seen to be significant in the short term, as a way of describing the current state of relations between mothers and children, and also in the longer term. It is important in the longer term because problems with attachment may have severe consequences; children who do not learn to trust and use their mothers as a secure base may have less confidence to explore and to engage in close relations with others (Bowlby, 1969).

Estimates of the security of children's attachments are usually based on their performance in a procedure known as the 'strange situation'. This puts children through a number of predetermined steps, designed to elicit anxiety and hence to encourage the display of their attachment behaviours. Children are brought into an unknown room and go through a sequence of comings and goings as mothers leave children on their own or with a stranger and as mothers return and are reunited with the children. Children's behaviour is noted and their security of attachment rated. This situation has been criticized for being unrelated to the everyday situations in which children find themselves and for failing to take into account children's previous experiences of separation. It also ignores the child's temperament, and it is sometimes argued that it is unclear whether attachment or children's temperament is being assessed. However, it continues to be used. This is in part because it is relatively easy to get different raters to agree on their judgments of children's attachment, making it a reliable measure. But it also has been shown to correlate with other measures of children's behaviour taken at the same time such as confidence in their home surroundings with their mother, a child-minder and an unfamiliar adult and also in the longer term. For example children who were securely attached as infants have better peer relations and perform better on problem-solving tasks later at school (Bretherton and Waters, 1985).

Attitudes to Childcare

A very different approach to mother-child relations is that which attempts to identify and measure parental attitudes towards childrearing or childcare. Research in this tradition considers how parents' (and usually mothers') attitudes may influence how they behave towards their children and their impact on children's development. Two kinds of attitudes or dimensions of childcare which emerge consistently from this research are the emotional relationship between mothers and children and how mothers control their children (Damon, 1983; Maccoby and Martin, 1983). The emotional relationship between mothers and children is usually classified as more or less accepting, warm, responsive or child-centred. Some mothers show greater warmth than others; they are more able or willing to show affection, they praise their children, accept their dependency or attachment needs and reason more with them. The second attitude concerning parental control is categorized as restrictive and demanding, permissive, or as giving autonomy to the child. Sears *et al.* (1957) found that permissive mothers, in contrast to more restrictive mothers, say that they are less concerned with issues such as good table manners, noise, neatness, obedience, aggression towards themselves and others, sexual play, and toilet training, and are less likely to use physical punishment.

Other investigators argue that we need to consider other parental attitudes or dimensions. Baumrind, for example, considers two further dimensions. These are clarity of parent-child communication (that is the openness of communication between parents and children, or the involvement of children in decision making and parents' willingness to give reasons for their disciplinary actions) and maturity demands (parental pressure to perform well) (Baumrind, 1967; Baumrind, 1973; Damon, 1983). From her research, Baumrind suggests that these dimensions cluster together to give three patterns of parental style which she labels authoritarian, authoritative and permissive. Most parents can be placed into one of these three categories.

Authoritarian parents are strict and controlling of their children's behaviour (high in control) and demand good performance from them (high in maturity demands). Their demands and restrictions are not discussed with children and few reasons are given (low in clarity of communication). When children deviate from the rules they are punished and parents show little warmth or affection (low in warmth).

Permissive parents (sometimes also labelled indulgent) take an accepting, tolerant attitude towards their children's impulses, including their sexual and aggressive impulses. They avoid asserting their authority or imposing controls or restrictions on their children's behaviour and they use little punishment (low in control). They also make few demands for mature behaviour, being fairly unconcerned about issues like table manners or polite behaviour (low on maturity demands). They prefer instead to allow children to regulate their own behaviour and make their own decisions as far as possible about issues such as bedtimes or watching television. Permissive parents tend to be moderately warm, although this can vary and some permissive parents are cool or uninvolved (moderate on warmth). Parental permissiveness often springs from a view of children as having self-centred impulses over which children have little control. In this respect permissive parents are similar to authoritarian parents. Authoritarian parents see such impulses as needing to be stamped out whereas permissive parents think that their free expression is healthy and desirable and are prepared to discuss these and other aspects of their childcare (high in clarity of communication).

Authoritative parents work on the assumption that parents have more knowledge and skill, can control resources and physically constrain their children if necessary and expect a fairly high degree of compliance and mature behaviour from their children (high in control, high in maturity demands). They tend not to be intrusive but are prepared to impose restrictions if they consider them to be necessary. Authoritative parents are also nurturant and respect their children's demands and points of view and are prepared to give their reasons for what they do or expect of their children (high in clarity of communication and high in nurturance). They believe that children are competent and should accept responsibility for their own actions.

Further information about parental style emerges from the research of Newson and Newson (1968). Mothers of 4-year-olds living in a Midlands town in the UK were interviewed about bringing up their children. For these mothers issues around compliance and control and their child-centredness were very salient. Compliance was salient because mothers' effectiveness is often judged on the basis of their children's good behaviour. Getting children to do as mothers want them to do recurs frequently in mothers' accounts. Mothers recognize the need to stay in control and to ensure that their children are reasonably obedient, but they also recognise the need to concede some autonomy to children by age 4. While over half (61 per cent) of mothers considered themselves to be easy-going, a substantial proportion (38 per cent) thought they were strict.

However, the interviews with mothers indicate that it is also necessary to consider the form of control mothers employ. Their choice of control technique is related to their beliefs about how control operates and their ideas of what is appropriate child behaviour (Goodnow, 1988). Some mothers consider that the use of physical or power assertive punishment is a valid way of controlling children and a necessary, if not an ideal, way of teaching them to respect the rights and possessions of others and the moral order of family life. Mothers who are prepared to employ smacking, shouting, forceful commands and threats tend to value compliance and obedience for its own sake. Other mothers use psychological forms of punishment such as threatening to withdraw love, praising, and reasoning with them. Reasoning is closely tied to an open style of communication in which the rules of behaviour are explained as well as why children are expected to conform. While such forms of control may seem less harsh, because they are based on personal knowledge of the child, their likes and dislikes and what has made children comply in the past, they are more effective than physical punishment (Becker, 1964; Walkerdine and Lucey, 1989).

Mothers' use of a particular style is related to a variety of factors. The use of reasoning requires that mothers believe that their children can understand what they are saying and that mothers are confident about talking an issue through. The pressures mothers are under may also influence their strategy. Mothers trying to clear up toys, prepare a meal and deal simultaneously with the demands of three children under 5 may use power assertive techniques (e.g. 'clear those toys up now because I say so'). On another occasion, the same but less harrassed mother may be prepared to negotiate with the children (e.g. 'OK, you can just finish that game and then you must clear up'). Mothers in different social circumstances, who have help with their children or a separate playroom, may not experience the same pressures and may, as a result, employ psychological strategies more frequently.

Another set of factors which needs to be considered are mothers' expectations, their perceptions and understandings of their children's behaviour and how strongly they feel about transgressions of particular rules (Goodnow, 1988). These ideas provide a structure for mothers' interactions with their children and their reactions to children's behaviour. Mothers with a strong sex role orientation, for example, respond negatively to aggression in their daughters which they perceive as inappropriate for girls but appropriate for boys (Bacon and Ashmore, 1985). Parents' reactions may also relate to their ideas about the causes of behaviour. For example, their reactions may depend on whether they think their children have behaved badly deliberately or whether they are ignorant of the rule they have broken. Behaviour perceived as wilful may elicit smacking whereas mothers may handle the accidental breaking of a rule by an explanation of what was correct behaviour (Dix *et al.*, 1986; 1989).

The other main dimension of maternal behaviour which Newson and Newson report with mothers of 4-year-olds is maternal responsiveness or child-centredness. By child-centredness they mean 'parents' recognition of the child's status as an individual with rights and feelings that are worthy of respect' (Newson and Newson, 1976: 312). Some mothers are more child-centred than others, with the proportion of mothers defined as child-centred depending to some extent on the questions asked. One question was about the extent to which mothers were ready to accept the child's reply that they were busy as a reason for not doing immediately what mothers wanted them to do. Over half (56 per cent) were willing to accept such a reply, if only temporarily, a further 13 per cent accepted but showed their disapproval of such reasons and the other one-third (31 per cent) said they insist on immediate obedience. When the question was about responsiveness to their children's demands for attention and affection, over two-thirds of mothers were rated as child-centred.

Relations between Parenting Styles and Development

Studies of childrearing attitudes are of interest because they point to ways in which mothers' behaviours towards their children differ. They also suggest how mothers may influence their children's development (for reviews see Damon, 1983; Maccoby and Martin, 1983). A warm, responsive relationship, a moderate amount of parental control and parental use of reasoning are associated with children's social and intellectual development. In Baumrind's study, authoritative parents were found to have children who were doing better on social, emotional and cognitive measures (instrumental competence). A parental mixture of a moderate amount of discipline, sensitivity to their children's needs but also demands for appropriately mature behaviour seemed to provide a context in which children developed self-esteem, competence, independence, resourcefulness, the motivation to do well, internalized control, an ability to engage peers and adults in a friendly and cooperative manner and popularity with peers. These effects continue into adolescence, especially for boys (Steinberg *et al.*, 1989).

In contrast, authoritarian parents tended to have children who were withdrawn, who did not take social initiatives, were less spontaneous, lacking achievement motivation and with low self-esteem, were shy and often uneasy around peers, and sometimes were aggressive and hostile. Children of authoritarian parents seemed to have little sense of their ability to control their environment and had, therefore, developed few positive strategies for doing so. These negative characteristics lasted into adolescence, especially for boys, their social and cognitive performance remained low and they lacked self-confidence in their relations with other young people (Maccoby and Martin, 1983). Children with permissive parents also tended to show low levels of instrumental competence, were aimless and impulsive with little self-reliance and self-control (Baumrind, 1967). The easy discipline and parents' acceptance of less mature behaviour provide a context in which children are not presented with clear expectations for behaviour and receive little feedback or reactions from parents about their social and intellectual performance.

Interestingly children with parents whose attitudes to parenting were very different, authoritarian and permissive, performed poorly on measures of instrumental competence. Baumrind (1973) suggests that while they may differ in their techniques of child management, both kinds of parents tend to shield their children from stress. Authoritarian parents do this by restricting children's activities and initiatives, with the result that children rarely encounter stressful events, and have little opportunity to learn how to deal with them. In contrast, permissive parents encourage their children to try out new activities. However, their parents' permissiveness means that children rarely have to cope with the consequences of their actions and hence they have less opportunity to learn how to deal with the negative reactions their behaviour elicits. In contrast to children experiencing these two types of parenting, children whose parents are authoritative are exposed to stressful events of their own making, but they are also expected to cope with the consequences of their actions. The problem solving skills they then develop enhance their self-esteem and promote more effective social interactive strategies.

Warm and moderately controlling parenting may be effective because children are encouraged to be compliant and to want to do what their parents say. When parents spend time with children and relations are close, children are more likely to discover what are the rules of behaviour and want to maintain their parents' approval. The threat of withdrawal of love is unlikely to be effective when there is not a great deal of contact or affection between parents and children. However, when parents respond to their children's individuality and allow them to take a part in decision making, children may develop a positive sense of themselves, a trust in others, and are motivated to behave well and to use others as a resource (Maccoby and Martin, 1983).

These studies point to ways in which parents' behaviour is associated with children's social and intellectual competence. However, we need to be cautious about assuming that it is parents' attitudes which are the cause of the results obtained. The studies are correlational and so the statistical links between children's and parental measures could come about for a number of reasons. Parents may behave as they say they do as a response to their children's behaviour rather than vice versa. Sears *et al.* (1957), for example, found that parents who were punitive tended to have children who were more aggressive. This could happen because when parents are very punitive, children learn that aggression is acceptable. Another explanation could be that when faced with very aggressive children parents tend to become more punitive. To know which of these, or other, explanations are most useful we need to consider how parents behave to other children in the family or to study families longitudinally to see which happens first, children's aggression or parents' punitiveness.

Observational Studies of Mother-Child Interaction

Studies of childrearing attitudes have been criticized because they focus on what parents say they do rather than on what they do. Parents may differ in the extent to which they reflect on what they do and can give accurate accounts. Studies which supplement interviews with behavioural measures find reasonable levels of consistency between the two kinds of measures (e.g. Baumrind, 1967; Dunn and Kendrick, 1982). Mothers' reports of their children's behaviour give us information about how mothers interpret and respond to their children's behaviour and what is considered to be appropriate behaviour for mothers and children in this society. Many of the assumptions and ideas about mothering developed in studies of mothers' attitudes subsequently informed observational studies. Through observation we can study

directly what is happening between mothers and children and come to understand the ways in which warmth, control, the clarity of communication and
maturity demands are translated into mothers' behaviour. Observations also
provide information about how mothers act as models or guides for their
children and how they facilitate the development of children's attachments
and instrumental competence.

Mothers' Behaviour with Young Children

Mothers' behaviour towards young children differs in a number of ways from
their behaviour to adults and older children. Stern (1977) noted a number of
distinctive aspects of mothers' behaviour to infants in the first six months. In
attracting and maintaining their infants' attention, mothers use exaggerated
facial expressions, with eyes wide open, eyebrows raised, and movements
which are slow to build up and are sustained for a long time. Mothers' speech
and vocalizations are also exaggerated, the pitch of their voice and their pace
are often extreme. Pauses between utterances tend to be long, they use many
repetitions, oohs and ahs and there is a high level of vocalizing together. This
'chorusing' is unusual in vocal exchanges with adults and older children and is
especially likely to occur with infants as interactions become more lively and
excited. Vocalizations are often accompanied by looking, again in contrast
with vocal exchanges with adults and older children where looking is limited
to brief glances or to the moments when the conversational 'turn' is handed
over to the other person. Mothers engage in prolonged mutual gazing with
young children and they tend to loom in very close. Infants can influence
their mothers' behaviour, encouraging interaction by smiling or gurgling as
mothers talk or by turning their heads away to avoid eye contact and prolonged stimulation (Maccoby and Martin, 1983; Schaffer and Crook, 1978).
Research demonstrates that mothers use the same signals with infants as they
use in their interactions with adults and older children to initiate, maintain
and terminate interactions. With infants, however, they have an exaggerated
quality which ensures they are easily perceived and contain little ambiguity.
This may serve to maximize the opportunities infants have to understand and
learn from what their mothers do.

During their second year children begin to talk and there is considerable
interest in the ways in which mothers and children use language to communicate with one another and influence one another's behaviour. Mothers'
language to children of this age uses a distinctive linguistic register, called
'motherese'. Mothers' language is short (about one-third of the length of the
utterances used to adults), it is simple and highly intelligible, with more
nouns, fewer verb forms, pronouns and embedded clauses than their language
to adults and older children. Mothers' pitch continues to be exaggerated and
their language is closely related to what children say, often responding to
children's utterances. Motherese is also very bossy, with a high proportion of
instructions and questions (Bates *et al.*, 1982; Power and Parke, 1986). Like
their behaviour to infants, mothers' language to 2-year-olds is structured in

ways which are likely to maximize children's understanding. Information is limited and expressed clearly and it is concerned with events and objects which are the focus of children's attention.

Modelling Behaviour

Interview and observational studies both point to mothers' provision of a model of appropriate behaviour. This may take the form of showing children how to label items, behave towards others or have a conversation. What mothers model depends on the age and competence of their children. As children's physical, social and language skills increase, they need to have different things modelled for them. What they need help with at one point may be well established three months later. In the first year infants point, look at objects and babble but these behaviour patterns are synchronized only towards the end of the second year. However, some months before this happens, mothers demonstrate synchronization in their own behaviour, pointing to objects as they label them, looking from the object to the child and back to the object. Mothers model the ways in which pointing can be used to draw attention to something of interest, and how pointing is more effective if it is accompanied by words (e.g. 'Look at this'). Mothers may also demonstrate how verbal and nonverbal aspects of communication go together. Mothers' verbal commands to younger children are more likely to be accompanied by nonverbal signals such as pointing which reduce the ambiguity of a complex message (Schaffer and Crook, 1978).

As children begin to talk, mothers model language for them, supplying them with information about relevant vocabulary, how language is segmented and how to build up sentences. They do this by repeating utterances in slightly modified ways or explaining things and talking to children using language which is slightly beyond the child's present level of competence. They encourage children to talk, to practise their vocabulary, to acquire new rules and express themselves appropriately. They ask questions to prompt children into talking, repeating and elaborating what children say and encouraging them to go beyond their present linguistic repertoire (e.g. Bates *et al.*, 1982; Kruper and Uzgiris, 1987). They encourage children to have conversations, by putting ideas into context and explaining what they are doing (Dunn, 1988; Goodsitt *et al.*, 1988). In their conversations with 4-year-olds, for example, mothers give children information about family members, family relationships, baby care and development and domestic matters, all in the context of ongoing family activities, imaginative play and story telling (Tizard and Hughes, 1984).

Sensitivity and Responsiveness

Observational studies have expanded ways of thinking about mothers' relations with their children by emphasizing the role of sensitivity or responsiveness. They show how mothers modify or time their behaviour in ways which are sensitive to their children's abilities, interests and moods. Mothers' behaviour with infants varies according to the infants' current activity. While their babies are feeding, mothers tend to remain inactive, but once they stop feeding, mothers begin to talk to infants and jig them up and down (Kaye, 1982). Mothers look at and talk to their infants when there is mutual gazing but their behaviour is slowed down when their infants look away (Stern, 1977). Mothers' behaviour also changes as children become more competent and take a more active role in social exchanges. Mothers of 24-month-olds allow children to regulate the topic of conversation more than mothers of 15-month-olds (Schaffer and Crook, 1978). Mothers ask more questions and request more information and contributions from children as they get older. In addition, what counts as an appropriate answer changes. For example, a mother who is prepared to accept as appropriate 'moo' or 'woof woof' when her child is 21 months may, six months later, expect the child to give a label, to correct themselves when they make a mistake and to contribute more actively to the conversation. Mothers take children's answers and position into account but increasingly expect children to consider mothers' viewpoints, moods and interests to wait for a 'good' moment or to find ways of making what they want to do interesting to mothers. The nature of mothers' conversations changes with their children's age and increasing linguistic skills. For example, when mothers read books to 18-month-old children, they concentrate on supplying labels for the pictures, at 2½ years they ask children questions about the pictures, such as the name of objects ('What is this?', 'What does a cat say?'). With children of 3 years and older they put the pictures into the wider context of other similar objects and the child's specific experience ('Do you remember we saw one at the zoo?') (Goodsitt *et al.*, 1988).

Wachs and Gruen (1982) in a review of studies of mother-child interactions suggest that different aspects of mothers' behaviour are associated with children's development at different ages. Infants up to the age of 6 months need visual contact and stimulation, but from 6 to 12 months social stimulation and interaction are more important. From 12 to 24 months responsiveness to children's social signs, verbal stimulation and encouragement of their exploration are linked to development. From 24 to 36 months it is responsiveness to children's verbal signals and from 36 to 48 months interaction with a variety of people and continued responsiveness to social signals and language which have greatest developmental significance. Their analysis suggests that the constituents of good mothering are various and ever changing but that mothers' sensitivity to children's interests and competence is an enduring theme. Sensitive mothers are seen to sustain their children's interest in topics, by changing or modifying their behaviour and their strategies to match their children's increasing competence.

Sensitivity is often viewed as the key feature of mothers' behaviour. It is commonly used to distinguish mothers as in Ainsworth *et al.*'s (1974) work on attachment and by psychologists working in a more cognitive tradition, e.g. Schaffer and Crook (1978) and Stern (1977). Being treated sensitively is seen as enabling children to trust others, acquire a sense of control over their environment and become cognitively competent. This approach is summarized by Belsky:

> In brief, it is sensitive mothering, evidencing appropriate responsiveness to infant cues, that appears to foster optimal development.... These findings strengthen the argument that sensitivity is THE influential dimension of mothering in infancy: it not only fosters healthy psychological functioning during this developmental epoch, but it also lays the foundation on which future experience will build. (Belsky, 1981: 8)

To be responsive and provide children with models and appropriate support for their level of competence, interests and preferences, mothers need to know their children well so they can 'read' effectively their children's cues. This degree of sensitivity requires that mothers and children spend considerable time around one another. As it is mothers, rather than fathers or others, who spend most time caring for young children, it is perhaps not surprising, therefore, that sensitivity and responsiveness are postulated as powerful mechanisms by which children's development is fostered by mothers. This contrasts with assumptions about the value of insensitivity and unpredictability in accounts of the influence of fathers and siblings (see Chapters 5 and 6).

Demands for Competence or Compliance

Research on attitudes to parenting and Baumrind's analysis of authoritative parental strategies stressed parental control and their demands for competence or mature behaviour. Sensitivity and child-centredness, while important, were viewed as only a part of the complex mix of behaviours which facilitate development. Sensitivity is a key factor in the early months, but as children get older and become more competent, they are more likely to resist their parents' suggestions and attempt to assert their own preferences and independence (Kuczynski *et al.*, 1987). In observational studies of 3-to-5-year-olds and in mothers' accounts of bringing up children of this age, issues around compliance and conflict become more salient at this age. Mothers are concerned to have cooperative children who perform well. They expect children to use words rather than gestures and pointing, to obey family rules such as having good table manners, saying please and thank you and waiting their turn, to play well with others and share toys and to ask for things without whining, to work at tasks, to hold conversations and answer questions intelligently, and to be independent and not to complain when they are left with others (Boulton, 1983; Newson and Newson, 1968; Tizard and Hughes, 1984; Phoenix *et al.*, in press).

Encouraging children's competence means sometimes viewing children's performance as inadequate and pushing them to do better. This may entail not being prepared to work at making sense of children's noises or to understand their viewpoint, or resisting requests for assistance. Tizard and Hughes (1984) and Dunn (1988) point to the ways in which confrontations between mothers and children may provide means to encourage competence. Tizard and Hughes (1984) studied the conversations between mothers and their 4-year-old daughters in their homes. These covered a wide range of topics and served a variety of functions. About 14 per cent of their conversations were concerned with control. Two topics were most likely to trigger conflicts. One was waste and damage (e.g. 'Don't spill it.', 'Be careful you don't break it.') and the other was manners, including table manners and children saying please and thank you. Families varied in the numbers of disputes observed. In some families between one-third and a half of the conversations contained at least one dispute whereas in others less than 5 per cent involved a dispute. During disputes mothers provided children with information about the physical and social world and about how to operate within it. In the course of one dispute about a broken bicycle, the mother told her daughter (a) about relative sizes by talking about how big children are too heavy to ride on small children's bikes, (b) about taking decisions for herself and not letting other children boss her around, (c) about mending bikes being man's work and finally (d) about how to persuade an unwilling father to mend the bike (Tizard and Hughes, 1984: 91). In about 60 per cent of the disputes observed, Tizard and Hughes (1984) found that mothers gave explanations; and they found that all mothers sometimes justified their demands or their refusal to comply with children's requests. In this way disputes provide children with opportunities for learning.

Dunn (1988) takes up this point in her analysis of disputes between mothers and 2 and 3 year olds and looks at the ways in which children are presented with information about their social world:

> Our conversational analyses show that the social rules of the world in which the children were growing up were continually discussed by their mothers: discourse on what was acceptable, what unacceptable, surrounded them, and these were conversations in which they were encouraged to take part.... This is a centrally important point. The moral order of their parents' world was conveyed to the children again and again in the repeated events of their daily lives. The messages, implicit in the emotional behaviour of the mother, explicit in her words, were about the moral concepts of the culture — messages in a deeply effective form. (Dunn, 1988: 73)

The moral issues discussed include the rights of others (who owns a toy, about taking turns, about letting someone join in a game) and also the basis on which people may be exempted from general rules (e.g. because they are tiny and therefore are not expected to eat their dinner properly or do not understand about taking turns). As children grow older, they increasingly come to use such rules to get their own way and to resist mothers' attempts to apply rules.

Highly Charged Emotional Atmosphere

As these accounts of confrontations indicate, mother-child relations are highly charged emotionally. Mothers restrict their children's activities and ignore their wishes, curbing their expressions of emotions and making them fit into adult routines. Children are frustrated by their mothers' constraints and at having to wait for things and may shout, scream and burst into tears if they cannot do what they want. Mothers get irritated by children's continuous demands, their refusals to do as they are asked and children's intrusions into adult activities (Boulton, 1983; Newson and Newson, 1968). Mothers and children also show one another a great deal of love and affection; their children's warmth, love and company are major sources of pleasure and interest for mothers. Their relationships are more intensively emotional than those between children and their teachers, childminders or providers of institutional care (Tizard, 1977; Tizard and Hughes, 1984).

A number of studies point to the benefits of an emotional context for learning. Mothers' willingness to accept their young children's emotions and to support their fears and anxieties may help children to understand their own and other people's feelings. Through experiencing their mothers' empathy and understanding, children learn that their viewpoints and feelings are acknowledged, are of interest and can form the basis of joint activity (Belsky *et al.*, 1984b; Walkerdine and Lucey, 1989). When mothers are tolerant of and willing to accept negative emotional behaviour, such as temper tantrums and food fads, and respond positively to their children's emotional distress, children are more socially sensitive (Roberts and Strayer, 1987). Reasoning is more effective as a strategy when mothers use emotional terms and let children know how they feel. Expressing their annoyance when children do not conform and their approval of altruistic behaviour seems to help children understand and make use of moral rules and conventions (Johnson and McGillicuddy-Delisi, 1983).

Mothers' expression of their feelings and their support for children's emotional expression may assist children's development of concepts about themselves and others. The expression of mixed emotions in someone to whom children are attached may provide a model of a person who has both good and bad qualities and may demonstrate that children are loved and valued even when they behave badly (Newson and Newson, 1968). This may help children to build up an understanding of themselves and others as complex and multi-dimensional people who act according to mood and situational factors (Damon, 1983). The highly charged emotional context of mother-child interactions may facilitate the development of understanding and demonstrates the close links between social, emotional and cognitive aspects of development.

Mothers' Influence on Development

Mothers' behaviour can influence their children in a number of ways. Mothers provide a model of competent behaviour and articulate the rules underlying behaviour. These are matched more or less sensitively and appropriately to children's competence. Mothers also make demands for competent or mature behaviour. Achieving the goals set by their mothers and being warmly approved for doing so may build up children's confidence in themselves and their ability to control their worlds. Mothers' sensitivity and responsiveness are associated with the development of cognitive and linguistic skills in their children, especially when combined with warmth and high expectations of their competence. These effects are demonstrated on a wide range of tasks, including intelligence tests, egocentricity and social sensitivity, language development and the understanding of social and moral rules (for reviews see Bates *et al.*, 1982; Belsky *et al.*, 1984b; Maccoby and Martin, 1983; Wachs and Gruen, 1982).

Mothers' influence operates through the close emotional ties they have with children. In this way children learn to trust, to gain a sense of themselves as able to control important people and events. They learn to be compliant, to relate to and operate successfully within their social worlds (Damon, 1983; Lay *et al.*, 1989). Trust and a positive self-image may enable children to learn from their experiences. Children who are poorly attached, who are fearful and anxious, may find it difficult to explore, to respond to initiatives and use people and events to further their own understanding and get their needs met. Such children, in turn, may elicit less stimulating, interested or sensitive behaviour from mothers and others.

Individual Differences amongst Mothers

There are considerable variations in mothers' behaviour toward their children and in their sensitivity. Mothers' behaviour may vary from hour to hour or day to day, according to how tired they are or the number of demands on their time and attention. But there are more stable variations which result from a wide variety of factors. These include mothers' personality or sex role orientation, their preferred interactional strategies, their confidence as mothers, and their current state including whether or not they are unwell or depressed (Baumrind, 1982). Children's gender, health, temperament and age also influence mothers' behaviour. Caring for a small and demanding baby makes different demands of mothers than caring for children who are older, more competent and more independent (Belsky *et al.*, 1984b; Pianta *et al.*, 1989). There is a considerable number of family variables which influence mothers' behaviour which are discussed in other chapters. These include whether or not mothers are bringing the child up on their own, their relationship with the child's father and the adjustments they are both making to
nds of children, whether they have a strong support network,
here are other children in the family, whether or not mothers are
outside the home, and cultural attitudes towards children.

Individual differences in mothers' behaviour have been considered from two perspectives. The first, which has been discussed, is how variability in mothering is experienced by children and what impact it has on their development. The second is how women experience motherhood and the influence of this on their relationships with their children. Women's experience of motherhood has received little attention from psychologists and therefore psychology has little to say about the variations in women's experiences, how these may be explained and how they may influence women's behaviour towards their children. There is however, some evidence about how mothers view motherhood (Phoenix *et al.*, in press). For many mothers the early months of motherhood are both exhilarating and potentially stressful. Kitzinger (1978) gives a graphic account of the daily life of mothers with young children and the repetitive and relentless quality of childcare as feeding, changing, bathing and tidying up follow one another in endless succession. The work of child-care brings mothers new responsibilities for their children's welfare (Antonis, 1981; Busfield, 1987). Women's reactions to this vary as Llewelyn and Osborne (1990) indicate:

> Whilst for some care-givers, responding to the needs of young children is delightful, if exhausting work, which enables them to get in touch with the nurturing they received as infants and to identify with the baby. For others, it is a frightening time of feeling overwhelmed by a complex bundle of demands which do not make sense and cannot be satisfied. (Llewelyn and Osborne, 1990: 174–5)

Variations in mothers' reactions have been studied by Boulton (1983). She interviewed mothers of preschool children who were living with fathers and whose financial circumstances were relatively comfortable. She found that a substantial proportion found some aspects of motherhood difficult. Half were irritated by the immediate situation of childcare and some felt that in becoming a mother they had lost their individuality and freedom and that childcare monopolized their lives. Help from fathers, while it demonstrated their commitment, did not substantially change women's perception of their situation. In contrast other women were more frustrated by the quantity of work and the conflict between doing housework and looking after children. For these mothers help from fathers was appreciated because it reduced their workload.

Another factor which influences women's adjustments as mothers is the relative isolation of many mothers in our society. Because women are generally not employed outside the home when their children are small, they have few social contacts and few sources of identity apart from motherhood. Especially in the early months, new mothers may have little contact with others and hence little emotional and practical support. Given their heavy workload and their isolation it is perhaps not surprising that for some women adjustment is difficult and there are high rates of depression and anxiety. Because motherhood is viewed positively as an identity for women, when women experience difficulties, they and others tend to seek explanations in terms of individual pathology, of hormones or women's inadequate personalities, instead of the amount and the nature of the work involved in being a mother (Antonis, 1981; Nicolson, 1986; Phoenix *et al.*, in press).

Analysis of maternal depression is one of the few ways in which the variability of mothers' experiences and adjustments have been recognized. Women who are depressed tend to be isolated, with less social support, and are less likely to have a confidant than women who are not depressed. They are also more likely to have experienced adverse life events such as difficult relationships and poor housing (Brown and Harris, 1978; Hinde and Stevenson-Hinde, 1988). Depression sometimes spills over into mothers' relations with their children, but this is by no means always the case and some mothers continue to have warm, sensitive relationships with their children. But relations with their children are often affected. Commonly, depressed mothers are irritable, controlling or punitive and more likely to express anger than non-depressed mothers. They tend to be less responsive to children and engage in less sustained social interaction. They are less likely to expand and extend children's contribution to interactions, probably because they are overwhelmed by their own condition and are unable to set aside their own needs and feelings (Belsky *et al.*, 1984b; Puckering, 1989). Depression often influences mothers' perceptions of their children, so that they tend to see children as unresponsive, demanding or difficult; characteristics likely to reduce mothers' involvement still further. Mothers' depression has an impact on children's development with children showing more emotional and behavioural disturbance and delays in language development (Puckering, 1989). Children may react to the low level of involvement and the negative perceptions of mothers by making fewer demands and initiating fewer interactions. As a result children and mothers may become progressively less involved with one another, and this low level of involvement may persist even when mothers' conditions change.

In Conclusion

We have discussed some aspects of mothers' behaviour with their children which psychologists view as significant for children's development. Mothers' behaviour shows considerable variation and we have considered the impact of this for children. Psychology has tended to ignore women's experiences as mothers so we have less information about the factors which may influence their behaviour and make them more or less sensitive, warm or demanding of mature behaviour. Nor do we know how mothers think or feel about being sensitive or child-centred and hence how this affects how they go about the tasks of mothering. Another reason for the lack of knowledge about what may influence mothers' behaviour is the predominant use in research of mothers and children on their own. This means that the wider contexts in which mothers bring up children and children develop are often neglected. In the following chapters we consider the wider family and the impact this has on children and parents.

Further Reading

DUNN, J. (1988) *The Beginnings of Social Understanding*, Oxford, Basil Blackwell.

From a series of studies of mothers and their young children in the home setting, Dunn considers the ways in which such intense family relationships provide a powerful context in which young children learn about themselves, other people and the rules underlying social interactions.

KAYE, K. (1982) *The Mental and Social Life of Babies*: *How Parents Create Persons*, London, Methuen.

A very detailed account of research on mother-infant interaction. Kaye uses this material to consider the different functions mothers serve for their young children and the ways in which they support their children's emerging sense of themselves.

MACCOBY, E.E. and MARTIN, J.A. (1983) 'Socialisation in the context of the family', in HETHERINGTON, E.M. (Ed.) *Handbook of Child Psychology*: *Volume 4*: *Socialisation, Personality and Social Development*, 4th ed., New York, Wiley.

An extensive review of the area which focuses on methodological issues such as the interdependence of measures obtained from children and mothers and how to decide whether mothers influence children or vice versa. A good review of research on childrearing practices and the factors which influence mothers' style.

PHOENIX, A., WOOLLETT, A. and LLOYD, E. (Eds) (in press) *Motherhood*: *Meanings, Practices and Ideologies*, London, Sage.

Psychology's treatment of mothers and their influence on their children's development is considered from the perspectives of childless women and mothers having children in different circumstances (e.g. old and young mothers, mothers with two children, mothers of boys and girls, mothers of deaf children). Findings are used to extend current psychological conceptualizations of motherhood to consider the variety of mothering experiences and practices and to point to limitations in current ideologies of motherhood.

SCARR, S. and DUNN, J. (1987) *Mother Care/Other Care*: *The Child-Care Dilemma for Women and Children*, Harmondsworth, Penguin.

Scarr and Dunn present an excellent critical analysis of psychological theories about mothers and children and in particular how theories make employment outside the home problematic for women. From the perspective of studies of childcare outside the home, they consider children's needs and how these can be met when mothers are employed.

SCHAFFER, R. (1977) *Mothering*, London, Fontana.

A good introduction (although now somewhat out of date) to ideas and research (including discussion of the methods employed) about mothers' behaviour around their children and the functions these might serve in terms of their children's development.

TIZARD, B. and HUGHES, M. (1984) *Young Children Learning*: *Talking and Thinking at Home and at School*, London, Fontana.

Mothers' conversations with their 4-year-old daughters form the basis of this book. The nature of the conversations and the cognitive and emotional richness of the underlying rules and understandings of the world are compared with laboratory-based studies of 4-year-olds in which children are viewed as far less competent.

Chapter 5

Beyond the Dyad:
Fathers, Mothers and Children

So far we have talked about the roles of mothers and the impact they have on their developing children. While in most homes it is the mother who is the principal caretaker, other family members, and especially fathers, also spend time with children. Initially when their children are small babies most fathers contribute little to childcare activities, but later from about 3 to 9 months fathers begin to get more involved and there is a slow increase in the frequency of their childcare activities, especially with sons, and this continues through to adolescence. Fathers are involved with their children, some more so than others, but most play with their children, interact with them and carry out some childcare activities. Given the amount of contact that fathers have with their children it would be surprising if they had no influence upon their development.

Despite the evidence that fathers spend time with their children, most research on child development has focused on mothers; indeed until the 1970s virtually all studies of parenting considered only the influence of mothers. The only studies to consider the impact of fathers were those focusing on psychopathology which considered father absence as a possible contributory factor in the emergence of emotional and behavioural problems in children and adolescents. Since the 1970s there has been a growing number of studies which have considered fathers as well as mothers as sources of influence in the development of children. As soon as fathers are considered as possible contributors to children's development, conceptions of family processes must be reconsidered; the dyad of mother and child becomes a triad of mother, father and child (or children) each of whom could influence the others in complex ways. For instance, considering only mothers' influence, the findings of attachment studies have been interpreted in terms of the quality of relationship with mothers influencing the development of cognitive skills. As soon as the possibility of fathers' influence is admitted this simple picture can no longer be accepted so readily; perhaps attachments to fathers are contributing to the picture somewhere. Once it is recognized that families do not simply consist of two people but of full family groups, complex models have to be developed that take into account the direct and indirect influence that each family member has on each other member.

Figure 1

Mother's Behaviour ----------> Child's Behaviour and Development

Figure 2

Mother's Behaviour   ---------->   Child's Behaviour
and Development   <-----------   and Development

Direct and Indirect Influences on Child Development

Early models of family influence considered mothers interacting only with a single child and the direction of influence was assumed to be one way; the child was considered to be influenced by the mother. For example in early accounts of child development it was assumed that the mother's linguistic style encouraged her child's development of language. In these accounts no consideration was given to the notion that other socialization agents might be active in encouraging the development of the child, e.g. grandparents or fathers, and equally no consideration was given to the possibility that linguistically advanced children elicited a different kind to language from their families than less linguistically advanced children. In these conceptions of the forces operating in child development consideration was given to the direct impact that mothers had on their children, as shown in Figure 1.

Bell (1979) argued that much of the developmental literature could be reconceptualized as the child's behaviours influencing its mother's behaviours; what the child did had a bearing on what the mother did. With the realization that children could influence mothers, the idea of reciprocal influence developed; both parties influence one another. The behaviour of neither mothers nor their children is static; how the child acts influences the mother and modifies her behaviour, and how the mother acts influences the child and modifies his or her behaviour. With this pattern of influence the behaviour of both parties constantly changes and evolves, as shown in Figure 2.

Unfortunately for this simple construction of family influence families do not consist of two members: they consist of many members, each mutually influencing the others, as shown in Figure 3.

As soon as the possibility of mutual influence is recognized as operating in the family then the behaviour of each family member can be seen to be influenced to differing degrees by the actions of each other family member, sometimes operating in unison, but sometimes exerting contradictory and conflicting pressures. For instance how the mother treats any one member of the family is influenced by her dealings with other members of the family. So the way in which a mother treats her youngest child is influenced by her experiences with the father, with her parents, with her other children and so on. This means that her parents, the father and her children each have an indirect influence on how the youngest child is treated. In this case the indirect influence is channelled through the mother. This channelling

Figure 3

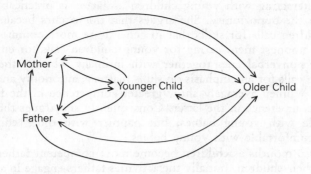

of indirect influence operates through all the family and applies equally to fathers, brothers and sisters and any other family member with regular contact. Of course the forces of influence are not restricted to within the family; friends, acquaintances, society at large all have an influence on how each member of the family behaves and so have an indirect influence on each family member. For instance if a mother is employed outside the home and has an argument with her boss she may return home at the end of the day feeling tired and depressed. This will have a bearing on how she responds to her children. Those children will have been indirectly influenced by their mother's boss even though they have never set eyes on the person. It is important to consider indirect influences on behaviour as well as direct influences in trying to understand what is going on in families. There is a high degree of interdependence within families and this must be recognized if the behaviour of any one family member is to be understood.

The issue of indirect effects on child development is an important one. Such effects are probably as influential as what family members do directly to the child. These indirect effects are discussed a great deal in theoretical reviews, but compared to direct influences on child development they have been neglected in empirical investigations. In the remainder of this chapter we will consider the direct and indirect influences of mothers and fathers on their children. To this end we will look at what fathers do with their children and then contrast this with what mothers do with children and consider the implications for children of these behaviours. Finally variations in parenting will be considered briefly.

What Fathers Do with their Children

How fathers behave towards their children is strongly influenced by their children's age and sex. For fathers there is more contact with children and more interest in children as they get older and become more competent. Father involvement in childcare is initially relatively high when the newborn first comes home, but usually this falls away dramatically as the father returns to work after any paternity leave he may have taken. Rossi (1987) argues that men avoid interacting with young children as far as is practicable whereas women grasp the opportunity. She argues that this occurs because the care of young children calls for skills that in general are more common amongst women than amongst men: caring for young children calls for empathy and sensitivity to nonverbal cues together with intimacy whereas the caring of older children calls for an emphasis on skills mastery, autonomy and cognitive achievement. Women averagely show greater competence in the former and men greater competence in the latter. Consequently she argues that men feel uncomfortable with young babies, but happier with older children, and women feel comfortable with young babies.

At about 3 months as children become more competent fathers begin to do more for their children. Initially the activities fathers engage in are playing, affectional displays and baby-sitting. The majority of fathers (80 per cent) play with their children of 3 months and more on a daily basis. Of the messier primary caretaking activities, feeding is the activity men are most likely to undertake regularly. Both mothers and fathers agree that 21 per cent of fathers are regularly involved in this activity. Father involvement in the other messy jobs is perceived differently by mothers and fathers, with fathers claiming to do more than mothers allow. For instance 14 per cent of fathers claim to change their infant's nappy at least once a day, but this is conceded by only 6 per cent of mothers (Moss *et al.*, 1987a).

La Rossa and La Rossa (1981) suggest that fathers assume an unreal incompetence when with young children, they are seen to be more clumsy with young children than in any other activity and because of their supposed incompetence are quickly relieved of childcare demands. In contrast, even first-time mothers act in an outwardly competent manner that may well mask their anxiety in their own competence. With second and subsequent children fathers continue to display incompetence. However they now have a legitimate excuse because the average father devotes more time to his older children, thus releasing more of the mother's time to devote to the young second-born. In their turn mothers are reported to be happy with this arrangement since it allows them to enjoy their (now) real expertise in caring for babies (Shapiro, 1979). As children grow older fathers gradually increase their contact up until 18 months at which time the average father shows a rapid increase in his availability. From this age onwards fathers become enamoured with the growing abilities of their 2 and 3 year old children. It is suggested that a further spurt in father availability occurs at around 6 or 7 years. At this age children become more rational and reasonable, they are less prone to apparently inexplicable temper tantrums and are easier to understand (Ross, 1982).

Gender of the Child

Studies in the UK and the USA show that the gender of a child has an important impact on the involvement of fathers but not of mothers in childcare and child-centred activities. In a review of US studies Lamb *et al.* (1987) show that fathers spend more time with boys, they play with them more and they are generally more involved. This difference in the involvement of fathers with sons and daughters can be seen immediately from birth. In one study fathers of sons stayed longer in the delivery room than fathers of daughters, they held sons for considerably longer, and talked much more to them, directing six times as many comments towards sons than towards daughters. Many of these comments referred to the newborn's sex, e.g. father to son 'Hello little fellow, you're here now' or 'that's it, let the world know you are here mate'. Even at this very early stage fathers were adopting the 'hail baby well met' style associated with fathers' greeting of sons. Their greeting of daughters as equally stereotyped, e.g. 'Thought you'd be a girl, you've been so obstinate'. In general mothers responded in similar ways to sons and daughters. When fathers were present, however, mothers made more comments about their daughters than they did when fathers were absent. This did not happen with mothers of sons. Mothers of daughters appeared to be trying to engage the father's interest in his daughter by drawing attention to various of her features and qualities (Woollett *et al.* in Beail and McGuire, 1982). In a cross-cultural survey of parents' preference for the sex of their first unborn child, Williamson (1976) reports that US families have stronger preferences for a son than do British families. In Britain fathers express a moderately strong preference for sons and mothers express a mild preference for sons as a first child, but both US men and women want their first child to be a boy.

In general as children become older fathers spend more time with them and show more interest in them, but this is especially true of fathers of sons. Indeed one longitudinal study of parents and their children found that fathers of boys showed increased involvement with increasing age from 3 to 9 years, but in contrast their contact with girls declined as girls got older (Radin and Goldsmith, 1985). In adolescence too fathers of girls interact less than fathers of boys and are more emotionally distant (Steinberg *et al.*, 1989). Differences in fathers' treatment of sons and daughters can be seen in their play with their children too. From an early age fathers engage in more boisterous play with sons than daughters. In contrast they cuddle daughters more. The more boisterous play with sons continues as children get older. As children become older fathers begin to stress the importance of preparation for a career and the value of occupational success, but they are much more likely to do this for sons. In situations where fathers are involved in teaching or problem solving with their children they are more concerned about successful achievement from their sons than their daughters. Achievements in mathematics are particularly stressed for boys (Hargreaves and Colley, 1986).

It is not clear why boys are so salient and important for fathers. Perhaps first-time fathers feel apprehensive about the new role that they have undertaken. They do not know what is expected of them and how to treat young babies. However, being male themselves they may feel that they have some insight into the needs of other males; in contrast, females are largely unknown. Given this, boys present one problem, their infancy, but girls present two problems, their infancy and their gender. Fathers feel more at home and knowledgeable about boys than they do about girls. In addition there is a traditional cultural value placed on maleness. Male roles are more valued in society than female roles.

Similarities and Differences in Mothers' and Fathers' Treatment of Children

Even though fathers are willing to get involved with their children, studies comparing mothers and fathers indicate quite clearly that the extent of fathers' involvement is limited compared to what mothers do. In most families mothers still retain primary responsibility for childcare and what fathers do is considered by them, and by mothers, merely as help. Moreover, when fathers engage in caretaking activities they tend to choose the clean easy jobs (e.g. fetching drinks and putting to bed) and avoid the dirty jobs, especially feeding and nappy changing. These clean jobs are not only easy but are activities that in contrast to mothers' child directed activities demand little attention, occupy little time and can be fitted in with other activities (La Rossa and La Rossa, 1981).

This profile of relatively little involvement by fathers is shown even in families that before the birth were egalitarian and avoided dividing home-making chores along traditional sex stereotyped lines. The birth of a first child is associated with a shift towards a more traditional division of family roles (Cowan and Cowan, 1985). This imposition of more traditional roles is often made by mothers who having relinquished their roles outside of the family in order to have children are then eager to ensure that there is no further erosion of their sphere of influence (Fein, 1976). This view is reinforced by Lamb *et al.* (1985) who present evidence showing that even in households where both parents are in paid employment, many mothers are happier to be overloaded by taking on the major caretaking role rather than relinquish their role as the child expert and apparently indispensible parent.

Not only do mothers and fathers differ in the amount of involvement with their children, but in some respects they treat their children differently too. An early longitudinal study illustrates some of these differences. Clarke-Stewart (1978) examined toddlers repeatedly between 15 months and 36 months interacting with both of their parents. She reports that even during those times when the father was in the home mothers gave more attention to their children and interacted with them more. Mothers touched children more than did fathers, talked to them more, engaged the child in more play with toys and objects, and disciplined their children more. More of the mothers' time was devoted to 'intellectual' pursuits such as reading to the child or playing with stacking toys. The only activity that fathers exhibited as much as did mothers was physical play and even here fathers' physical play tended to be in short bursts rather than the more enduring activities that mothers introduce. As the children grew older fathers spent more time with them and especially spent more time playing. The behaviour of the children tended to be somewhat different when with mothers and fathers. Children appeared to enjoy playing with fathers more than playing with mothers. During these episodes they were more cooperative, interested and engrossed in the activity. Most children sought their fathers as playmates in preference to their mothers. On all activities other than physical play mothers are more involved than are fathers. Nevertheless fathers interact in similar ways to mothers, they too talk and read to their children, and children are just as likely to be securely attached to their fathers as to their mothers. Mothers and fathers both exert indirect influences on their children. For instance when the father was in the house mothers were less responsive to their children and their children's attempts to interact were more likely to be ignored. Mothers talked to their children less, they initiated fewer play sessions and they were less positive and encouraging to their children.

A difference in parenting style that emerges from Clarke-Stewart's study is that fathers are much more involved in playful behaviours than mothers who are much more involved in caretaking. This is confirmed by other studies showing that when traditional working fathers interact with their children, they spend 70 per cent or more of that time playing and only 20 per cent of their time on caretaking activities. In contrast when traditional home-based mothers interact with their children they spend nearly half of that time engaging in caretaking activities (Power and Parke, 1982; Russell, 1983). In total mothers play just as much with their children as fathers but their play activities are spread through the whole day rather than being concentrated into a small part of it. Fathers' play tends to be highly variable and idiosyncratic so that fathers play differently from one another and also each father plays differently on different occasions, so the same games are not repeated in a predictable way. Although fathers' play is idiosyncratic there are nevertheless common features. Their play tends to be physically arousing including a lot of gross body movement, with rough-and-tumble elements, tossing in the air and bouncing around, and it tends to take place in staccato bursts. In contrast mothers' play tends to be more repetitive and so the child can anticipate what is going to happen and fit into the sequence of the game. Mothers tend to choose conventional games to play, games that are used by other mothers too. Mothers' play uses a lot of verbal stimulation and often has an obvious educational component, moreover their play is more likely to centre around and use objects. These characteristic play styles continue at least into the fifth year (Clarke-Stewart, 1978; Teti *et al.*, 1988). Fathers' play sequences are of a shorter duration than those of mothers. This is partly because fathers often play with their children while engaged in other activities such as reading the paper or watching the TV, switching between activities (La Rossa and La Rossa, 1981). These typical patterns of play adopted by mothers and fathers are found widely. US parents (Power and Parke, 1982), Israeli parents bringing up their children on Kibbutzim (Sagi *et al.*, 1985) and Swedish parents (Lamb *et al.*, 1988) all reveal similar differences between parents.

Despite some differences in mothers' and fathers' behaviour towards their children there are considerable similarities. Both mothers and fathers employ motherese when speaking to young children, using short simple utterances with repetitions and expansions of what the child has said. They both stress turn-taking in the games they play and in their interactions generally with their children. They both serve as attachment figures and attachment to mothers and fathers seems to have similar consequences for the child. For instance the more securely attached children are to a parent the more confidence they show in their dealings with an unfamiliar adult; this is true of attachments to either parent; however when children are attached to their mother they show more confidence than when they are attached to their father, and they show most confidence when they are attached to both parents (Main and Weston, 1981). Both parents encourage their children to play with sex appropriate toys, although this is something that fathers enforce more consistently than mothers. Similarities between the play of mothers and fathers have been observed in that both provide similar opportunities for visual exploration, relational and communicative play, object manipulation and the production of auditory and visual stimulation. In their play both mothers and fathers create a linguistically and intellectually enriching environment and throughout play both parents take the opportunity to develop their children's language, encouraging them to talk about what they are doing, asking questions and providing information. When children get older both mothers and fathers tend to enforce similar rules and have similar aspirations for their children. Moreover, they both encourage their children to be cognitively competent by providing stimulation that is developmentally appropriate. Thus as the child gets older both mothers and fathers maintain an interaction for a longer period, with more exchanges in each interactive sequence. Both mothers and fathers show the same developmental trends in their behaviour, increasing or decreasing the frequency of particular behaviours according to the child's developmental status. While one parent may exhibit slightly more of these behaviours than the other, what is noticeable is that they both produce all of them and they both change their production in similar developmentally appropriate fashions (Lamb *et al.*, 1985; Stevenson *et al.*, 1988; Teti *et al.*, 1988). One clear reason for similarities between parental behaviours towards their children is that to some extent they learn parenting skills from one another. Grossman *et al.* (1988) conducted a study of parents and their children from pregnancy up to age 5 years and showed that competent mothers have competent partners; they report that '. . . healthy, caring, warm, nurturant and skillful mothers in some way "instruct" the father in parenting skills'. The men themselves acknowledge this and report learning parenting skills from the mother.

Implications of Fathering for the Development of Children

A question that is raised about fathers and their influence on the development of their children is whether they have a unique role to play in child development. The behaviour of fathers that seems most obviously different from that of mothers is their characteristic style of play. Several theorists have considered that play might be uniquely important for fathers, determining their influence on their children.

Fathers' Play

Fathers spend a great deal of time playing when interacting with their children, but this play does not seem to be educational or to have any obvious developmental advantages for their children. But are there hidden advantages? Several possible benefits of fathers' play for children have been advocated. One suggested benefit is that fathers' play encourages curiosity and exploration and this in its turn encourages the intellectual development of children. One feature of play and particularly fathers' style of play is that it involves a lot of moving around and encourages children to explore their environment and try out new activities. Thus when they are with children fathers often encourage adventurousness and curiosity. In contrast mothers spend most of their time trying to restrict and contain their children's activities (Biller, 1976). One consequence of this style of behaviour is thought to be that fathers encourage their children to become more independent. Biller's conclusions are based on observations of fathers and mothers interacting with children up to 5 years of age. Studies of parents interacting with older children also stress fathers' continuing involvement in the development of independence (Hargreaves and Colley, 1986).

A second way in which father play may be beneficial is that it is non-repetitive and variable. It is therefore hard to predict what fathers will do next and to fit into their activities. Father play therefore presents children with problems to try and solve and to do this they have to be alert to any cue that fathers may present. The striving for understanding that is involved in father play helps to develop children's problem-solving skills. Such problem-solving skills are very important for later development and lay the foundation for successful interaction with peers and siblings and others. Such skills may also help protect the child in times of adversity (see Chapter 10). A rather similar notion has been suggested by Parke *et al.* (1989). They point out that if children are to enjoy the unpredictable physical play sessions with their fathers they have to learn quickly to communicate effectively with him to ensure that the play continues to be enjoyable and does not become boring because not in synchrony or confusing and frightening because too unpredictable. This means that they have to communicate efficiently their emotional reactions of enjoyment, fear or boredom. These expressions of emotion occur naturally, but it is suggested that the more children play with their father the faster they learn of the communicative possibilities of these emotional expressions and so begin to manipulate them. By learning to modify and use their own emotional expression they also learn to interpret the expressions of others. This is a necessary step in learning to take the perspective of others, and it is a skill that generalizes to new people and to new situations. Understanding what another person is thinking or feeling is important if sensitive interactions are to occur. This perspective-taking may be facilitated by fathers' style of physical play.

A further suggestion about the impact of father play stresses the possible indirect influence of father play on children. Lamb *et al.* (1985) suggest that fathers' play has little direct impact on their children; this play is not educational and does not practise any obvious skills. However one feature of fathers' play is that it can be fun; many children enjoy playing with their fathers and seek them out for further interaction and companionship. Lamb *et al.* (1985) suggest that the more that fathers play with their children the more that children like them and the more salient fathers become. As a result children grow up wanting their fathers to approve of them, they come to value fathers' opinions and want to be more like them. Fathers' attitudes then become important in indirectly moulding their children. If fathers value academic performance they will have children who are more strongly motivated to succeed academically. If they value assertiveness they will have children who attempt to be more assertive. Linked to this, fathers who are more playful with their children are more likely to serve as a model and their behaviours are more likely to be emulated.

It is quite possible that fathers' play does indeed serve a number of different functions, some or all of which may operate in any family, although not necessarily all at the same point in time. So for instance the modelling of behaviours may be influential when a child is still young and cognitively immature, whereas the adoption of more abstract values would only become apparent at a later age. The same parental behaviour, physical play, can have both direct and indirect influences on the developing child. Through the same activity fathers may directly influence the development of social problem-solving skills and of independence of behaviour, but indirectly encourage imitation and identification.

Complementarity of Parental Roles

In some respects mothers and fathers behave similarly whereas in other respects they behave differently. There have been suggestions that their behaviour serves different functions in child development. Fathers are thought to encourage the sex role development of their children, their independence, their perceptual and motor skills and the intellectual development of sons. On the other hand it is suggested that mothers encourage their children's language development, they offer emotional support and comfort, and they encourage the intellectual development of daughters. However, differences have probably been overstressed, since fathers and mothers both encourage similar developments in their children, but they may do so in complementary ways rather than in identical ways. Thus Clarke-Stewart (1978) shows that fathers encourage intellectual development by their playful behaviour and by their encouragement of independence whereas mothers encourage the same skills by their linguistic stimulation, their focusing on rule-bound, intellectually stimulating games and their use of objects during play. Just how influential each parent is depends in part on how they view one another. Lamb *et al.* (1985) looked at the effect of increased father involvement in childcare on the development of children. They believe that the impact of fathers on their children is mediated by the mothers' attitude to the fathers' increased involvement. If the mother wants the father to be more involved and if the mother believes that the father is acting competently then fathers have a strong influence. However they do not have such an influence if the mother does not wish to see the father involved or views him as incompetent.

The contribution of parents to their children's development will be considered further under the three broad headings of sex role learning, intellectual and socio-emotional development, and development of peer relations.

Sex Role Learning

Sex typing or the development of sex role identity is the process by which children learn that they are boys and girls and the behaviour, attitudes and motivations associated with sex role behaviour in their society. A large number of socialization agents contribute to this learning process including parents, the wider family, peers, teachers and the mass media. Parents contribute both directly and indirectly. They contribute directly by the way they behave to their children and the behaviour and attitudes that they demonstrate and model to children in their everyday lives. Indirectly parents influence sex role development by their control over the purchase and use of toys, control over television viewing and control over access to peers.

Parents care for, look after and play with their boys and girls in many similar ways, but their children's gender is an important determinant of their attitudes and behaviour. From an early age parents provide their children with playthings and also join to some extent in their children's play. By their choice of playthings and their style of play with their children parents influence their sex role preferences. Parents vary enormously in the extent to which they do or do not restrict their purchase of toys to gender appropriate toys. Even when parents provide their children with both same-sex and cross-sex toys they may defeat their attempts towards a non-sexist upbringing of their children by the way in which they then interact with their children and use those toys. In a laboratory study Caldera *et al.* (1989) found that neither mothers nor fathers actively encouraged play with same-sex toys or discouraged play with cross-sex toys. However, both mothers and fathers showed more enthusiasm when playing with same-sex toys and especially when playing with a child of the same sex as themselves; in this situation they could not only encourage gender appropriate behaviour but also model such behaviour to their child.

Parents are more protective of their daughters' well-being, encouraging their dependency and keeping them close to the family. Boys are allowed to play out more than girls and to go farther away from home, and are supervised less, and, as a result, have more traffic accidents. Girls are more highly chaperoned, they are encouraged to bring a friend home to play, and there is greater use of explanation. The patterns of interaction mothers develop with girls encourage a person-oriented rather than a thing-oriented approach. Girls are, therefore, more exposed to adult models and more susceptible to parental, and especially maternal, influence, hence their greater nurturance and superior verbal skills. In addition, their identity and self-esteem may be more closely bound up with their identification with their mothers. The birth of a sibling may have a greater impact for girls, as the close relationship between mother and daughter is disrupted by the new family member (Dunn, 1984; Hargreaves and Colley, 1986; Maccoby and Jacklin, 1987).

Boys are encouraged to explore, to achieve, to be independent and competitive. They play more aggressively, being both aggressors and victims of aggression more than girls. Boys are rarely allowed to deviate from typical 'masculine' behaviour; tomboyish behaviour is an acceptable option for young girls but deviation from behaviour considered appropriate for boys is 'sissy' and discouraged. Boys are more likely to have problems in school, with reading and speech difficulties and more emotional problems. After age 10 years they begin to do better than girls in visual spatial tasks and later in mathematical abilities (Maccoby, 1988).

There are considerable variations in mothers' and fathers' behaviour to their boys and girls, with some parents behaving in more stereotypical ways than others. These variations relate to parents' personalities and sex role orientation. Warm and nurturant parents are generally associated with more stereotypical sex role behaviour in their children. Fathers' absence, their coldness and being uninvolved may disrupt the learning of what is generally considered to be appropriate masculine behaviour by boys, result in lower achievement by both boys and girls and be associated with less successful heterosexual relationships in girls. Fathers appear to influence their daughters as much indirectly, by their attitudes and support for mothers' behaviour, as directly through their interactions with their daughters. The interactions between parents and children change continually, with expectations and re-actions redrawn as children grow and develop (Lamb *et al.*, 1985).

Intellectual and Socio-Emotional Development

A variety of longitudinal studies have shown that children's level of cognitive and socio-emotional development is associated with features of parental child-directed behaviour (e.g. Hinde and Stevenson-Hinde, 1988; Hwang *et al.*, 1989; Teti *et al.*, 1988). Relevant features are the provision of stimulation that is varied and developmentally appropriate, including: sensitive verbal stimulation, positive play behaviours using objects and toys, and responsiveness to children's social cues. These parental behaviours encourage the development of intellectual and cognitive skills, and they are associated with children who are psychologically mature and confident and secure in their dealings with others. Additional important aspects of parenting are parental warmth and the appropriate use of maturity demands. When children are young parental guided play with objects is associated with the development of exploratory skills and the imaginative use of objects. In contrast rough-and-tumble play (socio-physical play) is associated with social and communicative development. If fathers are highly available to their children and they display an authoritative parenting style their children are likely to be more friendly, independent and confident around other children and to be good at taking the viewpoint of others. Additionally, language development, the development of problem-solving skills and later academic attainment are all related to warmth of parenting, variety and pacing of stimulation, demands for mature behaviours and the use and consistent enforcement of rules. One further factor seems important for personality development and the growth of psychological maturity. Psychologically mature children and their parents are more likely to have greater access to social supports, particularly support from maternal grandparents. One reason why an extended social support network is advantageous is that this allows parents to introduce their children to a wide range of social partners of all ages. Parental attitudes are important too; children are more developmentally advanced when their parents have high expectations of them and when they have a positive image of their children. As children get older and more independent parental monitoring of their activities relates to their behaviour. Those parents who remain aware of what their child is doing both at school and during their leisure time have children who are more likely to perform well at school and less likely to display behaviour problems (Crouter *et al.*, 1990). The parental socialization behaviours viewed as optimal for intellectual and social development of sensitivity, warmth, variety of stimulation and appropriate maturity demands can be offered by either or both parents. There is very little evidence to suggest that either have a unique function. Comparisons of mothers and fathers bringing up their children as lone parents suggest that each can be equally successful in raising well adjusted, competent children (e.g. Santrock *et al.*, 1982; Zill, 1988; and see Chapter 7).

There is a tendency to view development as a highly canalized process; that, once it has started, its course is fixed within fairly narrow limits. This view emphasizes the idea that behaviours and skills exhibited at one time point are determined by what happened earlier rather than by what is happening now. Within this framework one would look for the origins of academic success in a 10-year-old in their early experiences, rather than in terms of what has been happening to them over the last month or two. However, the evidence from longitudinal studies shows only weak relationships between early parenting experiences and later child attainments, and this is especially true when there are changes in the child's experiences such as the divorce of their parents or the birth of a new brother or sister. The strongest predictions from parental behaviour to children's attainments are found when contemporaneous measures of both are taken. Children show rapid developmental gains if at that time they are receiving sensitive parental stimulation. Earlier sensitive treatment offers some, but rather limited, benefit.

Development of Peer Relations

Peers provide an important context for the development of children, they extend their range of experience and provide important new learning opportunities. Parents however have an important impact on the development of peer relations. Parents facilitate the development of peer relations both directly and indirectly. They do this directly by managing their children's social lives. Whether or not young children meet other young children depends largely on whether or not parents invite children into the house or take them to clubs and playgroups. When children meet others on a regular basis they learn how to interact effectively. With practice they get better at interacting and become more acceptable as companions. Children who first encounter peers when they are older show less age-appropriate interactive skills and have greater difficulty in becoming accepted and so benefiting from the opportunities that peer contact can offer.

A second direct influence on the development of peer relations is that parents typically monitor their children, especially their younger children, and intervene offering advice and instruction. In particular they stress such skills as turn-taking, sharing and cooperating, and in the event of a dispute they offer mediation. When 2-year-old toddlers play together they tend to need constant reminders of the required social rules. If parents leave toddlers alone together their interactions can quickly degenerate into disputes, fights and quarrels. Older children of 6 years also need help to establish harmonious interactions when they first encounter a new playmate and frequently require the intervention of a parent or other adult to smooth their route to cooperation. However, they can maintain harmony in the absence of an adult once the initial rule setting has been established (Parke et al., 1989).

Characteristics of parent-child interaction influence the characteristics of child-peer interactions. Children who are securely attached have greater confidence to explore new relationships, including those with age mates (Bretherton and Waters, 1985). Children who are successful in interacting with peers, who are helpful towards other children, communicate well, are confident, are willing to share toys and show originality and creativity in their play are likely to have mothers and fathers who are highly involved with them. This is especially true when parents are verbally stimulating, join in with their children's activities and steer the course of their children's interactions, but in a non-bossy way. Through interacting with parents children learn about turn-taking, about cooperation, how to initiate an interaction, how to maintain an interaction, and they learn about conflict resolution. All of these skills are generalized skills that transfer more or less effectively to other situations and to interactions with other partners. Pettit et al. (1988) suggest that enjoyable social interactions with parents lead to the development of good social problem-solving skills in children. They are better at assessing people and judging what they are feeling and thinking and hence judging how they are likely to behave in a variety of situations. If they develop good social problem-solving skills children are more likely to be accepted and popular with others of their age. However, if these skills are not developed children may become socially isolated. The importance of good social problem-solving skills and of good peer relations is discussed again at greater length in Chapter 10. Although parents can facilitate child-peer interactions, those interactions also require different skills from those that children use in interacting with parents. This is discussed further in Chapter 6.

Individual Differences

It is important to recognize that how mothers and fathers behave varies from family to family (Lamb *et al.*, 1985). Each parent develops their routines and activities within the context of the family as a whole; what fathers do is determined by what mothers are doing and vice versa. Fathers cannot spend a lot of time playing with their children if mothers take their children out on regular, long outings, keeping them away from the home at times when fathers are potentially available. Similarly mothers have no choice but to be the major caretaker if fathers remain at work or engaged in other out of home pursuits for the duration of the children's waking hours. The balance of what each parent does is negotiated implicitly or explicitly between them, and each couple arrive at a somewhat different balance. What mothers do is a balance between what they want to do and what other family members allow them to do or force them to do and the same is true of fathers. Each may end up doing more or less than they want with their children. Among the factors that may lead to individual differences in parental availability and behaviour the most frequently discussed are the quality of the relationship between the parents (e.g. Levi-Shiff and Iraelashvili, 1988), each parent's working role outside the family and their satisfaction with their occupation (e.g. Grossman *et al.*, 1988). Other factors considered are: characteristics of the children themselves such as their age, gender and temperament; characteristics and experiences of the parents including their attitudes to childrearing, their personality, their mental and physical health, how their own parents reared them; and the resources available to the family, such as social networks, supports and economic resources (Belsky *et al.*, 1984a; Radin and Goldsmith, 1985).

Relationship Quality

Several studies have considered whether the quality of the relationship between parents relates to their attitudes towards their children and their involvement with children. For the most part these studies have focused on the earliest period of the child's life. They reveal that the quality of the relationship has a very strong bearing on the involvement of both parents and especially on the involvement and warmth of fathers. For example Feldman *et al.* (1983) examined marital satisfaction in the third trimester of pregnancy and related this to father involvement later when the baby was 8 months old.

Fathers' marital satisfaction predicted caretaking, their satisfaction as parents and their involvement in play. Mothers' marital satisfaction during pregnancy was also highly predictive of fathers' involvement later. There is evidence also that relationship quality continues to influence parental behaviour towards children beyond the early days of parental role formation. Marital quality relates to fathers' attitudes towards childrearing and to the warmth of their behaviour. When the marital relationship is poor, fathers are less likely to confirm the appropriateness of their children's behaviour and so fail to encourage future appropriate behaviour. They are also more likely to be intrusive and interfere with their children's activities in an attempt to teach them how to carry out a task effectively. During periods of marital stress mothers are able to maintain more consistent reinforcement procedures than are fathers, but they too become more intrusive when attempting to teach their children (Brody *et al.*, 1986; Hinde and Stevenson-Hinde, 1988). Fathers who are happy with their marriages report more joy in their children and more interest in them whereas fathers who are unhappy in their relationship feel more anger and contempt towards their child. They also model negative responses for their children to copy. For both parents high marital harmony is associated with more positive, warm interactions with children. In their turn children are more compliant to parental requests and instructions. In contrast marital distress can lead to negative perceptions of children and to poor parent-child interactions. Indirect evidence for the lack of sensitivity of parents to their children when their own relationship with their partner is under strain comes from attachment studies. Children whose parents are undergoing temporary difficulties show a decline in their security of attachment to parents. When the parental relationship improves so does the security of attachment (Belsky *et al.*, 1984a).

Because of the link between relationship adjustments and parental treatment of their young children, there is interest in the determinants of relationship quality in the early months. Examinations of individual differences in marital or relationship satisfaction have revealed that the quality of the relationship before birth and the accuracy of prebirth expectations of the child and its impact on their lives are both major determinants of relationship satisfaction (Belsky *et al.*, 1986; Moss *et al.*, 1987a). In Chapter 2 we saw that the arrival of children could lead to a deterioration in the quality of the relationship between the couple unless that relationship was already a secure one. Relationships that are good before the birth of a child continue to be good and may improve. However relationships that are already weak are likely to be weakened still further by the birth of a child. Belsky *et al.* (1986) show that the determinants of relationship quality are somewhat different for mothers than for fathers. Looking at parents' marital satisfaction at 3 months they report that for fathers prenatal marital satisfaction is the best predictor. Of much less importance was the extent to which the reality of looking after the child was different from that anticipated. For mothers the most important determinant of marital satisfaction at 3 months was the extent to which prenatal expectations had been disappointed, followed by prenatal marital satisfaction and infant temperament. Parents often have unrealistic expectations of what their child will be like and how their presence will affect their lives. Belsky *et al.* (1986) comment on this:

> Parenthood is viewed by some as a means of bringing the couple closer together, of creating a shared interest for spouses, and of enhancing relations with extended family. Often unrecognised is the degree of real, and frequently stressful adaptation that goes on when an individual as dependent as a new baby is added to the family.

The reality of living with a child can come as a shock and new parents' romanticized view of parenting can not be sustained. Again Belsky *et al.* (1986) comment:

> When events deviate from what is anticipated, stress results and coping is required ... when events turn out less positive or more negative than anticipated, marriages change for the worse, whereas the opposite is true when events turn out less negative and more positive than anticipated.

The Belsky *et al.* (1986) study shows that child characteristics and especially their temperament and gender have an impact on relationship quality. Both mothers and fathers report their relationship to be less harmonious if the child is temperamentally difficult. Mothers seem to be more strongly influenced by temperament than fathers. It has been argued that infant temperament has an impact on marital relationships because a difficult child adds to parents' sense of overload and irritability. In turn this irritability will lead to marital conflict and so to a perceived decline in the relationship. In contrast the gender of children influences the way in which fathers, but not mothers, view the quality of their relationship. In the early months following the birth of a child, fathers of sons rate themselves as more satisfied with their partner than fathers of daughters. The label 'boy' or 'girl' has salience for men irrespective of the qualities that the child displays (Hinde and Stevenson-Hinde, 1988). The quality of the relationship between parents has an important indirect influence on the developing child and is a major determinant of observed individual differences in the quality of parenting and especially so for men. The principal determinants of relationship quality for parents are the quality of their relationship prior to the arrival of children and the accuracy with which they anticipated the changes children would make to their lives.

Parents' Employment

Constructions of normal families tend to assume that men are breadwinners and women involved in full-time childcare. But employment patterns may be more complex; mothers may work from home or outside the home on a full-time or, more usually, a part-time basis (Brannen and Moss, 1988); fathers may be unemployed or they may work from home; when both parents are working they may employ full-time caretakers such as nannies who may live with the family. Consequently, either, both or neither of the parents may be in paid employment. Fathers' and mothers' behaviour towards their children and their ideas about childcare may stem from their working lives outside the home (Bronfenbrenner, 1986). Two patterns of working arrangements are considered here, both of which involve the mother in working outside the home; dual earner families and role reversal families.

Dual Earner Families

In dual earner families both mother and father are in paid employment, usually outside the home. Dual earning families are headed by adults who combine the roles of wage earner, homemaker and parent. As such they often feel overloaded and tired. Concern about dual earner families focuses on two aspects: the adequacy of alternative care and the ability of working parents to provide adequate and sensitive care for their children. Part of the latter concern is that children have less contact with parents than they would if parents did not work. However, the time parents spend with their children is less critical for children's development than parental attitudes and their parenting style (Easterbrooks and Goldberg, 1984). Consequently, problems for children may result only if the experience of work adversely affects parents' attitudes and their relationship with their children.

Studies of dual earner families often fail to consider the importance of what the experience of work means to parents. For some parents work is a desired, stimulating experience, for others it is unwelcome and tedious. How parents view work is likely to be of great importance. It is possible for parents to be committed to both work and parenting. Parents who are committed to parenting make greater maturity demands, are warmer and more sensitive in their treatment of their children, and more authoritative than dissatisfied working parents. However, parents who are highly committed to both parent- and work are most likely to adopt an authoritative parenting style. Working parents who enjoy their work are likely to treat their young children more sensitively and warmly and to be on bettr terms with them during adolescence (Greenberger and Goldberg, 1989; Grossman *et al.*, 1988; Silverberg and Steinberg, 1990). Parents' working status need not detract from their commitment to parenting and may enhance it.

Despite the pressures on parents' time and energy it does not seem that children are parented very differently in dual earner families. Pedersen *et al.* (1982) found that mothers who were employed outside the home played with and stimulated their children more when they were home with them than did women who did not work outside the home. On the other hand fathers of these children spend less time than other fathers playing with their children. This is largely because the mothers in such families monopolize the time when both parents are at home with the children. Fathers in dual earner families are more involved in childcare and household tasks and are more likely to take sole responsibility for their children. Indeed the more mothers work outside of the home the more involved fathers become (Lamb *et al.*, 1988). In other respects children from dual earner families are treated similarly to other children. For instance working and non-working parents are equally likely to supervise their children closely, be aware of what their child is doing at school and in their leisure time and put pressure on their children to achieve (Crouter *et al.*, 1990). Children from dual earner families have a different balance of contact with parents including more experience of play with mothers but less with fathers compared with children in conventional families. However, there is no evidence that the parents' working experiences make them poorer parents and indeed if their work experience enhances their self-esteem they may become more confident and effective as parents.

Role Reversal Families
Several studies have looked at cases of so-called role reversal families where fathers remain at home and act as the principal caretaker and mothers work outside the home. This may happen because of fathers' unemployment, or because the mother has better earning powers than the father or it may reflect a commitment to non-traditional family relations. When fathers do take over as the principal caretaker they usually do so for short periods; less than a quarter of primary caretaking fathers act as such for more than two years (see e.g. Russell, 1983). The question asked in these studies is whether the experience of being the principal caretaker influences the way in which parents interact with their children. The principal caretaker has the responsibility of looking after children for relatively long periods in the day and has to fit childcare around housework and other activities. It is possible that how parents interact with their children is determined by their caretaking role rather than by their socialization experiences as men and women. If so women in paid work should behave like traditional fathers and men who stay at home to look after children should behave like traditional mothers.

One study to examine this was conducted by Radin (1982) on middle-class US couples with children aged between 3 and 6 years. Families with a principal caretaking mother were compared to families with a principal care-taking father. Primary and secondary caretaking fathers did not differ on their sex role orientation, nor their strictness in dealing with their children. Since secondary caretaking fathers were not at home long enough for their strict-ness to impinge on children, children of primary caretaking fathers perceived them to be more strict than children of secondary caretaking fathers. Primary caretaking fathers engaged in more cognitive stimulation and in more direct teaching of their children than did secondary caretaking fathers or primary caretaking mothers. In some respects primary caretaking fathers behaved differently towards their children than secondary caretaking fathers: having principal responsibility for children made fathers more concerned with en-couraging skills in a direct way. However in many respects their behaviour remained similar to that of other fathers: they still encouraged exploration and engaged in boisterous play. Other studies confirm that role reversal fathers behave essentially like other fathers but increase their production of certain behaviours (e.g. Field, 1978; Lamb *et al.*, 1982). In their turn the children who are looked after principally by their fathers show greater inter-nal locus of control and higher verbal intelligence scores. In contrast children who are brought up by a primary caretaking mother explore less and show more emotional dependence upon the mother. Growing up in a role reversal family does not appear to affect children adversely.

An Australian study of role reversal families reveals some of the costs and benefits to parents who choose this form of parenting (Russell, 1983). Primary caretaking fathers can benefit by forming closer relationships with their children and so feel more positively about them and their self-confidence can be enhanced by their perception of having taken on a new role successfully. However, there can be considerable costs in that they may spend much of the time feeling bored and they can feel starved of adult company. Also because they spend more time at home they may experience an increase in conflicts with their children. For mothers the principal benefit is the satisfaction that they may derive from their jobs, but there can be physical and psychological costs. The increased workload and tiredness resulting from their commitment to parenting and to work can be physically draining. Secondary caretaking mothers violate traditional expectations and assumptions of family life and hence they frequently feel guilty about relinquishing primary responsibility for the care of their children. They may regret the reduced contact with their children and for some their guilt may be fuelled by the belief that the father is not terribly good as a homemaker. The quality of the parents' relationship can be adversely affected with more conflicts, often centring around housework and childrearing practices.

In Conclusion

The introduction of studies of fathers has broadened our knowledge of family functioning and of some of the influences operating within families. One outcome has been to focus more attention on individual differences in parenting. From this has emerged the value of looking at marital relationships as a factor influencing mothers' and fathers' relationships with their children. Studies have focused predominantly on families with young children and so less is known about fathers' contribution to families when children are older. The influence of each family member on other members is determined by a complex of factors including how others in the family value and want to see that person having an influence, and factors external to the family such as parents' commitment to employment and other activities outside the family.

Further Reading

CROUTER, A.C., MacDERMID, S.M., McHALE, S.M. and PERRY-JENKINS, M. (1990) 'Parental monitoring and perceptions of children's school performance and conduct in dual- and single-earner families', *Developmental Psychology*, **26**, pp. 649–57.

Several studies have considered how parents' relationship with their children is affected by their working roles and in particular what happens when both parents work. This is an example of that type of study, showing that general attitudes towards parenting and the interest taken in children are independent of and more important than parents' working status.

GROSSMAN, F.K., POLLACK, W.S. and GOLDING, E. (1988) 'Fathers and children: predicting the quality and quantity of fathering', *Developmental Psychology*, **24**, pp. 82–91.

A report of a longitudinal study of families, where parents were recruited during the pregnancy and followed through until their child was 5 years old. The study considers how far fathering reflects enduring qualities of men and their partners and how far it is determined by their experiences at the time.

LAMB, M.E., PLECK, J.H. and LEVINE, J.A. (1985) 'The role of the father in child development: the effects of increased paternal involvement', in LAHEY, B.B. and KAZDIN, E. (Eds) *Advances in Clinical Child Psychology, Vol. 8*, New York, Plenum.

Reviews the contribution of fathers in the development of their children by looking at what happens when fathers increase their involvement. Direct and indirect influences of the father are considered by looking at the impact of increased involvement on the fathers themselves, on their partners and on their children.

LEWIS, C. and O'BRIEN, M. (Eds) (1987) *Reassessing Fatherhood: New Observations on Fathers and the Modern Family*, London, Sage.

A collection of chapters by psychologists and sociologists from Britain, North America, Australia and Sweden covering topics such as employment and fathering, role reversal families, lone fathering and divorce.

SILVERBERG, S.B. and STEINBERG, L. (1990) 'Psychological well-being of parents with early adolescent children', *Developmental Psychology*, **26**, pp. 658–66.

Most studies of parenting consider the impact of parents on their young children. This study is one of the few to consider older children and to consider the impact that children have on parents.

Chapter 6

Sibling and Family Relations in Childhood and Adolescence

In this chapter we widen the family perspective to look at family relations in childhood and adolescence. We will consider especially two kinds of family relations, those with siblings and those within families in middle childhood and adolescence. Research has tended to focus on first or only children, even though the majority of children have siblings, either brothers and sisters born to the same parents or stepsiblings as a result of the remarriage of one of their parents. Stepbrothers and stepsisters are discussed in Chapter 7. For many young children sibling relations are a major source of attachment and companionship which lasts well into adulthood.

Once children go to school their network of contacts expands and they spend a considerable amount of time away from their families. At this stage, psychologists focus predominantly on children's relations with peers and they are less interested in family relations. Discussions of parents' experiences also tend to focus upon the early years and there is less information about how parents feel about and relate to their children as they grow up. When children go to school, mothers engage increasingly in activities outside the home, including paid work. This brings changes in the lives of mothers themselves and in those of fathers and children who are often expected to take greater responsibility. With adolescence there is renewed interest in family relations. It is often assumed that as young people's relations with peers become more influential, relations within families deteriorate and are characterized by conflict, although much current research takes a more positive view.

Relations within Families

Families are now smaller than at most points in history. Just as many women become mothers as in the past but they have fewer children. Most families in the USA and the UK now have two or three children and this is considered to be the ideal family size, although there are still preferences for larger families in certain groups. The gaps or birth intervals between children have become smaller and birth intervals of eighteen months to three years are now most common. An exception to this is in reconstituted families, where children born into a second marriage may be considerably younger than their stepsiblings born into a first marriage. Because most siblings are of a similar age they tend to make good companions for one another. Older siblings can provide assistance to parents in caring for younger children. In some societies siblings are heavily involved in aspects of care for younger children and this happened too in western societies in earlier times, but is now less common (Dunn, 1984; Lamb and Sutton-Smith, 1982; Lewis and Feiring, 1984). Interactions in larger families differ from those in smaller families. With more children in a family there is less parental attention for each child and the amount of interaction between parents and children is less in larger families. This is to some extent compensated for by closer relations between siblings. Once older siblings go to school, younger children have greater opportunity for one-to-one relations with their mothers. In families with three or more children, there may never be a time when middle children are at home on their own with mothers. And this is also the case for twins. While children in larger families may be treated less sensitively, they can engage in a greater variety of interactions and they can observe and learn from the interactions of others (Dunn, 1984; Feiring and Lewis, 1984; Newson and Newson, 1976).

The experiences of parents and children differ, between families and within a single family. When first-borns are only children, they have their parents' total attention, but first-time parents are inexperienced and are perhaps anxious about childrearing. When there are other children in the family, first-borns have to share parents' attention. They do remain the oldest and hence in many respects the most competent children in a family. Second and subsequent children always have older children to show them how to do things, but they also have to share their parents' attention. For only children and last-borns there are no younger children to look after and control but as the youngest they may experience less pressure to grow up and become independent (Dunn, 1984; Lamb and Sutton-Smith, 1982). The parents of twins and triplets have two or more children simultaneously. The number of multiple births is small but increasing with the use of treatments for infertility such as IVF (see Chapter 3). In such families siblings are of the same age. If twins are identical they are also of the same sex and look very much alike. People find it difficult to distinguish between the two until they know them well. Being confused with their twin often makes it difficult for identical twins to acquire separate identities and a clear sense of themselves as individuals (Botting *et al.*, 1990; Lytton, 1980).

Families are also smaller now because grandparents and others are less likely to live with parents and children. Even when grandparents do not live in the same household, they may play an important part in children's lives. They can influence their grandchildren's development directly through the interactions they have with them. They may supplement parents' activities, providing similar care and control, but at the same time, they are often less concerned about discipline, and are thus more tolerant and willing to be led by children than are parents. Grandparents can also influence children indirectly through the support they offer parents. By looking after children or providing financial support, they may relieve the pressure on parents and result in children receiving more sensitive parenting (Tinsley and Parke, 1984).

The Birth of a Sibling

The birth of a sibling may be the first major change in the family experienced by young children. For parents the birth of a second child is probably less significant than that of a first child. They are already parents and so another child has less of an impact on parents' day to day activities, their identity and sense of themselves. However, a second child does alter family interaction patterns, requiring changes and realignments of relationships within the family (Kreppner *et al.*, 1982). Adjustments for mothers include having two children to look after, balancing their different needs and managing the relationships between them. A new sibling makes demands (often urgent and noisy demands) on parents' attention and energies and older children have to wait their turn. Parents deal with these demands in different ways. A strategy in two-parent families is for parents to divide the childcare tasks between them, with fathers taking charge of the older children while mothers look after younger children. Fathers often become more involved in childcare as a result of increased demands from first-borns when mothers are busy with a new baby (Stewart *et al.*, 1987). The birth of a second child can result in new constellations of relationships with mother and younger child or father and older child becoming particularly close. Parents also have to find a new balance between their marital and parental relations. This may take the form of recognizing that for some time at least parental activities take precedence or by calling on grandparents to help with childcare to give parents more time for themselves.

It is often assumed that older children feel jealous of the new baby and that their 'dethronement' create difficulties and stress for them. Research, however, suggests that the picture is much more complex. In a longitudinal study, Dunn and Kendrick (1982) followed a group of first-born children from about a month before the birth of a second child until younger children were 15 months old. From interviews with mothers and observations of mothers and children, there was evidence of some difficulties for first-born children. In the month after the birth, almost all mothers reported an increase in naughtiness. For more than half there was an increase in tearfulness and clinging, several were more withdrawn, had sleeping problems and difficulties with toilet training. Jealousy was also observed, especially when fathers and grandparents showed interest in the baby. Boys showed somewhat more problems than girls. These problems did not, by and large, persist. For a few children, however, their anxious and unhappy behaviour had not subsided by the time the younger child was 15 months and there was some increased reporting of fears and miserable or grumpy moods. But there were also more positive changes. For over half the children, the birth of a sibling was associated with increased independence. They wanted to dress, feed themselves, go to the toilet and play on their own. There was considerable interest in the baby; children talked about the baby, tried to cuddle, entertain, play with and care for it and were upset if the baby was distressed. These findings suggest that children's responses to the new baby were frequently mixed and complex, so for example, children who were affectionate to the new baby could also display jealousy.

The birth of a sibling changes the balance of the relationship between mothers and older children. There is a decrease in the time mothers and children play together and an increase in the number of confrontations. Mothers are less likely to initiate joint play sequences and respond to initiations from the child, placing greater responsibility on the child to start and maintain interactions. Before the birth of a sibling mothers' and children's conversations often focus on the children's activities and upon their likes and dislikes, but with the birth this focus of conversation changes. Now mothers and children talk about the new babies, viewing them as separate people with their own wants, intentions, likes and dislikes, and the new baby becomes a major focus of attention. Discussion about the new baby alters the ways in which many children talk about themselves. Dimensions and ways of describing people which were probably available to children beforehand become more salient when there is someone else with whom to compare themselves. Toddlers increasingly talk about themselves in comparative terms as big, competent and able to talk, walk and feed themselves. The birth of a different-sex sibling can mean that gender becomes very salient for children (Dunn and Kendrick, 1982).

There are considerable differences between families in the extent to which mothers and children discuss the wants and feelings of younger children. In some families mothers frequently draw older children's attention to the baby and involve them in discussion about caring for the baby, almost as if care were a joint responsibility, whereas in other families this seems to happen rarely. As well as involving older children in discussions about the younger one these mothers also have a somewhat different style of interacting with their children. They are more likely to give justifications for the demands they make of their children, to discuss people's motives and intentions and to use language for complex cognitive purposes. They are also more likely to enter into and encourage children's pretend games. This maternal style of interacting relates to the behaviour of older siblings. They help to care for the baby more, they are more affectionate towards the baby and they often refer to the baby's feelings, wants and interests. The closer sibling relations in these families usually persist as the children get older (Dunn and Kendrick, 1982).

Sibling Relations in Middle Childhood

As young children become more competent and more mobile, they are more able to participate in activities. With their increasing language skills they can join in verbal games. When they first begin to acquire language, young children are dependent on the support and scaffolding parents provide. When parents have one child to deal with they modify their behaviour and their language according to their child's level of competence (see Chapter 4) but there is less information about their ability to interact sensitively with two children. Woollett (1986) found that when two children were present, mothers continued to use different language registers with children of different ages, but the presence of an older child substantially reduced the amount of talk between mothers and toddlers. It seems difficult for mothers to maintain their supportive role in the face of competition from an articulate older child. In their turn younger children participate less when older siblings are present. As they become more competent language users, children are better able to enter into conversations between mothers and older children. Once they are able to do this mothers' relations with siblings begin to change and by middle childhood younger siblings get more attention than older siblings (Dunn and Shatz, 1989; Lamb and Sutton-Smith, 1982).

As younger children grow older, their siblings play with them, asserting their superiority by taking away toys or completing things younger children are trying to do. Older children also maintain their control by intervening in conversations and play between mothers and younger children, joining in or preventing further interaction between the two. When parents are committed to joint family activities they encourage children to play with their younger sibling, even though this means that parents have to monitor relations between the two children more carefully. Parents may encourage such alliances because when children play together parents have more time for themselves. However, sometimes alliances are formed, if only temporarily, against parents to object to parents' treatment of them. If sibling relations are poor, parents may need to be more involved in their activities to intervene when necessary. Because conflicts are often viewed negatively, having quarrelsome children may make parents feel they are incompetent or that they are not bringing up their children well. To avoid conflict between siblings parents may encourage them to engage in separate activities (Phoenix *et al.*, in press).

In middle childhood siblings provide children with important sources of companionship and a context for development which differs from that offered by parents. Parent-child relations may provide the basis for children's knowledge and respect for the rules of social order, whereas the roots of children's concern for equality, fairness and mutuality may be found in their relations with other children. Parents protect, look after, control and teach their children and they are committed to taking their children's viewpoint. As we have suggested in Chapter 4, psychological research stresses the value of maternal sensitivity and responsiveness. Children are dependent on parents and are expected to be compliant, respectful and loving, and to learn from them. In contrast relations with other children (both siblings and peers) are more reciprocal and symmetrical. Siblings engage in different kinds of activities with one another than they do with parents; there are more jokes, games, vulgarity, pretend and role play, and more imitation (Damon, 1983; Dunn, 1988). Siblings resemble one another in that their skills and power are comparatively limited, and they are often less able and less committed than parents to understanding and respecting one another's perspective. These differences can be seen in comparisons of children's play with mothers and siblings. Play with mothers tends to be more structured and has a clear educational feel. Interactive sequences are longer as mothers maintain the exchanges by responding to what their children do and say. Play with other children tends to be less structured and exchanges are shorter. Whining, tantrums, laughter, talking and demands for attention are more common in play with mothers and physical activity, aggression, negative commands, and yells are more common in play with children. Mothers and siblings participate differently in pretend play. Mothers act as spectators, offering suggestions and making comments but rarely involving themselves in the fantasy. Siblings, in contrast, participate, they are happy to role play as pretend people whether as mothers, fathers, babies, train drivers, policemen or real or imaginary friends (Lamb and Sutton-Smith, 1982; Stevenson *et al.*, 1988).

Similarities and Dissimilarities between Siblings

In the early years especially, there is an imbalance in sibling competence and behaviour. Older children use more complex language, their play is more skilled, they offer toys and take them away, they are more aggressive and also more sociable, and they comfort and praise younger children. Younger children tend to watch their older siblings, approach, follow and imitate them. They receive more physical and verbal aggression than older siblings and respond more positively to their siblings' behaviour. As they get older, the imbalance in skills and competence gets less and younger children take a more active part, initiating exchanges, becoming more aggressive, and using language to make requests, to command, tease, bribe and make territorial claims (Lamb and Sutton-Smith, 1982; Brody *et al.*, 1982; Dunn, 1984; Dunn and Munn, 1985; Newson and Newson, 1976). Older siblings act as leaders, controlling and managing interactions, and they encourage dependency. Increasingly this is resisted or challenged by younger siblings who do not always see their older sibling's help as useful or appropriate. Not surprisingly, therefore, mothers often see fights between siblings as a problem (Newson and Newson, 1976). In some families, younger children's competence outstrips that of their older siblings, especially when the older is handicapped (see Chapter 9).

But siblings are similar to one another in many respects. They live in the same family and spend a considerable amount of time together. They have the same parents, share the same space and resources, including toys and books, and have the same family pets and neighbours. And so they have a considerable amount of common history. In many families siblings spend more time interacting with one another than they do with fathers and even with mothers. When parental relations with children lack warmth or consistency or where there are marital problems, siblings may offer one another support. As they develop, the similarities in the competence of siblings and their social skills, interests and favourite activities are more apparent, especially when compared to those of adults. These similarities may be one reason why siblings get on well together and interact frequently with one another.

Reciprocity in Sibling Relations

Sibling interactions and relations tend to be reciprocal in nature. Compared with relations with adults, there is a greater balance in activities with both partners taking responsibility for initiating and maintaining the relationship. This can be seen in the frequency of imitation or coaction where children use imitation to build up and maintain interactions in a way they often find highly entertaining (Dunn, 1988). Imitative sequences begin in the first year when they often have communicative and emotional significance as this example suggests:

> Judy B puts her hand on the high chair where Carole (8 months) is sitting. Judy wiggles her fingers on the tray on the high chair. Carole watches. Judy wiggles her fingers; both continue to wiggle their fingers together, with mutual gaze and laughter. Three minutes later Carole, still in the high chair, wiggles her fingers on the tray, looks at Judy and vocalizes. (Dunn and Kendrick, 1982: 139.)

Initially, imitative sequences are started by children imitating their newborn siblings. These make up the majority of cases of imitation in the first eight months. Six months later, both older and younger children imitate one another and sibling relations in the second year are characterized by high levels of imitation. The frequency of imitation and the pleasure children get from it is thought to be related to the similarity or the 'like me' quality of siblings compared with adults (Pepler *et al.*, 1982; Dunn and Kendrick, 1982). In middle childhood siblings continue to engage in imitative activities. They act together with a meshing of interests, using imitations that are simultaneous (i.e. doing things together at the same time) and successive (i.e. one copies what the other has done). These could be a function of any rivalry between them, to show that they were able to do the same as their sibling but imitations often seem rather to express the close unity of children's lives and interests (Dunn, 1984).

The mutuality of sibling relations is also demonstrated in their considerable understanding of one another. Comments by 3-year-olds about siblings sometimes take the perspective of their siblings and are finely tuned to their wishes, such as 'He doesn't know you' (to observer), or 'Callum's crying because he wants his food cold'. Comments refer to a variety of states and feelings such as being hungry, happy, tired or cross. These comments suggest that 3-year-olds have a fairly sophisticated model of others and themselves as psychological beings (Dunn and Kendrick, 1982). This can perhaps be seen most clearly in their demonstrations of empathy and antagonism. To be effective these depend on children's ability to put themselves in the position of others. Such behaviour is common in 3-year-olds but even children as young as 14 or 15 months are sometimes able to move beyond their own perspective as the following example shows:

A 15-month-old was in the garden with his brother. The 15-month-old, Len, was a stocky boy with a fine round tummy, and he played at this time a particular game with his parents which always made them laugh. His game to come toward them, walking in an odd way, pulling up his T-shirt and showing his big stomach. One day his elder brother fell off the climbing frame in the garden and cried vigorously. Len watched solemnly. Then he approached his brother, pulling up his T-shirt and showing his tummy, vocalizing, and looking at his brother. (Dunn and Kendrick, 1982: 115–16.)

As they grow up, siblings continue to provide a context in which children are able to demonstrate mature cognitive behaviour. Young children are motivated to see their older siblings as separate individuals and to think of themselves in a similar way. Sibling relations provide one of the first contexts in which children demonstrate their ability to understand the feelings, intentions and needs of others. Perspective-taking with adults who are less similar or with whom children's relations are less intense is not observed until somewhat later. The evidence of perspective-taking and complex thinking in sibling relations lends support to psychologists such as Donaldson (1978), who argue that when situations make human sense, children can display levels of competence far in excess of those reported in laboratory-based studies. Children's ability to put themselves into the position of their siblings may be made easier by their similarity and their shared interests. But taking the perspective of others may also be facilitated because siblings are very salient to one another and there is an emotional urgency in their relations with one another. While parents' sensitivity is seen as having its basis in parents' willingness to put aside their own feelings, such holding back is unusual in sibling relations as Dunn (1984) indicates:

Young brothers and sisters love and hate, play and fight, tease and mock each other with devastating lack of inhibition. Some quarrel and bicker constantly, others are inseparable, affectionate companions, others veer between happy cooperative play and fierce aggression. (Dunn, 1984: 11.)

Children express positive feelings towards their siblings and show warmth, assistance and support, and they respond to their siblings' distress. These expressions of positive emotions increase as children get older. But more negative emotions are also common. Children are provocative and hostile, they hit and pinch one another, take toys, annoy, and tease one another (Dunn, 1984; Lamb and Sutton-Smith, 1982).

In general, siblings continue to be important as companions and playmates for one another. Conflict, jealousy, sharing, companionship and ambivalent feelings between siblings continue as children grow into middle childhood and adolescence. Disputes with siblings about social rules and obligations continue to be important for the formation of ideas about social rules as well as the development of skills of argument. However, there are changes with younger children becoming more assertive and exchanges taking on a more verbal character. In addition, older children become less available as they develop friendships with children of their own age at school. The close relations between siblings are often modified once one of them starts school and they spend less time together. As siblings go to school and develop friends of their own at school, shared experiences are reduced (Dunn, 1984; Dunn and Kendrick, 1982; Dunn and Stocker, 1989; Lamb and Sutton-Smith, 1982).

Individual Differences in Sibling Relations

There are large individual differences in families, with some siblings getting on much better than others. In some families both siblings express considerable hostility to one another and in other families considerable warmth. In yet others there is an imbalance with one sibling showing mainly positive and the other mainly negative feelings (Dunn, 1988). A number of factors have been associated with individual differences, including the gender of siblings and the age gap between children. Same-sex siblings get along with one another somewhat better. This may be related to the increasingly disparate interests of boys and girls in middle childhood and in parents' treatment of them. Parents are less consistent in their treatment of different-sex siblings and emphasize the differences rather than the similarities between them. With same-sex siblings parents stress their similarities and siblings tend to see one another as companions and playmates. Sometimes a small gap means, as with twins, a similarity of interests and greater warmth and closeness. But it can mean greater discord and jealousy. A larger age gap can result in fewer shared interests but also fewer arguments (Abramovitch *et al.*, 1986; Dunn, 1984; Lamb and Sutton-Smith, 1982).

There seems to be some continuity in sibling relations from early childhood. Siblings who are more positive about one another at age 6 tend to be those who had been more friendly towards their siblings four years earlier (Dunn, 1984). This continuity may stem from siblings having similar interests and personalities and also from continuities in their mothers' behaviour. Some mothers facilitate the development of good relations between children more than others. When mothers have very close relations with one child, children's relations with their siblings tend to be less positive. This may happen because a new baby disrupts an intense relationship between mother and older child. Mothers may influence sibling relationships by their support for the developing relationship between children. In families where mothers discuss the new baby and involve children in decision making, subsequent relations between older children and their siblings are more likely to be warm and friendly. Mothers may also discourage close sibling relationships by stressing the differences between children and encouraging competitiveness. This is most likely to happen with different-sex siblings.

The overall level of parental behaviour seems to have a less profound effect on sibling relations than the disparity in treatment children receive. Big discrepancies in mothers' responsiveness to their two children have a negative effect on sibling relations although in some families such discrepancies may be compensated for by fathers' relations with children. These discrepancies in mothers' behaviour may have particular significance in one-parent or divorced families (Bryant and Crockenberg, 1980; Dunn and Stocker, 1989; Hinde and Stevenson-Hinde, 1988; Lamb and Sutton-Smith, 1982).

Sibling relations are also associated with mothers' interventions in conflicts and quarrels. Mothers vary considerably in how much they get involved in quarrels between siblings. Mothers are likely to react when older children hit younger children and are more likely to prohibit older than younger children. When mothers intervene frequently, children are more likely to behave negatively towards one another. Conflicts in the family are also influenced by children's relations with fathers. When the relationship between first-borns and fathers is close before the birth of a second child there are fewer problems and conflicts with mothers after the birth. Fathers in such families may buffer older children against any problems they experience when younger children are born (Dunn, 1984; Dunn and Munn, 1986).

Large individual differences characterize sibling relations in middle childhood where relations vary in their intensity, warmth and closeness. As children form relationships outside the family, sibling relations are put on a more voluntary basis and in some cases become minimized, particularly when relations have been poor. Some 5 and 6 year olds play frequently with their siblings, but others play hardly at all. Koch (1960) found that a quarter of siblings said they quarrelled constantly, while a third said they hardly ever quarrelled. Some preferred their sibling as a playmate, whereas others preferred a friend. Few children were indifferent about having a sibling: a third said they would prefer to be without one but the rest claimed it was better to have a sibling. The reasons children gave for liking their siblings included the help they received, the protection siblings offered when children went to school, and the comforts and companionship they provided. Those who felt they would be happier without a sibling said siblings were bossy and they and their sibling frequently quarrelled.

Older children provide a powerful and salient model for their younger siblings based on the similarity in children's interests and levels of competence. For most children siblings are an ever present and a highly charged aspect of family life. Children are direct participants in some family relations and interactions. However they are also observers of other interactions and they overhear what is happening around them between other family members. They monitor the interactions between parents and other children, sometimes getting involved and transforming dyads into triads. In this way children are presented with a variety of models about how others behave, the explanations they give, and how they ensure the compliance of others. And by listening to others (and especially siblings who resemble them in many respects), children learn that other people, their motives and intentions, their needs and wishes, constitute a substantial part of people's conversations.

Family Relations in Middle Childhood

The dimensions devised by psychologists to describe childrearing with young children are also relevant with older children, although the ways in which parents manifest qualities such as warmth and sensitivity, how they control children and what they demand as mature behaviour change with their children's age. As they get older, children are expected to show greater control over their expression of impulses. The ready expression of impulses may be tolerated in toddlers but during middle childhood children are increasingly expected to delay gratification and get their needs met in socially acceptable ways. This can be by asking for things or waiting their turn rather than snatching them. It also means not crying or having a temper tantrum because they cannot do what they want. The issues which concern parents change, with mothers expressing concern about children's rudeness, cheek and bad language at 7 years. Children are also expected to express their feelings or impulses in line with their gender, so that, for example, boys are allowed to express aggression more freely than girls (Newson and Newson, 1976).

Children's increasing language skills make them more adept at verbally resisting parents and more able to find reasons why they should not do what is asked of them. These strategies may be as irritating or frustrating to parents as the whining and temper tantrums of younger children, but parents need to deal with them in different ways. Distraction and suggestion are less powerful once children get to middle childhood, but verbal strategies can be used more. Mothers' use of verbal explanations and justifications demonstrates a continuing concern with using discipline not merely as a way of controlling children's present behaviour, but in the pursuance of longer-term goals (Kuczynski *et al.*, 1987). These may include teaching children the value of compliance and reciprocity and respect for the feelings of others. Smacking and physical punishment are still used by parents, alongside other techniques, often as an impulsive response to children's defiance. But smacking is effective only as long as children are willing to accept it as a legitimate form of control. If they resist or retaliate, smacking may escalate rather than reduce unacceptable behaviour (Dix *et al.*, 1986).

By the time children reach age 7 mothers spend less time playing with children and the nature of their contact changes. Mothers of 7-year-olds are less likely than mothers of 4-year-olds to get involved in play. But children's greater conversational skills and their clearer sense of themselves make the time they spend together more enjoyable for many mothers who feel that their children provide them with more companionship as they grow up. This is especially so with daughters. Daughters are more likely to be home-based than sons and by age 7 many have developed interests which mothers enjoy sharing (Llewelyn and Osborne, 1990; Newson and Newson, 1976).

Parents' approaches to childcare vary as a function of their structural position. Middle-class mothers report using more democratic and verbal means of control. Working-class mothers are more likely to act in an authoritarian way and are less likely to use verbal means of control. They tend to use words to threaten and bamboozle children into obedience rather than to

explain the rules underlying social behaviour. Children in working-class families are less able than those in middle-class families to identify with or operate
effectively in school (Arnot and Weiner, 1987; Newson and Newson, 1976).
Such differences are usually seen as resulting from parents' behaviour,
although the links are very complex. Parents' behaviour, their beliefs and
expectations, and the meanings they impart to their children's behaviour stem
from as well as influence their children's lives. Parents' attitudes and the
behaviour they encourage in their children result from their experience of
being middle or working class, black or white, rich or poor. But these
attitudes also provide a powerful framework within which they evaluate their
own and their children's behaviour.

The styles parents employ are associated with variability in social and
intellectual competence in middle childhood. The use of reasoning, consistent
discipline and the expression of warmth have been found to be positively
related to self-esteem, internalized control, pro-social attitudes and intellectual
achievement although once children get to school their intellectual performance and their relations with others are also influenced by teachers and peers
(Hwang *et al.*, 1989; Maccoby and Martin, 1983). Parents' relationships with
their children continue to be important but they are increasingly supple-
mented by those with other people. Parents, and especially mothers, continue to be the major source of affection and intimacy for children, they
support and enhance children's self-esteem and provide help and support. The
close emotional ties between parents and children, their continuity and shared
history, give parent-child relationships their potential for conflict and storms
as well as warmth and intimacy. But children also find satisfaction from other
relationships, such as those with grandparents, siblings, friends and teachers
(Buhrmester and Furman, 1987).

Going to School: Links between Family and School

Once children go to school they live in separate but interrelated worlds with
the family continuing to provide a central context for development. For many
children contact with the world outside their families starts early if they are
looked after by grandmothers or nannies, or go to playgroups and nursery
classes (Lewis and Feiring, 1984; Tizard and Hughes, 1984). Going to school
allows children to become more independent although parents continue to
control many aspects of their children's lives. In their choice of an area in
which to live, the school children attend and the activities in which they
engage, parents provide a general framework within which children make
friends and they supervise their children's friendships, although boys are
increasingly free of parental surveillance (Hargreaves and Colley, 1986). In
addition, children's self-esteem and their sense of personal efficacy derived
from experiences in their families, influence how they relate to other children
(Damon, 1983).

Parents are expected to prepare children for the wider world. This involves passing on cultural expectations and beliefs, and teaching children how to behave acceptably. Children are expected to apply rules and moral principles learned in the family to other settings but also to modify their behaviour to suit a variety of situations. Children who behave badly in their families may be forgiven and continue to be loved but the same behaviour may lead to their rejection by peers or teachers. Learning to operate within these different contexts is important for children. It is also important for parents, and especially mothers, that children behave well in the wider world. Acceptable behaviour from children indicates parents' success, achievement, and sometimes their acceptance by their community (New and David, 1985; Newson and Newson, 1976).

Children move from one world to the other, keeping parents in touch with what happens at school, who they play with, what they enjoy and what they worry about. This makes considerable demands of children's developing cognitive skills and exerts pressure for other-perspective taking as children try to tell others in the family about things that have happened to them at school in ways their family can understand. How much mothers in particular encourage children to make these links between home and school depends in part on how mothers are adjusting to their children being at school and forming relationships with other people. Some mothers respond positively but others miss the companionship their children provide and their involvement in their children's worlds. This happens especially when the youngest child in a family starts school. Some mothers are concerned about pressures which are increasingly brought to bear upon children, often demanding conformity and high achievement (Llewelyn and Osborne, 1990). Teachers often supplement parents as sources of authority and information, but sometimes their values and expectations conflict with or undermine those of parents. For example, parents bringing up children on their own may find they have to help children to cope with feelings of marginality induced by assumptions at school that all children live with a mother AND a father. Black or Asian parents may have to help their children deal with the racism children encounter at school (see e.g. Arnot and Weiner, 1987).

Children take their home life into school. There is considerable evidence that family variables including parents' values and attitudes towards education, their expectations and support for children's developing competence and their educational achievement all influence children's performance at school, as measured by vocabulary, IQ, reading ability, problem-solving skills, exploratory behaviour and social competence (see e.g. Damon, 1983; Pettit *et al.*, 1988). Schools generally take little notice of family relations although siblings may be compared with one another, or in the case of large families treated as a group, e.g. as 'the Browns'. Schools may also provide children with the opportunity to talk to other children and to adults about problems they are experiencing at home. Good relations at school may act as a buffer against some of the difficulties associated with stresses such as divorce of their parents (see Chapter 7) and may also alert teachers and others to problems such as abuse (see Chapter 8).

Family Relations in Adolescence

Children's entry into the world beyond the family is accelerated during adolescence. In adolescence young people have considerable freedom to make day to day decisions, such as about clothes or how to spend their time and money, to take responsibility for themselves and make decisions about education, work and political beliefs, to make new relationships outside the family and to develop a coherent identity. Some psychological research stresses the magnitude and the disruptiveness of changes in adolescence compared with those in middle childhood. These changes are seen as initiated or propelled by physical changes or cognitive development or by the pressures on young people to move into the adult world, including the world of work, and to separate themselves physically and emotionally from their parents. Whatever their cause, as young people become more independent and more involved with peers, relations within their families are assumed to become difficult (Coleman and Hendry, 1990; Damon, 1983). In their search for autonomy and an identity or clear sense of themselves, young people are seen as pulled in one way by peers and media presentations of 'normal' teenage behaviour and in other ways by parents and other sources of authority. The strategies or defence mechanisms young people employ to cope with different expectations and pressures are thought to result in conflicts between young people and their families (Coleman and Hendry, 1990).

Studies of family relations do not support such a gloomy view. Parental relations with young people indicate that parents continue to be major sources of information, attachment, affection and esteem. Young people generally retain strong and positive feelings towards their families and home life and feel that they communicate well with parents. They tend to share their parents' values and attitudes towards many moral and political issues and often turn to parents for guidance especially about important academic, career or personal choices. Relations with parents become more reciprocal during adolescence. Young people continue to defer to their parents' knowledge but increasingly they believe that they have a contribution to make to family decisions. Close relations with parents are associated with higher self-esteem and better adjustment for young people (Armsden and Greenberg, 1987; Damon, 1983; Montemayor, 1983).

An important aspect of young people's identity relates to their gender and their sense of themselves as young men and women. The formation of gender identity has different implications for boys and girls. For boys the major shift in gender identity comes in the preschool years when they are encouraged to become independent and assertive. For girls, the major shift comes later. During childhood appropriate female behaviour encourages both dependence and independence, so girls may be assertive, competitive and achievement-oriented. However, at adolescence expectations for girls change. To continue to be viewed positively, girls have to abandon or disguise competitiveness and assertiveness. This shift means giving up direct achievement and accepting achievement through their relationships with others, in adult life as wives and mothers. During adolescence, girls begin to under-achieve as they recognize that in our society being 'too' clever puts at risk their appropriate gender identity (Coleman and Hendry, 1990; Lees, 1986; Llewelyn and Osborne, 1990; Sharpe, 1976).

Young people's development of gender identity is linked to relations with parents, especially when young people see parents' behaviour and in-terests as similar to their own. Boys who view their fathers positively are more likely to want to engage in activities with them. Girls who feel close to and similar to mothers who work outside the home are more likely to share their ideas about work and to be independent and highly motivated and to score well on measures of social and personality adjustment. Mothers and fathers have somewhat different ideas about childrearing; fathers encourage independence and assertiveness whereas mothers encourage more interperson-al behaviours such as politeness and manners. Parents' aspirations for their children depend upon their gender; parents see social behaviour and polite-ness as more important for girls and independence as important for boys (Power and Shanks, 1989).

A small but significant percentage of young people have difficult rela-tionships with their parents (Rutter, 1980). Many conflicts within families tend be about relatively minor matters, especially around topics such as make-up, dating, leisure activities, and music. Even when there are conflicts about such issues, young people and parents do not generally consider that their underlying relationship is poor (Coleman and Hendry, 1990). This may be a reflection of fairly realistic expectations of young people and their parents; they do not expect relations to be perfect and entirely free of conflict and therefore are not too disappointed when they encounter some difficulties.

Managing Conflict

Even when conflicts do occur, they tend not to undermine family function-ing. Conflict can be accommodated partly because most disagreements have as their focus relatively superficial aspects of young people's relations with their parents rather than basic values and attitudes. Another reason is that young people's and their parents' concern and respect for one another provides a framework within which issues can be worked out or contained. One way in which conflict is contained is by limiting discussions to relatively unconten-tious topics and keeping 'hot' topics which would cause conflict to discus-sions with grandparents, friends and teachers (Hunter, 1985; Montemayor, 1983). When there is discussion of difficult topics such as sexuality, sexual behaviour or drug use, discussion tends to be superficial. While this reduces the potential for conflict, it does mean that parents are frequently in a rather poor position to inform, advise or support young people.

The extent of conflict in families and the way it is managed varies considerably. Some parental styles encourage close relations between young people and their parents while others may escalate tensions and conflicts. For example, parents who are very strict or who employ an authoritarian style may succeed in containing conflict only as long as young people accept parents' authority and are willing to be controlled in this way. In middle childhood, children sometimes object and retaliate if they dislike parents' behaviour or consider it to be unfair or inappropriate. The potential for retaliation is increased in adolescence. Young people can demand explanations from parents and can argue effectively when they think their parents are wrong. Close friends provide them with insight into how other families operate and may feed their sense of grievance as they compare their parents with those of their friends. In addition, as sons grow bigger and stronger than parents (and especially mothers), control techniques based on parents' physical strength are impossible to maintain. Conflict between mothers and sons is lessened by middle adolescence suggesting that by this stage most parents have acknowledged and come to terms with their sons' increased autonomy and power (Steinberg, 1981).

In contrast, parents who are more authoritative, who discuss things with children and involve them in family decisions, may find that the techniques they used in childhood continue to be workable and they have fewer problems. Adolescents who are provided with experience of decision making under parental supervision and who receive explanations from parents are most likely to be independent, to want to be like their parents, to mix with friends who are approved of by their parents, and to perform well at school (Coleman and Hendry, 1990; Steinberg *et al.*, 1989). Young people themselves express a preference for democratic and authoritative solutions to some family issues, such as what time they should come home at night, although they are prepared to accept more authoritarian decisions about domestic chores (Coleman and Hendry, 1990).

Family Adjustments to Young People

Families differ in their adjustments to adolescent members. Factors which may influence the quality of relations between young people and their families are parents' beliefs about the course of development and their willingness to accept and acknowledge young people's independence (Savin-Williams and Small, 1986). Some families are slow to change and may resist the 'new' person and their new interests and find it hard to appreciate that their scruffy 10-year-old has become a squeaky-clean 13-year-old who spends hours in the bathroom or that their scatterbrained 13-year-old has become a cool and organized 17-year-old. But even so, families may still get it wrong because parents and young people often have contradictory ideas and expectations of one another. Parents' expectations of young people are not static and consequently their treatment may swing between demands for obedience on one occasion and leaving young people to make their own decisions the next. Parents' attempts to let go and encourage independence may be welcomed by young people on one occasion but on another parents may be accused of being insufficiently interested and supportive. Young people do not always respond well to increased autonomy, for example boys sometimes resist the increased responsibility and decreased supervision of their activities when mothers take up employment outside the home (Coleman and Hendry, 1990).

Changes in adolescence have an impact on all members of the family and everyone has to adjust to the growing and maturing person. This may involve complex patterns of interaction as parents and young people mutually influence one another. How easily parents make adjustments and support young people depends in part on events in their lives. Some parents enjoy the changes in their relationships with young people. They respect the greater competence of young people and their help in the home or with the care of younger children and enjoy sharing adult interests with them. Parents may value their children's increased independence because it gives them opportunities to develop interests of their own. But other parents find their children's maturity and independence threatening, in part because of what it indicates about their own age and position in the family. Realization of the passing of time may be particularly difficult for parents if other aspects of their lives are unsatisfactory (Llewelyn and Osborne, 1990). Parents who are preoccupied with their own worries or are going through divorce may be less sensitive to what is happening in young people's lives (see Chapter 7). But there are other changes which influence relations in families with young people, including maternal employment outside the home, job change and redundancy for parents, grandparents coming to live with the family, and older children leaving home.

Although siblings are seen as an important part of the family system in childhood, there is less information about sibling relations in adolescence. They can be fairly fraught, with young people reporting a higher rate of conflicts and quarrels with their siblings than with parents or friends (Fogelman, 1976). As the first child reaches puberty and becomes less family-based, they may have less in common with other siblings and there may be less contact between them. However, when a second or subsequent child reaches puberty they may begin to have more in common and get closer again. When parents and children have difficulty about emotionally laden subjects such as sex or the use of drugs, siblings can sometimes provide reliable and consistent support. Grandparents provide an extra source of adult support and sometimes can help mediate relations between young people and their parents (Lamb and Sutton-Smith, 1982; Tinsley and Parke, 1984). In general, families retain their influence and significance for young people. The changes young people undergo have far-reaching consequences for themselves and other people in the family and alter family dynamics and patterns of interaction. Families provide a context in which young people work through many of the changes and adjustments in adolescence but in doing so they change the nature and experience of family life for other family members.

Relations with Peers in Adolescence

From an early age children are interested in one another and many psychologists consider that play with peers is an important impetus for development (e.g. Damon, 1983). For many children the opportunity to interact in recip-rocal ways with people similar to themselves is first encountered in sibling interactions. Only children and children whose sibling relations are not close, may experience reciprocal relations in their play with peers. Close rela-tionships with other children provide alternative sources of interaction and support for young people (Berndt and Perry, 1986). It means interacting with people with whom there is no common family history and with whom they do not have long-term relationships. It means, for example, playing with children who do not know family members and pets, who do not observe the same rituals around birthdays and do not have the same toys and interests. In addition it may mean getting to know children who come from families with different expectations and beliefs around, for example, what are considered appropriate activities for girls and boys. A close friendship is associated with greater confidence and a more positive self-image. Peer relations may act as a strong support particularly when relations with parents are difficult or when parents, because of difficulties in their lives, are less available (Coleman and Hendry, 1990; Mannarino, 1978).

Peer relations change somewhat during childhood and adolescence. In middle childhood friendships are segregated according to gender; boys play with boys and girls play with girls. Often there is little contact and few shared interests. This may be a result of the different play styles and distinctive cultures of boys and girls. Boys' groups are more hierarchically organized and concerned with dominance; boys interrupt one another and use commands and threats. Girls' groups are more concerned with socially cohesive functions so that girls tend, for example, to express agreement with what a speaker has said and they pause to give others a turn. Girls have more intense relation-ships and those relationships provide them with greater intimacy, affection and self-esteem than do boys' friendships. These characteristics reflect stereo-types of gender identity which schools, books, sport etc. generally reinforce (Bryant, 1985; Hargreaves and Colley, 1986; Maccoby, 1988). Gradually during adolescence heterosexual relations become more important and the em-ergence of sexuality leads to more sustained and intimate heterosexual rela-tions (Buhrmester and Furman, 1987; Damon, 1983; Maccoby and Jacklin, 1987).

Peer relations are characterized by greater reciprocity and equality than are those with parents. There is more sharing, explaining and mutual under-standing than with parents who tend to supply information and allow young people less opportunity to express their viewpoints (Hunter, 1985). Peer relations are particularly important in terms of current events and activities. They give young people opportunities to experience and verify alternative views about interpersonal relationships (Younnis, 1980). Learning to get on with and have good relations with others are important skills and ones which are related to young people's social acceptance. In their relations with peers, young people learn to cope with rejection and loss which result from the end of a friendship and the need to build up the confidence to make new friends (Hartup, 1983; Rubin, 1980).

Mutuality in friendships is based on intimacy and involves the apprecia-tion of the reciprocal nature of the activities, abilities and personalities of friends. Friendships provide a forum for self-revelation in which young people can share their feelings and opinions with others without fear of them being used against them (Younnis, 1980). Through close friendships, young people become aware of the uniqueness of other people and through their understanding of their different viewpoints, they may overcome the egocentricity which characterizes adolescent thinking (Coleman and Hendry, 1990).

Friendships and peer relations reduce young people's emotional dependence on parents. In many respects parents support these friendships and their attitudes and values are not often in opposition. Developing reciprocal and mutually supportive relations with peers may feed back into relations with parents and siblings. Recognizing the value of thinking about how things look to other people in their relations with their peers may be used with profit in their relations with parents and siblings. And seeing and learning about friends' relations with families may help them to appreciate their own families.

But young people's peer relations may be a source of concern and conflict. The interest of many parents (and psychologists) in peer relations stems from concern about the ways in which peer group pressure can encourage anti-social behaviour. Social pressures from friends and peers are important factors influencing young people's behaviour with alcohol, tobacco, and other drugs (see e.g. Chassin *et al.*, 1986; Morgan and Grube, 1989). Involvement in such activities may provide young people with an identity and gives them a sense of being mature and grown-up people as well as a way of being accepted by others. This would seem to be particularly important when relations with parents are poor and young people cannot use parents as sources of information about the risks of drug abuse. In addition, engaging in anti-social behaviour may be a way of separating themselves from their parents and forcing parents to recognize that they are grown-up. However, some parents encourage young people in drug abuse, providing them with access to cigarettes, alcohol and other drugs as well as encouraging positive attitudes to drug use (Chassin *et al.*, 1986; Coleman and Hendry, 1990; Montemayor, 1983; Morgan and Grube, 1989).

Another aspect of behaviour which may cause concern and conflict between parents and young people is sexual behaviour. Recent concern with young people's sexual behaviour focuses on HIV/AIDS and public health campaigns around 'safer sex' and the use of condoms (White *et al.*, 1989). Media campaigns have brought such issues into the public domain and increased the awareness of some parents of the value of talking to young people about sexual matters generally, although it is not clear to what extent raising these issues means that parents and young people can discuss them more easily. Attitudes to sexual behaviour have changed considerably, but there is still a general assumption that getting pregnant and becoming a single parent creates a major source of tension and conflict between parents and young people. Women who become mothers when they are young and single are seen as problematic, medically and socially, and their children are considered to be at risk. However, many young mothers see motherhood more positively. It provides them with an important source of adult status and one which, given the kinds of work in which they usually engage, does not interfere with their careers. Many young women have good and supportive relations with their parents (and especially their mothers) who provide them with considerable assistance once their babies are born (Phoenix, 1991).

In Conclusion

Relations between children differ in many respects from those between children and adults and provide different incentives and pressures for development. But parental and sibling relations are not independent of one another. Parents manage children's interactions and influence the nature of sibling relations. Through their encouragement of relations between siblings and their interventions in quarrels, mothers (and probably fathers, too) set the scene within which sibling relations develop. In their turn, relations between siblings may influence how parents view themselves and whether or not they think of themselves as effective parents.

Family relations continue to provide a powerful context for development in middle childhood and adolescence, as children move into the wider social world. Relations with friends and their experience of life at school become increasingly important. They provide different ways of interacting with and relating to people and they may have somewhat different implications for children's development. Young people's experiences in their social networks feed into their interactions and relations within their families, just as family experiences influence how children operate in the wider world. In many respects the attitudes and values children develop in the outside world reflect those in their families. But as they grow older, discrepancies and conflicts between family and other values and practices are of increasing concern.

Further Reading

COLEMAN, J.C. and HENDRY, L. (1990) *The Nature of Adolescence*, 2nd ed., London, Routledge.

A good review of a variety of psychological studies of adolescence including work on identity formation and young people's relations with their parents.

DUNN, J. (1984) *Sisters and Brothers*, London, Fontana.

A review (using some interesting historical material) of studies of sibling relationships during childhood, of the nature of influence between siblings and the impact of sibling relations for children's development.

DUNN, J. and KENDRICK, C. (1982) *Siblings: Love, Envy and Understanding*, London, Grant McIntyre.

An account of longitudinal study of mothers and 2- to 3-year-old children as a second child is born into the family. Changes in the relationships and interactions between mothers and children are reported as well as the emerging relationships between children and their younger siblings. The impact of the nature of mother-child relationships on the development of sibling relationships is discussed.

DUNN, J. and SHATZ, M. (1989) 'Becoming a conversationalist despite (or because of) having an older sibling', *Child Development*, **60**, pp. 399–410.

Most studies of language acquisition stress the importance of a sophisticated language user who is committed to making sense of and supporting children's emerging language and conversational skills. Here the advantages and disadvantages for children's language development of overhearing language which is not addressed to them and the development of strategies for entering conversations between mothers and older siblings are discussed.

LAMB, M.E. and SUTTON-SMITH, B. (Eds) (1982) *Sibling Relationships: Their Nature and Significance across the Lifespan*, Hillsdale, NJ, Lawrence Erlbaum Associates.

Reports on a large number of studies of sibling relationships. Studies concentrate mainly on North American childhood, but there are chapters on sibling relationships in adulthood and sibling relationships cross-culturally.

TINSLEY, B.R. and PARKE, R.D. (1984) 'Grandparents as support and socialization agents', in LEWIS, M. (Ed.) *Beyond the Dyad*, New York, Plenum.

The reasons why psychological approaches to families rarely extend to grandparents are considered and evidence about grandparents' influence is presented. Grandparents can influence children directly through the nature of their relationships with grandchildren, acting as substitute parents or as playmates without the everyday responsibility for children. They may have an indirect influence through their support for the parental relationship or by providing feedback about parenting. Relationships between children and their grandparents depend to a large extent on the age differences between them and on grandparents' fitness and hence their ability to get involved.

Chapter 7

The Family in Transition:
Single Parenting, Family Breakup
and Reconstituted Families

The assumed norm for family life is that children are reared by two parents, their mother and father. Much of the material earlier in this book has discussed ideas within the framework of a stable intact family with both parents present. However, for many children this is not the family life they experience. Many children are brought up for some part of their childhood by a single parent, usually their mother. For a variety of reasons some children spend some or part of their childhood in the care of foster parents or experience institutional care. Other children continue to be reared within their family but the family composition changes. Change to the family may involve the addition or loss of children. The change in family functioning brought about by the birth of children is discussed in Chapters 2 and 6. Other changes in family structure occur as 'parents' are removed from or added to the family. Parents may be lost through their death or through family breakup. Single parents may take on new partners introducing step-parents and possibly stepsiblings. Any change in the family makes adjustment demands of all members. Changes can cause uncertainty and unhappiness, but can also be a stimulus to growth for family members. Different individuals experience changes within the family differently and the same individual experiences those changes differently at different points in time. This chapter considers two transitional family states, families following breakup and step-parent families.

Families Headed by Single Parents

In many western societies a large number of children are living in single-parent families at any one time. In the UK in 1988 16 per cent of the families with dependent children were headed by a single parent (OPCS, 1989). The remaining children were living either with both natural parents, a parent and a step-parent, or with adoptive parents. Figures from US Census returns show 21 per cent of children in single-parent households (Laosa, 1988). Children can live in households headed by a single parent for a variety of reasons. Mothers may never have married or cohabited, one parent may have died or a two-parent family may have broken up. In the UK a quarter of births are to unmarried mothers and the figures from the USA show similar rates. Many unmarried mothers are young, but, in the UK especially, these figures include an increasingly large number of older non-married, but cohabiting, mothers (Butler and Golding, 1986; Wicks and Keirnan, 1990). In the UK widow and widower headed households account for less than 2 per cent of households with dependent children. Family breakup is much more common with 9 per cent of families in the UK and 15 per cent of US families headed by a divorced or separated parent. Breakup rates of unmarried cohabiting couples are harder to monitor and so the true figures for separated parents may be higher.

Looking at these statistics in a different way, figures from the USA show that 38 per cent of the children born in the period 1965–9 were not living with both natural parents by age 16 years. It is estimated that 50 per cent or more of children born in the late 1970s will spend some time in a single-parent family before they reach the age of 16 years (Bumpass, 1984; Hofferth, 1985). Projections for family breakup in the UK are much lower; it is anticipated that about 70 per cent of British children will continue to be brought up by both parents, although in many cases the parents will remain unmarried (Wicks and Kiernan, 1990). Most children do not remain in a single-parent household for all of their childhood. The projected average time spent in a single-parent US family is six years for white children and eleven years for black children (Hofferth, 1985).

Family Breakup

As has been indicated family breakup is relatively frequent and many children have to adjust to the discontinuities in family life and routines as parents separate and divorce. However, some families are more likely to break up than others. Cohabiting couples are more likely to split up than married couples, couples without a background of religious belief and women whose own parents separated are more likely to experience the breakup of their own relationships. Other factors are: children being conceived soon after the start of a relationship or being unplanned; mothers under 20 years of age, and parents having low educational achievements and poorly paid jobs (Ferguson *et al.*, 1984; Haskey, 1987). The characteristics of families who are most likely to break up explain in part the apparent effects of family breakup on the children involved.

Custody Arrangements

Following family breakup more than 80 per cent of children are looked after by their mothers, although this is affected by the age and sex of the children. Fathers have custody of boys, and especially adolescent boys, more frequently than of girls and they are least likely to have custody of girls under the age of

2 years. Recently there have been moves in both the UK and the USA to make joint custody arrangements, so that the children of divorcing parents maintain contact with both parents. As part of that move there is also greater emphasis on conciliation and divorce counselling in an attempt to minimize post-divorce conflict and disagreements. However, the evidence suggests that changes in the legal arrangements are not reflected in the living arrangements of families post-divorce. Children generally live with one parent and have few overnight stays with the other parent. Only a small percentage of children spend large amounts of time with both parents (Maccoby *et al.*, 1988). In general children do not see a great deal of their non-custodial parent, although there are marked individual differences. Mothers are better at maintaining regular contact than are fathers when they are the parent without custody. In 44 per cent of families there is no contact at all with the non-custodial parent. However, in about 20 per cent of cases the non-custodial parents see their children once a week or more (Furstenberg, 1988). Contact with the non-custodial parent declines with the passage of time with fathers showing a more marked decline in the frequency of their visits than mothers and contact with daughters declining more rapidly than contact with sons (Hetherington *et al.*, 1982).

Adjusting to Changed Family Circumstances

Hetherington (1979) has pointed out that divorce is not a single event, but a sequence of events which she splits into four phases: disequilibrium in the family prior to breakup, disequilibrium and disorganization after the divorce, development of coping strategies and routines within the new family framework, and emergence of a new equilibrium.

Families do not usually break up without any warning. For some time before they separate most couples are aware of a deterioration in their relationship that is frequently expressed in terms of arguments and conflict in the home. Conflict and tension in the family is distressing for all family members. In Chapter 5 we discussed the importance of good relationships between parents for ensuring their consistent and sensitive parenting. Because of deteriorating family relationships prior to the breakup it is likely that children already suffer adverse consequences, and that these accelerate with the breakup.

The Immediate Response to the Breakup

Hetherington (1979) suggests that there is disequilibrium and disorganization after the divorce. Even when relationships have become unsatisfactory their termination calls for adjustments on the part of all family members and those adjustments take time and draw heavily on emotional resources. Consequently, the year following family breakup is a period when family members are unlikely to function well. At some point during this time most men and women feel depressed, incompetent, angry and rejected. Adjusting to the changes following separation are almost as difficult for the initiator of the separation as for the non-initiator (Pettit and Bloom, 1984). After one year of separation 60 per cent of men and 70 per cent of women regret the separation, although the separation is viewed much more positively later with less than a quarter of men and women still regretting the breakup by the end of the second year. For both partners the development of new close relationships helps with the speedy adjustment to the breakup and to a more positive view of post-separation life (Hetherington *et al.*, 1982).

For the majority of custodial parents the first year of bringing up children on their own is demanding; most report experiencing task overload with too much to do and too little time and energy available. They report being socially isolated, receiving little support with parenting and working longer hours (Weinraub and Wolf, 1983). Their social isolation usually does not occur immediately, but after a few months. According to Hetherington *et al.* (1982), in the first few months following the breakup friends and relatives tend to rally round and the parent has plenty of contact with adults, but this declines. One reason for this is that custodial parents may feel depressed and so do not seek out friends. As the contacts with adults decline, their world tends to become more restricted to interactions with children or about children. Custodial parents tend to be poor at maintaining consistent routines for themselves and their children and established routines may be disrupted by the breakup. Thus the average custodial parent is less likely to read to children or to play with them, they are less likely to get their children to school on time and are more erratic in getting their children to bed (Hetherington *et al.*, 1982). In addition, for the early years following the separation custodial parents make fewer maturity demands of their children. In part this arises because parents find it easier to do tasks for their children rather than requiring the children to do the task themselves. In the short term it is easier to put a child's toys away rather than nagging a child to do it. Although this might be quicker in the short term, it gives children less opportunity to become competent and contribute to household tasks placing more of a load on parents longer term.

During this early period children tend to respond negatively to the changes in their lives. Children of all ages show initial depression, unhappiness and anxiety. In addition, they become inattentive to others and more socially withdrawn, not entering into interactions with their friends and family as readily as before. Younger children also display more clinging, whining, complaining and aggression and are less compliant, refusing to do things that they are asked to do. This is true for both sons and daughters. After about a year girls usually show a marked improvement, but for sons the apparent improvement is less. Even after two years boys are more socially isolated, less cooperative and more obviously unhappy. In the year following separation, one of children's common fears is that they will be abandoned by the custodial parent. They also fear ridicule from their friends and peers; at this time self-blame is common too (Kurdek, 1988). In the following, second, year of the separation all of these fears and anxieties decrease.

The average immediate disequilibrium following breakup does not affect all families equally. Factors such as the level of conflict pre-separation and the availability of social supports will modify these early reactions.

Longer-Term Reactions to the Breakup
Once the initial adjustments have been made by custodial parents their sense of well-being improves. Additionally, with the departure of the ex-partner consistent routines may be re-established or, in the case of families who had experienced large amounts of conflict, routines may be established for the first time. This is especially true when daughters are involved. The majority of mothers feel positively about daughters, they feel close and affectionate towards them and in tune with them. In contrast their relations with boys are frequently problematic even six or more years after the breakup. Mothers tend to spend less time with sons than daughters and report feeling less rapport with them and feeling less close to them. They also report having poor control over their sons: their requests are frequently ignored and when this happens mothers tend not to pursue the request. Interactions with sons involve a lot of complaints and nagging and mothers are more likely to enter into angry and lengthy exchanges with them. However, both sons and daughters are allowed more responsibility and independence than children of the same age from intact families. As part of this, mothers monitor their children less, and they are less likely to know where children are or who they are with. In addition these children are more likely to be left unsupervised when the mother is away from the house. On this regime, girls report that they feel they are growing up faster than they would have done had the family stayed together; they also report being satisfied with their relationships with their mothers. For their part boys frequently recognize that they are making life difficult for their mothers and admit that they behave aggressively and engage in anti-social acts (Hetherington, 1988).

Although custodial parents usually feel better adjusted by the second year, there is evidence that family breakup has longer-term influences on some aspects of children's functioning. These can be seen in children's increased aggressiveness and non-compliance and their poor impulse control and underachievement (Hetherington, 1988). In a twenty-six-year study of a British sample Wadsworth (1985) reports on the long-term adjustments of a large sample of women who were brought up as children in homes broken by either the death of a parent or the breakup of their parents' relationship and compares them to women who were brought up as children in intact homes. Both groups of women from broken homes described their childhoods as less happy than did women from intact homes and as mothers they were less warm and demonstrative with their own (first-born) children. Both men and women show some long-term lowering of educational attainment and men brought up in a single-parent family tend to remain socially and economically disadvantaged (Wadsworth and Maclean, 1986). According to Hetherington (1988) differences in the performance of children from broken and intact homes occur because custodial parents experience difficulty in maintaining their routines; they are not shown in those cases where the custodial parent is able to maintain consistent and sensitive routines.

Children from intact homes tend to perform better at school than children from single-parent homes (Hetherington, 1988; Wadsworth and Maclean, 1986). The simplistic interpretation of these findings that the loss of a parent leads directly to impaired performance may be incorrect. These two groups of families vary in a number of ways which might give rise to the difference in their performance. The most obvious difference is that children from single-parent families tend to come from a lower socio-economic background. Averagely children with less well educated and poorer parents do less well themselves at school and score less well on standardized tests. The poorer performance of these children could then be due to the absence of a parent or to the social background of their parents. When account is taken of these confounding variables there is only a modest difference in academic performance that is due to the disruption of the family, although children who are less than 6 years old at the time of the breakup show more long-term effects on their academic performance (Furstenberg, 1988).

In the short term girls cope better than boys, but it is in the longer term that effects of family breakup on girls are more apparent. In adolescence girls from broken homes are more rebellious, show higher rates of depression and experience more difficulty in their heterosexual relations than do children from intact, non-divorced homes (Hetherington, 1988; Wallerstein *et al.*, 1988).

The Extended Family

When parents separate, children frequently lose contact with the non-custodial parent's family. This is more likely to happen where the absent parent does not maintain contact with the family. However loss of contact with one line of the family may be offset by an increase in contact with the extended family of the custodial parent, especially with grandparents who may offer increased support and help. In many cases the family goes to live with the parents of the remaining parent. Examination of the living arrangements of families shows that 13 per cent of families headed by a divorcee live with the children's grandparents compared to only 1 per cent of intact families (Furstenberg, 1988). Grandmothers in particular are likely to become more actively involved in childrearing; setting and enforcing rules, offering emotional support and so on. Boys especially seem to benefit from this involvement, forming better relationships with both their grandmother and mother (Wilson and Tolson, 1988). They experience a direct benefit from the nurturant support of grandmothers, but also an indirect benefit in that when grandmothers are present mothers feel less stressed and more relaxed and respond more positively to their sons. For girls the opposite is true: they think that their mothers are more involved with them when the grandmother is less involved. Probably one reason why girls do not see the same benefits is that when they live with a lone parent they have more responsibility and a special position within the family that may be undermined if another adult becomes involved.

Changing Family Experiences

Family breakup involves a number of changes in the lives of all remaining family members. Most obviously the family composition has changed, the same group of people no longer live together. However, additional changes occur. The self-image of each family member changes. They can no longer view themselves in quite the same way but have to come to terms with the loss of the non-custodial parent and the new routines and patterns in their lives. Additionally most families are worse off financially as the same income has to be stretched to support two households and they may experience environmental changes, no longer living in the same physical location surrounded by the same familiar belongings. Any of these changes could have an impact on children and their parents and could contribute to ease of adjustments following family breakup.

Family Income

On average, family breakup leads to a lowering of family income, in many cases quite drastically. Single-parent families make up a large proportion of the poor in Britain (Mack and Lansley, 1985). In the USA divorce leads to a marked and enduring drop in income, on the money spent on food and household expenditure, while remarriage usually leads to a marked improvement in family income (Weiss, 1984). It seems that family breakup has a twofold impact on the development of children: a direct effect of the loss of a parent and the loss of the family identity and an indirect impact through lowered family income. The greater the financial hardship following family breakup, the harder are the adjustments for all family members and the more adjustment problems are shown by children. Their emotional well-being, their school performance and their social acceptance by peers can all be affected (Guidubaldi and Perry, 1984). Family income has an impact probably through changes in the child's routines and the custodial parent's satisfaction with and confidence in their parenting abilities. Parents who are preoccupied with family finances will find it harder to be attentive and responsive to their children. Children who suffer minimal loss of material resources and who are able to maintain pre-divorce routines do not show impairment in their cognitive, emotional and social functioning. Because of financial problems custodial parents may seek paid work outside the home. If the change in the working status of the parent occurs soon after the breakup this presents another change in routines for all the family. This has been associated with a further increased incidence in behaviour problems, especially aggressiveness, bedwetting and school refusal (Hetherington *et al.*, 1982). While most families are worse off financially following family breakup, there are exceptions where the ex-partner withdrew more from the family budget than they contributed. In these cases the improved financial circumstances of the family may bring benefits.

Family breakup results in some degree of environmental change. Frequently family breakup leads to changes in housing, often with the family going to live with the custodial parent's own parents. House moving may result in considerable environmental change, especially when the move takes the family to a new geographical area. It has been suggested that the greater the environmental change, the greater the stress for children, the more adjustments they have to make and the more depression, aggression and social withdrawal shown (Hetherington *et al.*, 1982).

Quality of the Relationship with Each Parent

One reason why children may be adversely affected by the separation of the parents is that they also experience changes in the nature and quality of parenting. In the first two years following the breakup, custodial mothers make few maturity demands of their children, they communicate with them less, show fewer signs of affection and are inconsistent in their disciplining (Hetherington *et al.*, 1982). This inconsistent disciplining takes the form of restrictive rules that are poorly enforced. Children's compliance and non-compliance both tend to be ignored, so the children receive inadequate feedback about the appropriateness of their behaviour. The more stressed the custodial parent in the aftermath of the breakup the more inconsistent they are likely to be in setting and enforcing rules and the more anti-social behaviour their children display (Forgatch *et al.*, 1988). Furthermore, parents who are stressed and/or depressed tend to perceive their children as behaving less well than they really are and so have a lowered tolerance of them. In part this occurs because when they are preoccupied with their own difficulties parents attend less to their children and the behaviours they then notice are usually inappropriate or anti-social. Parents then misperceive these behaviours and consider them characteristic of their children's behaviour. This perception of the child as deviant leads the parent to increase their attempts at authoritarian control. In turn this leads to more conflict between the two, as parents adopt increasingly ineffective management strategies (Brody and Forehand, 1988). The more adversely affected the mother's behaviour the more adversely affected is the child's behaviour, encouraging a declining interactive spiral between the two. If they occur, these changes in the quality of parenting operate alongside the loss of the non-custodial parent and can contribute to children's uncertainty. Children make the best adjustment to divorce when they are provided with an organized, predictable environment which includes having clearly defined and consistently enforced rules.

Following the breakup, contact with the non-custodial parent usually declines although some mothers and fathers continue to see a great deal of their children and to be highly involved. Regular contact with the non-custodial parent and good relationships with both parents protect children from the emotional disturbance often shown (Black, 1984). At the time of the breakup, departing parents may influence children's development (Hetherington *et al.*, 1982). For instance the warmth, maturity demands and techniques of disciplining employed by departing fathers all relate to measures of their children's cognitive ability and sex role development. But a year later these fathers no longer influence children's performance. Fathers cease to have a direct influence and they also lose their power to buffer or protect children from a poorer relationship with the mother. However good the relationship with fathers they cannot contribute to children's resilience unless they are available on a regular basis (Furstenberg and Seltzer, 1986).

Individual Differences in Adjusting

There are marked individual differences in the reactions of parents and children to family breakup. One factor is the sheer quantity of changes that have to be tackled at one time; the more changes, the more difficulties are experienced by families. Other moderating factors include the amount of conflict experienced and the sex and age of children.

Family Conflict

Conflicts occur periodically in all families, although different families express their conflicts in different ways and find different ways of resolving them. Conflicts that are not resolved quickly can be upsetting for the whole family, even for children as young as 1 year (Cummings *et al.*, 1981). Moreover, the more frequently that anger and fights occur the stronger the distress (Cummings *et al.*, 1984). Persistent family conflict is associated with conduct disorders and emotional difficulties in children and adolescents (Furstenberg and Seltzer, 1986; Rutter, 1978; Werner, 1989). In addition to the distress experienced by children when they witness it, family conflict may have an indirect influence on children. When there is conflict between them parents may become preoccupied with the difficulties in the marital relationship and so less available and sensitive to the children. The parenting of mothers is less influenced by marital conflict than that of fathers. One frequent response of fathers in high-conflict homes is to adopt more punitive disciplinary techniques with their children (Stoneman *et al.*, 1989). Poor quality parenting can add to children's distress.

The way in which conflict is resolved may be more crucial than the levels of conflict experienced. If conflicts are usually resolved by a compromise between the parents, children are better adjusted, exhibit more pro-social behaviours and have higher self-esteem. In contrast if conflicts are usually left unresolved or are resolved by the one parent verbally or physically attacking the other, children show lower self-esteem and engage in more aggressive behaviours and fewer pro-social behaviours (Camera and Resnick, 1988). The cause of the conflict may also influence the reaction of children. Disagreements about parenting strategies may be more problematic for children than those about non-childrearing issues such as finances. Parents who argue about non-childrearing issues but agree about childrearing are less likely to have children who are aggressive and display behavioural problems (Camera and Resnick, 1988).

An increase in conflict is frequently associated with family breakup. The breakup may be preceded by conflict and conflict may escalate following the breakup, as parents argue about custody arrangements and so on. Some of the difficulties experienced by family members before, during and after family breakup are linked to their experience of conflict. Years before family breakup occurs children, and especially boys, who are exposed to marital conflict may show the kinds of behaviours which children display in the immediate months following the breakup. Poor impulse control, high aggression and high activity levels can all be observed (Block *et al.*, 1986; Cummings *et al.*, 1984). The more conflict family members encounter the more difficulties they are likely to experience in coping with the demands made of them on a daily basis; exposure to conflict can create difficulties whether it occurs before, during or after breakup.

Boys appear to be more susceptible to parental disharmony than girls (Hetherington *et al.*, 1982). One reason for this may be that parents try to shield girls from conflict and argue less when girls are around (Hetherington *et al.*, 1982). Boys tend to be more demanding of attention and require more direct control than girls. When parents are stressed they become irritated by the demands of boys, perceive them negatively and so become less sensitive (Bronfenbrenner *et al.*, 1984).

An issue that is frequently raised when there is conflict is whether children fare better in intact families or in families which break up. There are costs and benefits associated with either. Children are capable of loving even parents who abuse them and separation represents a loss of a known and predictable element in their lives. Despite this, most evidence points to the advantages of removing children from conflict. Children of conflict-free divorce are usually better adjusted than children of conflict-ridden marriage or divorce. Girls from conflict-free divorce tend to be indistinguishable from girls of conflict-free marriages, although boys are adversely affected even when the divorce is conflict-free, but not as adversely affected as they are by conflict in marriage (Furstenberg and Seltzer, 1986: Hetherington *et al.*, 1982).

Family breakup can bring an improvement in the quality of parents' relationships with their children when it leads to a reduction in conflict. In their study, Hetherington *et al.* (1982) reported that 20 per cent of non-custodial fathers reported an improvement in their relationships with their children after the breakup. This improvement occurred, they claimed, because prior to the breakup the conflict with their partners occupied them so much that they gave little attention to the children. With the removal of the conflict they could concentrate more on their children and build up better relationships. However, family breakup does not necessarily lead to a reduction in conflict (Hetherington *et al.*, 1982). Following the breakup parents may use the children as sounding-boards for their anger and frustrations with the former partner.

Children's Gender

In childhood boys appear to be more adversely affected by family breakup than girls. This difference may be more apparent than real and result from differences in the way that boys and girls express their distress, with boys' expression of distress being more visible than that of girls. Boys demonstrate more externalizing behaviours such as aggressiveness, poor attention, delinquency and anti-social problem behaviours. In contrast girls are more likely to express their distress by internalizing behaviours such as anxiety, withdrawal and depression. Boys' behaviours are highly visible and their reaction cannot be overlooked, but girls' behaviours may impinge less on their caretakers (Zaslow, 1989).

Over and above these differences in the expression of distress, boys do show a more adverse reaction, especially when they live with their mother as the lone parent. In part this may result from their experiences with peers. The deterioration of children's behaviour with the stress of family breakup overflows into relationships with peers. Following the breakup, children become less socially competent, initiating fewer interactions and responding less positively and acceptably to their friends. As a result they become more socially isolated. Within a few months their sociability returns and they seek to renew social contacts. For girls these social inititations are received positively and they are quickly reabsorbed into their previous social networks, made up largely of other girls. Boys are not so well received by their former friends, mostly other boys, and so they remain socially isolated or seek companionship from those who will accept them, and in practice that is same-aged girls or younger boys. The rejection experienced by boys from their peers can add to their unhappiness. This rejection does not occur with new classmates if boys move school about one year after the breakup (Hetherington *et al.*, 1982).

Boys show a more adverse reaction when they live with their mother as the lone parent, but girls fare worse in cases of father custody and when they are in a family with a stepfather. In the long term girls may be especially adversely affected by the loss of their mother, particularly if they experience other adverse life events too (Bifulco *et al.*, 1987). Maternal loss is associated with an increased incidence of clinical depression. Bifulco *et al.* (1987) argue that women without a mother are more likely to receive inadequate parenting and so are less likely to develop the resources that allow them to cope with adversity. Lowered self-esteem may also be a contributory factor. The conclusion seems to be that children cope best with family breakup when they are cared for by a custodial parent of the same sex (Peterson and Zill, 1986; Santrock, *et al.*, 1982).

Age of the Child

Kurdek (1986) suggests that the short-term reactions of children to the separation of their parents vary as a function of their age. Infants and toddlers up to 2 years show their distress by failing to form secure attachments. Preschool children are most likely to worry about their own contribution to their parent's departure, to believe that the separation is temporary, and to be confused by a parent assuring the child of his or her love yet moving away. These children tend to be the most frightened and confused. The next age group (6 to 8 years) can understand that their parents might be incompatible and incapable of living together. They want to see their parents reconciled but also realize that this is unlikely and can see the benefits of the reduction in family conflict. The next age group (9 to 12 years) are most likely to experience conflicts of loyalty and also to be ambivalent about both parents and to view their home and family environment negatively. Adolescents aged 13 to 19 years can see positive outcomes of the divorce in terms of their own increased sense of self-reliance and responsibility and positive personality changes for parents.

In the longer term it may be older children who have the greatest adjustment problems. Ten years after the separation young children can remember little of their pre-divorce lives. They perceive themselves as having a close relationship with their mothers and they are optimistic about their own futures. They also plan to get married themselves later and expect their own marriages to last. Children aged 9 to 18 years at the separation show fewer signs of distress at the time of the breakup. However, ten years later these adult children of divorce look back on the breakup as a time of great personal unhappiness. They consider the divorce had a powerful influence on their lives and see their idealized childhood as having been snatched away from them. There is still a yearning for the family to be reunited and this feeling is stronger amongst children who were older at the time of the breakup (Wallerstein *et al.*, 1988). Children from broken homes may look inappropriately for explanations of any current unhappiness in terms of family breakup whereas children intact homes have to find alternative explanations if they feel unhappy and dissatisfied with their lives.

Positive Outcomes of Family Breakup

In talking of divorce and/or family breakup, there is a tendency to dwell on the negative side, but there can be positive features. The most obvious is that breakup can reduce conflict within the home. In the longer term children from broken homes frequently see themselves as more mature and sensitive, and as having benefited from the extra responsibility they took on. A further advantage is that it can bring custodial parents and their children closer together as they come to rely increasingly on each other for emotional and social support. Siblings can also become closer, especially sisters (Hetherington, 1988; Kier and Fouts, 1989). One benefit of sibling relationships at this time is that they may offer proof that fidelity, intimacy and enduring love are possible in relationships despite the counter-example of their own parents' relationship (Wallerstein *et al.*, 1988).

Family breakup can provide the impetus for growth in the separating parents. Wallerstein *et al.* (1988), reporting on parents ten years after the separation, suggest that women who were under 30 at the time of the breakup show most gains and that in general women show more growth than men. Amongst the benefits for women can be the impetus to develop a satisfying career which is then associated with increased self-confidence and sense of maturity. In the long term, new relationships may prove to be more satisfying than the old ones. Men report fewer changes resulting from the divorce and from any new relationships since the divorce.

Reconstituted Families and Step-Parenting

The large majority of single parents take on a new partner at some time, so many children who spend time in a single-parent family experience also life with a step-parent. For instance, 80 per cent of mothers who are unmarried at the birth of a child subsequently marry (Hernandez, 1988). Similarly, the majority of divorcing parents remarry, especially younger parents and those with custody of fewer children (Hernandez, 1988). About 10 per cent of children at a given point in time are living with a step-parent as well as one of their biological parents, but it is thought that about 30 per cent of children spend some part of their childhood living in this type of family.

Because mothers most frequently have custody of children following family breakup, step-parent families are most usually stepfather families. There are more than four times as many stepfather families as stepmother families. The family composition of stepmother and stepfather families is somewhat different. For instance, families headed by a biological father and a stepmother are more likely to include boys than girls, indeed only a third of the children living in such families are girls, whereas families headed by a biological mother and a stepfather have equal numbers of boys and girls (Zill, 1988). Stepmothers are more likely to bring children with them to a new relationship and to start a new family with the new partner, so children in these families are more likely to be required to form relationships with stepsiblings and cope with siblings born into the new relationship.

The introduction of a step-parent and any stepsiblings calls for major adjustments by all family members. The whole dynamics of a family change when new members are introduced; new relationships have to be forged and old relationships renegotiated. The custodial parent has to learn to live with the new partner while at the same time coping with parenting and children's reactions to the presence of the new parent. The step-parent has simultaneously to learn to live with a new partner and to learn to be a parent to the stepchildren. The children have to cope with their developing relationship with the step-parent and to learn to share their custodial parent's attention with the step-parent. Additionally, children have to recognize that their custodial parent is a sexually active and desired figure. Hetherington *et al.* (1982) report that children age 9 to 15 years seem to have the most difficulty in coping with this. Not surprisingly second marriages frequently falter early on. The most common cause of difficulties is that the demands of parenting allow too little time for the couple to get to know one another. As a result parents tend to view the marriage as less cohesive, more problematic and more stressful than do parents in first marriages (Bray, 1988).

The Impact of Step-Parenting on Children

A step-parent may change families in ways that are beneficial, e.g. by improving the finances of a family and hence reducing problems associated with poverty. A step-parent can help to improve the experiences of children by their direct interactions with the child or through the support they offer their partner. This support can be in the form of direct help with childcare or indirectly by influencing their partner's self-esteem, offering advice about childcare and offering reassurance that the children are being cared for effectively. On the other hand a step-parent may bring changes which can be problematic for children.

There are some small but consistent differences between children from step-parent and intact families (Zill, 1988). Compared to children from intact homes, children from both single-parent homes and step-parent homes show more problem behaviours, including anti-social destructive behaviours, verbal and physical aggression, poor attention span, high levels of anxiety, social withdrawal and depressed mood; they perform less well at school and they miss more school because of illness. There are somewhat more problems amongst children in stepmother families. This is associated with the introduction of the stepmother rather than with the previous experience of being brought up by fathers on their own. It would seem that the introduction of a stepfather presents different adjustment challenges to children than the introduction of a stepmother. In stepmother families the new parent takes over the principal child management role. Managing someone else's children invites comparisons and increases the opportunities for disagreement and arguments. Children compare stepmothers with memories of the dead or departed biological mother and the parenting of the father when he was the lone parent. Frequently these comparisons are unfavourable as children tend to romanticize their past experiences. Stepmothers are seen as less fair and affectionate than biological mothers (Ganong and Coleman, 1987) and as a consequence stepmothers frequently report experiencing coping problems (Smith, 1990). Most of the literature on step-parenting focuses on the problems experienced by parents and children. These studies usually examine step-parent families soon after their formation. The studies reveal that there are usually some short-term difficulties, but if the family remains together most of these problems are resolved.

Factors Associated with Children's Adjustments
Some families absorb a step-parent better than others. In a large-scale survey of step-parents it was found that the children who adjusted worst to being in a step-parent family had poorly educated, badly paid parents, had a living but absent mother, had new half or step brothers and sisters and were either very young or into adolescence at the time of the initial family breakup (Zill, 1988).

Some children in step-parent families continue to have contact with their absent biological parent. Contact with the biological parent can influence their relationship with both the custodial parent and step-parent by introducing loyalty conflicts. Such conflicts of loyalty are especially likely when there is continuing hostility between the two biological parents (Furstenberg, 1988; Brand *et al.*, 1988). Boys are better than girls at maintaining good relationships with their stepmothers and biological mothers. When they have contact with mothers, girls tend to have worse relations with their stepmothers (Brand *et al.*, 1988). Stepmothers are most readily accepted when the biological mother has died, or, if she is still alive, when children do not see her. The acceptance of stepfathers is not influenced by these considerations, reflecting their more peripheral role in most households.

Step-parent families are frequently blended families with the new family including new children as well as a new parent. Additionally, new couples often start a new family so that half brothers and sisters are introduced quite quickly into the family. Children then have to adjust to one or more stepsiblings, or half-siblings. This clearly increases the number of new relationships and provides scope for personality clashes, conflicts, perceived injustices and other sources of family tension. In many households this would appear to happen and the presence of a stepsibling or half-sibling is associated with more behavioural problems. Children are happiest when they do not have to share their custodial parent's attention with other new children.

Adjustments of Boys and Girls over Time

There is some evidence of gender differences in response to step-parenting but these are affected by the factors discussed above such as ages of children at the time of the breakup and remarriage, and the sex of the step-parent, and reactions differ at different stages in the history of the new family. The benefits to children of their parents' new relationship or remarriage can be slow to emerge. Within the first five years of their parents' remarriage, stepchildren exhibit more behavioural problems than other groups of children and this is true even when the children have good relationships with the step-parent (Furstenberg and Seltzer, 1986). This may be affected by the sex of the child. Boys show more rapid improvements. Bray (1988) studying stepfather families reports that within six months of the remarriage boys aged 6 to 9 years show increased intellectual performance, their vocabulary increases and their arithmetic skills improve. Boys benefit from remarriage, but most of the benefit comes from an improved relationship with the custodial parent and not from the new relationship with the step-parent. Daughters, however, do not seem to benefit in the same way. Even two years into the marriage they still show unhappiness; mothers have less control over them and conflict with daughters increases. Daughters become demanding, hostile, coercive to both their mother and the stepfather. Things improve after two years but girls remain antagonistic to both parents and are more disruptive (Hetherington, 1988).

With remarriage the behaviour of the custodial parent to their children changes. Mothers become warmer in their interaction with their children and more consistent in their behaviour, but also more demanding of good and mature behaviour from children. It takes most stepfathers quite a while to become effectively involved with their stepchildren. Initially they show low warmth and low involvement. They do not attempt to monitor the child's activities or to control them and they make few maturity demands. In the first two years, stepfathers see themselves as working hard to present a pleasant face to their stepchildren. With the passage of time stepfathers become more responsive to sons and slowly become more involved in setting and enforcing rules and more authoritative in their treatment of sons. In turn boys become more accepting of their stepfather and they show fewer behavioural problems. In long-lasting remarriages boys frequently report good close relationships with their stepfather; they see him as someone to respect who is supportive and whose advice is sought. With girls, stepfathers find it hard to get involved and to establish good relationships. They tend to become impatient with them and the number of angry exchanges increases. Stepdaughters see their stepfathers as unreasonable, hostile and punitive. Many stepfathers find it hard even after long periods of remarriage to develop good relationships with their stepdaughters. The better the relationship between the parents the less secure daughters feel and the more difficult they are, but in contrast boys cope better the more cohesive and emotionally bonded their mother and stepfather are (Bray, 1988; Brand *et al.*, 1988; Hetherington, 1988). As with first marriages, the better the marital relationship between the parents the more positively the step-parents feel towards their children (Brand *et al.*, 1988).

The Wider Family

The marriage of a lone parent has implications for the developing child who has to adjust to a series of changes in the immediate family. However, remarriage also has implications for the child's contact with the extended family. Hetherington (1988) has examined sibling relationships in families where remarriage has taken place. Early in the remarriage, girls seem to cut themselves off from their families and are distant from their siblings. It is important if sibling relations are to improve that parents are fair and consistent in their treatment of all children. When parents treat one child with less warmth and affection, and more coercion, punitiveness, irritability and restrictiveness than another, siblings are likely to be aggressive, rivalrous and unaffectionate to one another.

Most non-custodial parents see less of their children following the introduction of a step-parent into the family. If the non-custodial parent reduces contact with his or her children it is likely that the grandparents on that side of the family will also reduce contact (Furstenberg, 1988). Moreover because lone parents frequently live with their own parents remarriage can mean setting up a separate household and hence a reduction in contact with the custodial grandparents too. While contact with natural grandparents may wane this may be offset by the introduction of a new extended family in the form of the parents and relations of the step-parent. Furstenberg (1988) reports that stepgrandparents frequently adopt the grandparenting role enthusiastically and children up to the age of adolescence tend to be accepting of these new steprelatives.

Failure in Remarriages

The demands made on a couple by children can allow them insufficient time and energy to solve any initial interpersonal problems in their new relationship. Moreover experiences with hostile children may be so negative that they offset any pleasures that the adults find in each other's company, swinging the balance against continuing the relationship. Remarriages on average are less cohesive than first marriages and conflict occurs frequently. Causes of conflict often centre around the children, their behaviour, how to respond to them, and money spent on them. Consequently, such marriages fail more frequently than first marriages. If the couple do split up this leads to a repeat of the experience of family breakup. Furstenberg (1988) reports that one child in ten experiences two or more family breakups before the age of 16 years.

In Conclusion

Family breakup and the marriage of a single parent call for adjustments to be made by all family members and these can be problematic in the short term. However, being a member of a single-parent family or of a reconstituted family need not be problematic in the longer term. The majority of children growing up in both types of household are well adjusted and cope well. All individuals have difficulty coping with change and the greater the changes the harder life is for them and the more likely they are to show some behavioural problems. Furstenberg (1988) has shown that marital transitions, whether it be the marriage of a parent or the divorce of a parent, involves change to which children and parents have to adjust. The more transitions experienced, the more coping demands are made of the individual. If marital transitions are accompanied by other changes such as a decline in material resources, they present more problems. Children and adults also cope best when they know that is expected of them. Children who show the best adjustments are those who can maintain predictable routines and have clear rules set for them (Hetherington *et al.*, 1982). This environment can be provided by single mothers, by single fathers and by step-parents equally effectively (Lamb *et al.*, 1985; Zill, 1988). The changes introduced by marital transitions may be positive changes, for instance family breakup may remove the family from abuse and conflict while remarriage may lead to an improvement in the material well-being of a family and to improved educational attainment of children. Children do not need two parents for effective development. Having said that, it is easier for parents bringing up children when they have some support for parenting and to help solve problems as they arise. Step-parent families can become cohesive, providing supportive environments offering security and close relationships for all the family, but achieving this can require time and patience.

Further Reading

HETHERINGTON, E.M. and ARASTEH, J. (Eds) (1988) *The Impact of Divorce, Single Parenting and Step-Parenting on Children*, Hillsdale, NJ, Lawrence Erlbaum Associates.

Brings together a collection of reports of US research currently examining factors influencing children's reactions to family breakup and the introduction of a step-parent and stepsiblings. Issues considered include cultural and ethnic differences in expectations and social supports. The chapters focus mainly on problems associated with transitions in the family, so beware of drawing over-pessimistic conclusions.

PARKINSON, L. (1985) 'Divorce counselling', in DRYDEN, W. (Ed.) *Marital Therapy in Britain, Vol. 2*, Milton Keynes, Open University.

The author of this chapter considers the extent to which couples experiencing difficulties in their relationship consult professionals (other than solicitors and doctors). She finds widespread reluctance, even when relationships have reached crisis point. The aims and potential benefits of divorce counselling and conciliation are explored through some case examples.

WALLERSTEIN, J.S. and BLAKESLEE, S. (1990) *Second Chances: Men, Women and Children a Decade after Divorce*, London, Bantam Press.

This book draws upon the years of experience that Wallerstein has gained researching family breakup and providing counselling. The subjects of this research are those families who do experience difficulties with family breakup. Consequently clinical and counselling insights are offered for this group. However, these observations do not apply to the many families who manage the breakup with only minimal distress or even relief.

ZASLOW, M.J. (1989) 'Sex differences in children's response to parental divorce: 2. Samples, variables, ages, and sources', *American Journal of Orthopsychiatry*, **59**, pp. 118–41.

Reviews the evidence that boys are more adversely affected by divorce than girls. She finds discrepancies in the evidence, but boys living with a mother who has not remarried do indeed seem to respond more negatively, both immediately and over a period of years. However girls living with stepfathers or with custodial fathers fare worse. Boys and girls express their distress to divorce in different ways with boys' distress being more immediately visible.

Chapter 8

Child Abuse within the Family

Studies of parenting point to the different ways in which parents care for their children. Some parents are more sensitive and show more affection and some control and punish their children more than others. In this chapter we consider parenting which steps outside the acceptable range and is abusive.

What is Meant by Abuse?

There are many definitions of abuse but most distinguish between physical, sexual and emotional abuse (Browne *et al.*, 1988). Physical abuse is where a parent (or someone else caring for the child) physically hurts, injures or kills a child. This can involve hitting, shaking, squeezing, burning, biting, giving a child poisonous substances or inappropriate drugs and the use of excessive force when carrying out tasks like feeding or nappy changing. Sexual abuse occurs when adults seek sexual gratification by using children. This may involve vaginal or anal sexual intercourse, engaging with the child in fondling, masturbation or oral sex, or encouraging children to watch sexually explicit behaviour or pornographic material. Neglect and emotional abuse is the failure by caregivers to meet the basic essential needs of children, like adequate food, clothes, warmth and medical care including leaving young children alone and unsupervised. In addition, children's psychological and emotional needs may not be adequately met, for example, there may be constant lack of love and affection, threats, verbal attacks, taunting or shouting. Abuse may be limited to one of these categories: parents may, for example, neglect their children but not resort to physical or sexual abuse. But often the different forms of abuse go together: for example, a father who sexually abuses his children may also abuse them physically and their fear of being beaten may help to ensure their silence about the sexual abuse. Another form of abuse which is sometimes recognized is that of children who witness interparental violence, often their mother being beaten by their father (Emery, 1989). Some children attempt to stop their parents' violence and become involved themselves. When parents stay together, the effects of this form of abuse for children's development have to be balanced against the possible impact of divorce.

There are few reliable estimates of the extent of child abuse. As people are more willing to acknowledge its existence and it is taken more seriously, so the rate of reporting has increased. In the UK in 1986–7 the National Society for the Prevention of Cruelty to Children helped over 50,000 children and it is estimated that over 100 children die in the UK each year as a direct result of abuse and neglect (Browne *et al.*, 1988). The extent and the intensity of abuse experienced by children varies. For some, abuse may be continuous over a number of years, whereas others are abused for a shorter time, often at a time of family crisis. In some families, parents abuse only one child whereas in others all the children are abused. The impact of abuse may also differ, with physical abuse having somewhat different consequences than sexual abuse or neglect. Abuse may have few lasting effects on one child but there may be severe and long-term effects for another.

What these forms of abuse have in common is that they result from distortions or disruptions of parent-child relations, a lack of respect for the needs and the vulnerability of children and an abuse of power by adults. To understand how and why parent-child relations become abusive we need to study the dynamics of family relations and the wider context in which parenting takes place (Browne *et al.*, 1988). We do this by considering in more detail two kinds of abuse, physical and sexual abuse.

Child abuse is studied by a variety of professional groups, each with somewhat different interests and concerns. Psychologists look for characteristics of abused children and their families, the family dynamics associated with abuse, and the effects of abuse, and they work with children who have been abused. Discussion of such issues throws light on some assumptions about how children and parents should relate to one another, what are acceptable and non-acceptable ways of expressing anger, affection and sexuality and of controlling and disciplining children. Other professionals have somewhat different agendas around child abuse. Doctors, for example, are interested in ways of detecting abuse. Lawyers are concerned with the nature of the evidence children provide about abuse. And social workers who provide services for children who have been abused are interested in the advantages and disadvantages of removing children who have been abused from their families.

Physical Abuse

The National Society for the Prevention of Cruelty to Children has helped over 9 million children in the hundred years since it was founded in the UK, clear indication that child abuse has a long history and is not a new phenomenon. Attempts to understand physical abuse have focused on parents, on children and, more recently, on family dynamics.

Parents who Abuse

A considerable amount of effort has been invested in trying to identify the social and personality characteristics of parents who abuse. It was often assumed that they must be psychologically disturbed, but there is little evidence that parents who abuse can be clearly distinguished from those who do not or that there is an 'abusive' personality. A number of characteristics are found more frequently, including low self-esteem, depression, hostility, low tolerance of frustration, insensitive parenting, inability to put the child's needs before their own, lack of information about child development and unrealistic expectations of children's behaviour. Other researchers look at social and demographic characteristics. They seek to identify the causes of abuse not in the personality of abusing parents but in the context in which they parent, including the social and economic context. Parents who abuse are more likely to be young, from large families, unemployed, and of lower socio-economic status, and to live in poor housing. They are more likely to have a criminal record, to be in poor health or have psychiatric problems and to have had unhappy childhoods and been abused themselves. Many abusing families are isolated with little social support, parents are more likely to have poor marital relations and many abused children live with stepfathers (Browne *et al.*, 1988; Emery, 1989; Herzberger and Tennen, 1986; Wolfe, 1985).

It is often difficult to know to what extent such factors are implicated in abuse itself or merely in the frequency with which it is reported. Parents who are unemployed or those with housing problems have more contact with social welfare agencies and hence their cases of abuse are more likely to become known. In contrast, middle-class families and families with fewer problems tend to have little contact with welfare agencies and are in a better position to keep abuse from public notice. Findings about the social distribution of abuse may also influence the expectations and hence the perceptiveness of those in a position to detect abuse. Believing that someone they are visiting has many of the characteristics outlined above may alert social workers to the possibility of abuse but make them less likely to identify the signs of abuse in other families (Hallett, 1988; New and David, 1985). Doctors' judgments about whether or not a child is being abused have been found to be related as much to the family's social class or ethnicity as to the physical evidence (O'Toole *et al.*, 1983).

Characteristics of Children who are Abused

It has been argued that some children are more susceptible to abuse than others. Young children are more at risk of physical abuse than older children; over half of the reported cases occur to children under 4 years, with children under 2 years at greatest risk (Browne *et al.*, 1988). What is it about young children which makes them more susceptible to abuse? Young children are dependent on their parents and need to attract their attention and communicate with them to get their needs met. Some children do this in ways which induce negative reactions from parents. For example, children who whine or have temper tantrums may irritate parents and elicit more hostile responses than children who express themselves more positively. Such children may find that as they get older and can do more for themselves, they make fewer demands on their parents or they may find ways of communicating which parents find more acceptable and hence are less at risk of abuse. On the other hand, for some children age may increase their vulnerability as their increasing demands for autonomy and to do things for themselves may trigger anger and abuse from parents who like to control their activities (Martin, 1976).

As they grow up, children's understanding increases and this may help them find more successful ways of getting their needs met and coping with a difficult home environment (Herzberger and Tennen, 1986). They may become more sensitive to signals which indicate when their parents' tolerance is low and hence can predict better when to make demands and when to keep quiet. Children also begin to have more contact with people outside the family. This may enable them to evaluate their parents' behaviour and to attribute their abuse to their parents' unreasonableness or to current family difficulties rather than merely to their own 'badness' or refusal to behave well. People outside the family may also act as confidants and give children support.

Boys are somewhat more likely to be physically abused than girls (Browne *et al.*, 1988). Children's sex may be important because of parents' expectations about gender roles and appropriate ways of relating to boys and girls (Hargreaves and Colley, 1986; Newson and Newson, 1986). Some children may spark off abusive incidents, in part at least, because their parents consider that they are behaving inappropriately. Boys who are whiney or cry a great deal may irritate parents whereas similar behaviour in girls may be tolerated because they consider it acceptable for girls to be fearful. Conversely, aggressive and angry reactions may be more difficult to tolerate in girls.

Another characteristic which has received attention is the child's temperament. Children who cry a great deal and are difficult to soothe, who do not sleep, who are irritable or demanding, and those who are fussy feeders, make heavy demands of parents. Their parents may feel that they can never get their childcare right and this may undermine their confidence. Temperamental differences may help to explain the higher rates of abuse sometimes found in studies of handicapped children, children born prematurely or of low birthweight (Browne *et al.*, 1988; Friedrich and Boriskin, 1980).

'Goodness of Fit' or Meshing Child and Parent Characteristics

A number of child characteristics have been linked to child abuse. But just as there is no distinctive profile of abusing parents, so there is none of the abused child. Many studies are retrospective and consider the temperament or behaviour of children only once they have been abused. In such cases it is difficult to distinguish between difficult child behaviour which triggers abuse and difficult behaviour which stems from children's experience of abuse. Better designed research suggests that the relationship between abuse and child factors such as illness, temperament or handicap is complex. There are different routes by which children come to be abused but, in general, child factors may be less important than parents' reactions and beliefs about children's behaviour (Belsky, 1984). The parents of many handicapped children, for example, recognize that their child will develop slowly and so modify their expectations. In addition, parents' perceptions of whether their children are difficult, poor sleepers or cry a great deal do not necessarily relate closely to observations of their behaviour (Starr, 1988; Stratton and Swaffer, 1988). This means that we may need to think less in terms of the characteristics of children or parents and more in terms of the meshing of the two sets of characteristics. We need an explanation of child abuse which considers how parents respond to children AND how children respond to adults. The same child may elicit different reactions from parents according to whether they consider the child's demands for attention acceptable or not and the motives they attribute to children. A continual stream of questions may be seen on one occasion or by one set of parents as an indication of a child's curiosity and hence to be encouraged. On another occasion parents may view the same behaviour differently as, for example, an attempt to prevent them looking after a younger child or to delay going to bed. And children also respond to parents' control and abuse differently: some children may respond in ways likely to reduce their parents' anger or physical threats, but others, by their reactions, may aggravate or escalate parents' anger and aggression (Belsky, 1984; Browne *et al.*, 1988).

To understand abuse we need to consider the wider context of family interactions and to identify patterns linked with abuse. These may include the expectations of parents about what are appropriate ways to behave towards children, what to expect realistically of children, how to make sense of children's behaviour and how to ensure a reasonable level of compliance. Families do not operate in a vacuum. Parents' ideas about children and childcare and their perceptions of their children's behaviour are influenced by the ideas of their community and the wider society. The norms prevalent in a society are used by parents to define what they consider to be desirable and acceptable goals and ways of parenting (Kessel and Siegel, 1981; Korbin, 1981). It has been argued that positive media portrayal of violence helps to reinforce views about the acceptability of violence in families (Gordon, 1986). In this ideological context, parents may feel able to justify their behaviour in terms of generally acceptable norms of childcare such as 'spare the rod and spoil the child' or 'fathers being the head of the household' or in terms of other people's behaviour: 'Everyone does it'. In addition, family functioning needs to be seen in terms of family circumstances. As has been suggested, abuse is more common in families who are already experiencing problems with housing, employment and health. The stress these generate may be increased for some parents by their personal or social circumstances, such as marital breakdown or a history of being poorly parented themselves (see

Chapter 10). It is not surprising, therefore, that current approaches to child abuse consider that a number of social, situational and psychological factors interacting together are implicated in abuse. We consider two aspects of family functioning which may help us to understand abuse: relationships and interactions between family members, including discipline and control; and the support available for families.

Relationships within Families

There is a great deal of diversity within abusing families, just as there is among families who function well, and family patterns change over time. Analysis of family life and interactions indicate a number of ways in which interactions may become abusive, and also how parents at risk of abusing children may become warm and sensitive parents. In many families the everyday tasks of childcare have the potential to erupt into defiance and resistance on the part of children and anger and aggression from parents (Frude and Goss, 1980; Newson and Newson, 1968). Young children have the power to arouse strong feelings even in parents who do not abuse their children. (Grahah (1980) found that over half of the mothers she interviewed repoted feelings of anger towards their 1-month-old babies. They were especially likely to feel angry when they were tired and unable to placate their babies when they cried. Mothers whose babies had been small at birth or had suffered minor illnesses were somewhat more likely to say they felt angry, indicating the difficulties mothers may have in caring for small and vulnerable babies. Mothers' anger was often related to their ignorance of what was the cause of their babies' crying and of how to soothe them. Their feelings were sometimes exacerbated by the reactions of other children. Dunn and Kendrick (1982), for example, report the higher incidence of confrontations with pre-school children when mothers were breastfeeding younger siblings.

Having high standards and expecting mature behaviour of children is seen as beneficial for their development (Baumrind, 1967) (see Chapter 4). But when parents' standards are unrealistically high, or their means of ensuring children's compliance is very harsh, children may be abused. Such parents may expect physical competence well in advance of their children's age and get angry when children wet their beds or do not feed themselves properly. Their expectations of children's cognitive, social or emotional development may also be inappropriate. They may expect a sophisticated understanding or expect children to be responsive and meet the parents' needs for love and attention. If children do not behave as they expect parents may assume that they are 'playing up' and that the parents are entitled, and even obliged, to express their disappointment by punishing children.

Discipline and Control

Ideas differ about how parents should deal with naughtiness and transgressions of rules. In some communities and some families children's compliance is insisted upon and smacking is seen as an appropriate way of punishing children whereas others prefer more psychological forms of control (Browne *et al.*, 1988; Korbin, 1981; Newson and Newson, 1968; Walkerdine and Lucey, 1989) (see Chapter 11). Many acts of abuse begin as attempts to discipline children and there is a fine line between firm discipline and abuse. In some families aggression is an inevitable part of family life. There is an association between marital and child abuse, suggesting that when fathers are violent to mothers, the violence may carry over into parents' relations with children (Wolfe, 1985). This approach sees abuse not as a deviant form of family interaction as much as one end of a continuum, with firm but loving discipline at one end and abuse at the other, as the 'unacceptable face of legitimate parental control' (New and David, 1985). Some parents start by being firm but, if children continue to disobey, they escalate their level of punishment.

Many parents smack their children. About half of the mothers interviewed by Newson and Newson (1968) said they smacked their 4-year-olds reasonably or fairly often. Mothers thought that their smacking was triggered by a number of factors. One was their own temperament; some mothers saw themselves as quick-tempered or as not very patient especially when they were tired. Mothers sometimes smacked when children did something which frightened them such as reaching for a hot pan or rushing out into the road. Lastly, mothers felt that their smacking was associated with an interaction between mothers' state and children's behaviour, for example by children doing things which were irritating when mothers were very busy or under stress (Frude and Goss, 1980; Newson and Newson, 1980).

Parents who abuse their children use more control and especially control based on their power, such as threats and humiliation, rather than using approaches that gain compliance through explanation or appeals to children's interests. Herzberger and Tennen (1986) found that interactions in abusive families were more negatively tinged, and that parents' treatment of their children was inconsistent and cold and lacked empathy. However, as Wolfe (1985) argues, we cannot assume a simple and straightforward punitive regime in abusing families. The interactions between abusive mothers and their children are sometimes warm and sensitive. Rather, abusing families may be characterized by a greater proportion of aversive to positive interactions and the balance between the two may depend on factors external to the parent-child relationship, such as a family crisis. This suggests that we need to look not just for gross quantitative differences in parents' behaviour but also for more subtle qualitative differences.

Parental control and discipline may be modified according to children's reactions and parents' understandings of those reactions (Newson and Newson, 1968). Children may respond to conflicts with parents by withdrawing into themselves or becoming more obedient. Parents' control may thus be softened because quiet children are less likely to be noticed and hence to trigger anger which erupts into abuse. However, if children's silence is seen as sulky or critical of parents, it may irritate parents and encourage further abuse. Some children respond to anger and physical abuse in a like manner, returning their parents' anger or attacking them physically. Such behaviour may shock parents into acknowledging that their behaviour is unreasonable or it may escalate the violence. How children react seems to be related to their age, position in the family, temperament and personality and this may explain why some children are more likely to be singled out for abuse.

Support for Parents

Parents with good social support are less likely to abuse their children. This support can take many forms, with partners being the major source (Wolfe, 1985). Women with close family support may be less dependent on their partners. It is thought that one of the benefits of such support may come through the provision of information about what is appropriate and acceptable behaviour in children. Parents who are concerned about some aspects of their children's behaviour or how to manage unacceptable behaviour can talk to partners, close family or friends. However, abusing parents are often isolated from their families or other parents and have little opportunity to talk to others about what irritates and upsets them, and how best to deal with naughtiness and their own feelings of anger or powerlessness in the face of resistance from children (Belsky, 1981). Other benefits of good support may come through assistance with childcare and through enhancing mothers' sense of well-being and general competence. Mothers who feel competent and positive about themselves are more likely to be able to appreciate and respond appropriately to their child's individuality. In addition, their confidence means that mothers may be better placed to reflect on their childrearing practices and to modify them in the light of their own and other people's experiences and their children's responses (Belsky *et al.*, 1984b). For some mothers employment outside the home is a major source of support (Sharpe, 1984). Mothers who work outside the home have greater expectations of their children and make greater demands on them for mature and competent behaviour (Belsky, 1984). Fathers' employment may also provide them with support but there is little evidence about how fathers' employment influences their parenting (Bronfenbrenner, 1986).

We have discussed a number of factors associated with child abuse. They all give some clues about why children are abused but they leave many questions unanswered. One attempt to go beyond current thinking is that of Belsky (1984) who assesses the comparative weightings of three variables. These are the child's characteristics (temperament, health etc.), parents' personal resources (personality, levels of nurturance and child-centredness) and parental support networks. Abuse is more likely when children are difficult, there is little or poor parental support AND when parents' well-being is low. Belsky argues that of the three variables, child characteristics are the least important, citing evidence from studies of premature and sick children. In spite of the problems the parents of such children experience, there is little evidence that premature and sick children are any more at risk as long as parents are well supported. When there is good social support, the development of such children is not compromised. Personal resources are seen as the most crucial factor. This is partly because they influence parental warmth and willingness to take the child's perspective. But they are also important because they influence the support parents can call on. Parents who are confident, socially skilled and more 'other-centred' are likely to have more supportive family, friends and colleagues at work than parents who are isolated and depressed.

Family approaches to child abuse indicate the myriad of ways in which families operate and abusive relationships may develop. This emphasizes the value of moving away from explanations of abuse based on the personal characteristics of parents or children. Taking such an approach means that children are less likely to be blamed for eliciting abuse or parents for being bad parents and encourages researchers to look for ways of helping children and parents involved in abuse.

Consequences of Physical Abuse

Interest in physical abuse and its impact on children stems from an immediate concern about the physical and emotional risks for children of being in a violent relationship and also the longer-term effects on children's development. An obvious first consequence of physical abuse is the injury children receive. Sometimes injuries are substantial, requiring hospital treatment. Indeed it is sometimes the fact that children are brought to hospital as well as the nature of their injuries that arouses suspicions. When injuries are severe they can cause disfigurement, brain damage and stunted growth (Browne *et al.*, 1988). There is no single behavioural or emotional set or pattern of reactions to abuse; children respond in many different ways (Herzberger and Tennen, 1986). Some children are devastated, withdrawn and depressed. Others become hypervigilant for future aggression. And yet others survive with their sense of dignity and esteem intact, their emotional life is not impoverished and they remain responsive to others. In the 'strange situation', for example, some abused children show signs of insecure attachment, but the behaviour of others suggests ambivalent or even secure attachments (Main, 1980). In addition, children's behaviour varies in ways that do not tie in easily with the nature or the extent of their abuse. One factor which may influence how children react is their understanding and interpretation of events, including how far they blame themselves and how far they blame the abusing parent; children who blame their parents may focus their anger on parents rather than themselves. But children's reactions to distressing events vary considerably and there is no reason to expect that this would not be the case with abuse (see Chapter 10).

A variety of longer-term reactions to abuse has been reported. The experience of abuse, especially if children come to believe that they deserve the punishments they receive, may result in low self-esteem and depression (Herzberger and Tennen, 1986). The process whereby abused children come to have low self-esteem is extremely complex. It has been suggested that low self-esteem is a result of their failure to achieve goals set by parents. But their failure reduces their motivation to achieve other parental goals, thereby losing an opportunity for more positive relations with parents. Low self-esteem may also result from a lack of social skills, which isolates children from alternative sources of support. The distortion of relationships within the family and children's wariness of adults may make it difficult for them to form good relations with people outside the family (Browne *et al.*, 1988). Some abused children have a negative view of their parents and other adults whom they see as unwilling to reciprocate kind initiatives (Herzberger and Tennen, 1986). They tend to be more aggressive and more likely physically to assault other children and hence other children may be less willing to play with them and have them as friends (Herzberger and Tennen, 1986). Their lack of close relationships and insecure attachments may increase the risks of abused children abusing their own children, but the majority of children who experience abuse do not become abusing parents (Emery, 1989; Main, 1980).

Sexual Abuse

Sexual abuse is a more recent 'discovery' than physical abuse. In 1981, when cases of sexual abuse were first recorded in the UK, they made up 3 per cent of the total number of cases of abuse reported, but had risen to 31 per cent by 1986. Most workers in the field believe that there is still considerable under-reporting. Because of the low rates of reporting, we do not have a great deal of reliable information about the incidence and nature of child sexual abuse (CSA). The data we have come from a number of sources. There are a few large-scale studies looking at rates of CSA in the population. We also have information from adults who, sometimes as part of therapy, reveal their experiences of sexual abuse as children. CSA is also known about through reports to the police, doctors and welfare agencies. Welfare agencies sometimes become aware of children who are abused as a result of investigations carried out for other purposes. These sources provide some information, but there are still many unanswered questions (Browne *et al.*, 1988; La Fontaine, 1990).

From the data we have, it would seem that the majority of children who are sexually abused are girls. This contrasts with physical abuse where boys are somewhat more likely to be abused. Some workers believe that larger numbers of boys are abused than we know about and that this is an area of considerable under-reporting. Children of all ages are sexually abused; abuse has been reported in children from a few months upwards. La Fontaine (1990) found that almost half the cases seen in one hospital in the UK were under 12 years. There is a higher rate of reporting of CSA by adolescent than by younger girls (Browne and Finkelhor, 1986; Browne *et al.*, 1988).

The profile of abusers is also somewhat different for sexual abuse. Both men and women physically abuse children but most sexual abusers are men. Fathers and stepfathers are the largest category of abusers but others include grandfathers and other family members, neighbours and other men known to children as well as strangers. There have been few attempts to identify the characteristics of abusers. Kempe and Kempe (1978) considered that fathers who abuse are introverted and socially isolated and La Fontaine (1990) that they are unwilling to take responsibility for their actions.

Sexual abuse involves the use of children and young people for the sexual gratification of adults and takes a number of forms. Anal intercourse, vaginal intercourse and kissing, touching and other forms of sexual contact where intercourse is not attempted are most commonly reported. Sexual abuse is sometimes accompanied by physical abuse; children may be held down and hit as part of being sexually assaulted and they are sometimes hit or threatened with violence to ensure they do not disclose the sexual abuse.

Detecting Child Sexual Abuse

Detecting sexual abuse is a major current concern. Detection of CSA is more contentious than that of physical abuse, although it is not clear whether this is because of the relative inexperience of workers in the field or because people are still shocked about CSA and do not want to recognize its existence. Sexual abuse may go on for years, hidden within the close family. This may be because there is considerable pressure on children not to reveal that they have been abused. Most people feel very uncomfortable about CSA, as the commotion in the UK around recent cases reveals. One way of dealing with shock is denial and this is commonly employed around sexual abuse. Those who are abused often deny that it has happened and memories of the abuse may be forgotten for many years. Those who abuse children often deny what they have done or deny their responsibility. Welfare professionals, the police and the general public often refuse to accept that sexual abuse happens because they find it so upsetting. CSA is upsetting because it violates basic assumptions about the vulnerability of children and about families as safe places and about parents as committed to the care and protection of children. It also reveals in a particularly crude form the power of adults over children and how parents may be prepared to put their own needs before those of children (Browne *et al.*, 1988; La Fontaine, 1990).

Children are not considered capable of giving their consent to sexual activities and so their feelings and the quality of their relationship with the abuser are not considered in cases of CSA. The emphasis is on looking for evidence that abuse has taken place. Various kinds of evidence are considered. Medical practitioners examine children for physical evidence of abuse. This may involve bruises on children's arms or body where they have been held down, damage or soreness to their anus or vagina or evidence of an infection resulting from abuse. Behavioural indications are also looked for. Children who are sexually abused, like those who are physically abused, display a variety of emotional reactions. Examples of reactions which alert workers to the possibility of abuse include being frightened of having a bath or going to bed because these are times when children have been abused, sexual precociousness resulting from having been involved in abuse and a frozen watchfulness. These may be noticed and reported by family members, welfare agencies or by teachers (Kitzinger, 1989). Sometimes abuse comes to light through children's reports. Children do not always find it easy to admit they have been abused, and this might be especially so for boys. Children may fear that people will think less of them or blame them if they know what they have been doing. They may have been threatened by the abuser. Abusers sometimes ensure children's silence by entering into conspiracies, such as 'Don't let's tell anyone our secret' and children are reluctant to break their promises. Children may be deterred from reporting abuse because in the past people have responded with disbelief or anger and they have discovered, as their abusers predicted, that telling can be dangerous. If the abuser denies the abuse, it is the child's word against that of the abuser, although it is generally considered that young children rarely make up stories about abuse. The last form of evidence is the admission from the abuser. Without the abusers' admission, it can be difficult to get a successful prosecution and so the police are often not keen to bring a case to court. However, when welfare agencies feel that there are strong reasons to suspect abuse, children can be taken into the care of local authorities (Browne *et al.*, 1988; La Fontaine, 1990).

Consequences of Child Sexual Abuse

CSA is sometimes seen, like physical abuse, as part of a continuum, with kissing, hugging and other acceptable forms of affectionate behaviour at one end and abuse at the other. This suggests that abusers usually start by being affectionate with children but at some point they slip over the edge into unacceptable behaviour. Some abuse does seem to take this form. The implications of such a view for parents', and especially fathers', involvement in childcare is that they need to be vigilant about their behaviour and especially how they express affection. There is another view which suggests that there is clear demarcation between sexual and non-sexual behaviour. According to this approach, abuse cannot be explained in terms of abusers letting their affection get out of hand but as abusers using children for their own gratification. Accordingly, one way of preventing abuse is for fathers to get more involved in childcare, so they get to know their children as individuals in their own right. By establishing close relationships, fathers may respect children more and are less likely to use them for their own sexual purposes. They may also learn that they cannot impute their own motives to children, and become more sensitive to children's expressions of fear, reluctance or dislike of what they are asked to do (Finkelhor, 1984).

Child sexual abuse is seen largely as a family affair, as La Fontaine (1990) suggests:

> Children are most often abused in houses where they live, by the people with whom they live. These are the significant facts. Domestic life throws adults and children together in conditions of intimacy which make opportunities for abuse much more frequent and much

easier to conceal even from other members of the household. (La Fontaine, 1990: 151)

Abuse distorts relationships within families in a number of ways. To abuse their children, fathers and stepfathers need to ignore their children's feelings or to view them according to their own perspectives. Children may appear to enjoy their special relationship with fathers and the extra attention they get because they are 'Daddy's pet' (Browne *et al.*, 1988). This may make it difficult for children to express their fears or their dislike of the abuse and children's silence or lack of complaint may be interpreted as compliance or their willingness to participate. When they talk about abuse later, children who were abused often mention feeling powerless to stop what was happening (La Fontaine, 1990). They may relate this to their fathers' physical size and strength but it is sometimes expressed in terms of their fear and guilt at being involved in activities they know to be wrong but which they do not know how to stop. This sense of powerlessness has its basis in reality and is increased by the privacy of the family which gives parents control over many aspects of children's lives.

CSA takes its toll on children in a number of ways. Children exhibit fears and phobias, hostility and anger, sleeping and eating disorders, guilt and shame (Browne and Finkelhor, 1986). Children are sometimes so engrossed with surviving and keeping the abuse secret, that they have little opportunity for childlike activities. Children who are abused are sometimes reported to have poor social skills, experience problems at school, and display a seductiveness or precociousness which may put them at risk of further sexual abuse (Kitzinger, 1989). Emotional problems are more likely when children are abused by fathers than by grandfathers or more distant family members or people outside the family. This may be because fathers have greater power and control over their lives but also because being abused by people they trust involves greater betrayal (Browne *et al.*, 1988).

For many children disclosure can be costly. Their fears of how others will react may be one reason why children are unwilling to report abuse. The costliness may relate to the feelings such an admission may generate in the family, especially if the abuse is made public and the father is prosecuted or the child is taken into care. Other family members including siblings may be angry at the disruption of family relationships and family life caused by the disclosure. Jealousy between siblings about the 'special' attention one child has received may come to the fore, although occasionally children work together to protect and to support one another (Browne and Finkelhor, 1986; Browne *et al.*, 1988; La Fontaine, 1990).

Abuse as a Challenge to Views about Family Life

The discussion in this chapter has, by and large, treated physical abuse and sexual abuse separately. There are, however, a number of ways in which they resemble one another and point to similar ideas about family life and its consequences for children and their development. Physical and sexual abuse both involve complex patterns of behaviour. There are few simple, clear cut patterns of abuse; no obvious characteristics by which abusers may be easily recognized and few obvious indications that allow us to say with confidence that a child had been abused. Diversity characterizes the ways abuse occurs, is viewed by parents and children, and affects children's (and parents') sense of themselves and their relationships with one another. This underlines the complex nature of family relations, but makes for difficulties in detecting and hence ensuring that abuse is stopped as quickly as possible. Our ability to listen to children, to make sense of the indications of abuse and to reach the right conclusions are influenced by the ideas we all have about family relationships.

Physical abuse and child sexual abuse both challenge common-sense ideas about children and families. Children are seen as vulnerable, physically and emotionally, and one of the main functions of parenting is to provide a safe and sensitive environment in which children can grow and develop. They also challenge notions of families as committed to meeting equally the needs of all their members. Abuse points to the ways in which parents may use their power destructively and how children's needs may be subordinated to those of parents. It brings out clearly the ways in which children may be considered the property of their parents who control their lives.

While things are going well, the privacy of the family is maintained and parents' power over their children is seen as benign, serving children's best interests. Breakdowns in family functioning and in families' ability to care for children, point to the ways in which family life is regulated by outside agencies. One of the most heated arguments around child abuse cases centres on the rights and responsibilities of parents versus those of welfare agencies and the circumstances in which agencies can, in children's best interests, remove them from families. Unfortunately, all too often, the rights of children (and their physical safety) get submerged in battles between adults (La Fontaine, 1990).

There is considerable debate about the best ways to deal with abuse. Prosecuting abusers and putting children into care may stop the abuse and punish abusers but may in themselves create yet more problems for children. Concern around abuse and especially sexual abuse has focused on detection rather than on ways of handling abuse that are minimally disruptive and damaging for the parents and children involved. A better way may be to seek ways of supporting families and trying to improve parent-child relations (Browne *et al.*, 1988).

In Conclusion

In many families parenting is not sensitive and responsive to children's needs and children are exposed to experiences which put their physical and psychological health at risk. A number of aspects of family life may be damaging to children; we have discussed two here, physical and sexual abuse. Abuse of children is more likely when families are under stress and other relationships are unsatisfactory. The emphasis in research has been on identifying children and families at risk. But we also need to examine factors which increase children's resilience and their ability to cope with abuse and so help them to grow and develop in spite of their experiences. We also need to find ways of providing support and constructive assistance for families in which abuse has taken place.

Further Reading

BELSKY, J. (1984) 'The determinants of parenting: a process model', *Child Development*, **55**, pp. 83–96.

In this article Belsky considers abuse as an aspect of parent-child relationships. Three sources or systems of influence on parent-child relations are discussed: those from the individual parent, from the individual child and from the broader social context, such as marital relations, social networks and occupational experience. One system may help buffer another, so that abuse is more likely when there are problems in two or three of the systems.

BROWNE, K., DAVIES, C. and STRATTON, P. (Eds) (1988) *Early Prediction and Prevention of Child Abuse*, Chichester, Wiley.

A substantial collection of current studies (including many British studies) of physical and sexual abuse. The collection looks at prevalence, identification and prevention of abuse, which is seen as an issue for the families as well as for individuals.

LA FONTAINE, J. (1990) *Child Sexual Abuse*, Cambridge, Polity Press.

An interesting and thoughtful review of research on child sexual abuse. By considering the reactions of press, Parliament and public opinion in general as exemplified in reactions to, for example, events in Cleveland in 1987, La Fontaine provides a powerful setting for addressing questions about the prevalance, cause and best ways to deal with child sexual abuse.

Chapter 9

The Health of the Child: Prematurity, Illness, Handicap and the Family

In Chapter 2 we discussed some of the adjustments adults make as they become parents and we saw that men and women make better adjustments the closer their experiences are to those that they had envisaged. The more predictable the experiences, the smoother the transition. Unfortunately, the process is not always smooth and predictable; difficulties can arise that impose heavy burdens on family members. Among these are threats to the well-being of children, including prematurely born and sickly babies, later childhood illnesses and the development of handicaps both physical and mental. The impact of these events on the well-being of the family is discussed here.

Prematurity

Babies who are premature and of low-birthweight differ from full-term infants in a number of ways. They are smaller and more vulnerable to illnesses. Parents describe them as less physically attractive and less pleasant to interact with than full-term infants and their high-pitched cries can be irritating and disturbing (Frodi *et al.*, 1978). The smaller the premature or low-birthweight baby, the more likely it is to be slow developing and show some intellectual and cognitive impairment; a birthweight of three pounds or less can result in significant deficits in later reading, language, arithmetic and spelling, as well as in measured IQ. However, this only occurs in 15 per cent of cases; despite being small and vulnerable the remaining 85 per cent recover well (Kopp and Krakow, 1983).

Premature babies may have to remain in special care after birth until they are sufficiently healthy to be handed over to their parents' care. This can mean that babies remain in special care for six weeks or more, so that the mother returns home from hospital without her baby and parents have less opportunity than normal to practice their parenting skills. In consequence parents, and especially mothers, begin to lose confidence in their ability to cope, particularly as they know that they have a delicate child to care for. This anxiety can be reduced although not eliminated by encouraging parents to carry out simple caretaking activities while the infant remains in special care (Leifer *et al.*, 1972). Later when premature babies are with parents they can be more demanding than full-term infants: they tend to be harder to feed, they sleep less regularly, and moreover they provide less distinctive cues to guide parental behaviour and are less responsive (Field, 1987). As a result these babies are harder to interact with and it can take longer than normal for parents to become attached to them. Prematurely born babies are initially developmentally delayed. How quickly they recover and catch up depends on their home environment. Children from stable and stimulating home backgrounds show rapid recovery, but those from unstable backgrounds frequently show impairments up to six or seven years later (Werner and Smith, 1982).

The birth of a premature or low-birthweight infant is often stressful for parents, who can be angry, shocked and upset. Mothers report crying more, feeling guilty and helpless even when the infant is seen as being at low risk (Trause and Kramer, 1983). Mothers are more upset than are fathers both immediately and into the first year of life; their major concern is for the infant and its welfare. Fathers' concerns tend to focus more on the mother and on her well-being and ability to cope. Predictably, the emotional upset experienced by parents is related to the health status of the infant and mothers are more likely to report alienation from ill premature babies than from healthy premature babies (Pederson *et al.*, 1985).

In the short term the birth of a premature infant may prompt fathers to become more involved than usual; they are more likely to get up in the night to console their infants and to do 'messy' jobs such as bathing (Yogman, 1985). It seems that this increased father involvement occurs because fathers believe that the mother is unable to cope and that they can help and so is most likely to occur when the health of the baby is poor (Parke and Beitel, 1988). Although fathers may carry out more caretaking when a baby is premature, they play with them less. Neither parent interacts in the same way as they do with full-term babies (Yogman, 1985). Fathers of premature babies show less of their typical physical staccato play and interactions are of shorter duration. Mothers talk to premature babies more than to full-terms, but they show less expressive affectionate behaviour. Mothers interact with their premature infants at a greater distance than they do with full-term children. For the first two years mothers pick up premature babies less and hold them further away from their bodies, on their knees rather than cuddled close to the body (Leifer *et al.*, 1972). The reduced interactions between fathers and prematurely born infants probably occurs because the infant is small and seen to be vulnerable and so not able to withstand the vigorous stimulation normally offered. Mothers' altered interaction patterns are likely to reflect the less responsive nature of premature babies. Mothers talk more to the premature infant in order to attract its attention but the reduction in expressive behaviour is taken by many to be a sign that parents are not emotionally attached to their infant.

In Chapter 8 it was seen that children born prematurely or of low birthweight are sometimes found to be more likely to be physically abused by their parents than are full-term healthy babies. The explanation offered by many for the increased levels of abuse is that the vulnerability of the infant and its stay in special care have resulted in a failure to form affectionate attachment bonds. While this may be a contributory factor it seems that the social and economic status of parents of prematurely born babies may be more important. Mothers of prematurely born babies are more likely to be young, poorly educated, on a low income, and socially isolated. These factors lead to difficulties in coping financially and emotionally with their lives, and so when their children are irritating they over-react.

Physical and Mental Handicap

Some children exhibit handicaps and disabilities which affect their development and so they require more care and attention to help them achieve optimum levels of social and intellectual development. Together with the stigma frequently associated with disability this means that families caring for handicapped children have different demands made of them than do other families. Regardless of the type of handicap, many parents of handicapped and difficult children report high levels of family stress. The stress of adjusting to a handicapped child and living with the demands made by the child's handicaps have particularly strong and frequent effects on job performance, the maintenance of friendships, and marital harmony, and parents frequently report problems with housing (Palfrey *et al.*, 1989). The handicapping conditions most frequently studied are Down's syndrome, developmental delay, cerebral palsy, spina bifida, blindness and deafness. Although handicapping conditions vary substantially there are common adjustment problems to be faced by the families. For instance Holroyd and Guthrie (1986) compared the reported stressors listed by mothers of children with three chronic childhood illnesses: cystic fibrosis, neuromuscular disease and renal disease. In every case financial implications of the disease were mentioned. Other problems mentioned were the perceptions of others and the stigma attached to handicap, and the constraints placed on family activities. To give a clearer account of the impact of a handicapped child on the family, one illustrative handicapping condition, Down's syndrome, is considered in detail. Because Down's syndrome is normally diagnosed at birth it represents a relatively straightforward case for examining the reactions and adjustments of the family. Other handicapping conditions frequently are developed or become apparent only later and the family may have to live with growing doubts about the child until the condition is confirmed. In the case of developmental delay this uncertainty may be prolonged for a considerable time.

Down's Syndrome and the Family

There are two interlinked issues that are considered here. The first is to what extent the family contributes to the level of disability of the handicapped child, either by facilitating development or hindering development. The treatment that handicapped children receive might add to the level of handicap independently of the primary handicapping condition. This is referred to as secondary handicap. For instance parents may not talk to blind children very often about things happening around them because they know that their children cannot see what they are talking about. If they do this the parents deny their children the linguistic stimulation young children generally receive and benefit from. The second issue is how the family adjusts to a handicapped member and what factors facilitate or hinder those adjustments.

Children with Down's syndrome are born with a chromosomal defect in which the individual usually has an extra chromosome or part of a chromosome giving them forty-seven instead of the usual forty-six. The disorder is characterized by physical features that facilitate early diagnosis such as the shape of eyes and head and often the presence of a long crease across the palm of the hand. They frequently have heart defects that result in early death or require early surgery. Because of this it is difficult when the condition is diagnosed to give a firm prognosis about the child's chances of survival. Children with Down's syndrome may also have physical and mental handicaps. In particular they may suffer from poor coordination and muscle control which may lead to difficulties in walking or supporting their bodies. Again the extent of this physical disability is very variable. Intellectually, children with Down's syndrome are very variable with some becoming severely retarded while others achieve at the lower end of the normal range. Once again no clear information can be given to parents about the likely extent of their child's handicaps at the time the condition is diagnosed.

In general the behaviour of a baby with Down's syndrome in the first six months of life is very similar to the behaviour of any other baby (Woods *et al.*, 1984). However, after six months normally developing babies begin to show major developmental advances and pull ahead rapidly. From a year or so the rate of developmental gain of non-handicapped children slows down and while continuing to pull ahead developmentally they do so at a slower pace.

Despite the variation in the levels of development of children with Down's syndrome, there are some common features. They have difficulty communicating with others and in particular they are poor at making and maintaining eye contact. This results in them missing nonverbal cues provided by others and in their turn they produce inadequate nonverbal feedback. They do not vocalize, point or gesture much, they persist for shorter periods with an activity and require greater stimulation than other toddlers to elicit a response (Huntington and Simeonsson, 1987). Turn-taking tends to be poor and so there are more interactional clashes. This creates difficulties for their caregivers who would normally pick up on the activities of the child and try to develop interactions from them (Jones, 1977). As they get older they become more competent although their rate of progress tends to be slow. By their middle childhood many are developing reasonable self-help skills and are able to eat unaided and so on (Carr, 1988). Speech tends to continue as a problem area although in other areas of communication they do better (Mundy *et al.*, 1988).

Secondary Handicap

Interactions between children and their caregivers are influenced by the characteristics of the child. Inevitably handicapped children make a different contribution than non-handicapped children. Depending on its precise nature the handicap may interfere substantially with efficient communication. Because children with Down's syndrome frequently provide limited or misleading feedback it can be difficult for the caretaker to demonstrate sensitivity despite all their efforts (Jones, 1980). Handicapped preschool children become more verbal and more responsive to others when their communications are consistently responded to by mothers and when their mothers centre interactions around the child's activities (Mahoney, 1988). Initially this is how most parents attempt to interact with their handicapped child, with most of the early interactions being child-initiated. But because parents are anxious to interact as much as possible they often treat non-intentional behaviours as if they were deliberate and so many attempts by parents to encourage their child to interact fail. As a result parents become discouraged and abandon this approach. Instead they become more directive, interfering more and trying to encourage the child to interact or to try out new activities. Rather than encouraging the child to develop further the limited skills that it has already, they try to impose new activities on the child (Cunningham *et al.*, 1981; Hooshyar, 1987). Unfortunately, the new strategy they adopt is less effective in encouraging development than the one they abandoned.

Another reason for parents responding less to children's activities is that they do not want to interrupt their child when it becomes involved in an activity. Handicapped children have limited attention spans; they do not often become engrossed in an activity. If the child is going to develop well it has to learn to attend to things going on round about it. When parents see that their child has become engrossed in an activity they want to encourage that concentration of attention and do not want to distract the child. Although parents do this for the best of motives they then miss an opportunity of talking to their child about the things that interests it and of playing with objects that have attracted its attention. Such interchanges encourage the child to learn about language and about the importance of turn-taking. In this way they also learn to attend to people and to anticipate their actions and reactions. Because parents do not want to interrupt their children when they are engrossed in something, parents of handicapped children talk to them less than do mothers of non-handicapped children, they have fewer physical contacts and fewer expressions of affection (Levy-Shiff, 1986). Unwittingly, parents may be hindering development. The cycle of interactions that leads to secondary handicap can be broken. Intervention programmes introduced for parents of children with Down's syndrome have been effective in changing parental interactive styles and children have made developmental gains. Intervention programmes that focus mothers' attention on the areas of competence of the child rather than on areas of incompetence are particularly effective (Woods *et al.*, 1984).

Family Adjustments

When parents are told their child has Down's syndrome they display reactions similar to those associated with bereavement (Gath, 1978). The loss they suffer is of the normal healthy child they expected. Parents have clear images of what their child will be like and their actual child does not conform to those images. Parents lose their idealized non-handicapped child and this calls for adjustments on their behalf. It is only when they have adjusted to the loss that they can come to appreciate the child in its own right as it really is.

The reactions to the discovery that the child is handicapped consist of shock, disbelief and anger, especially anger directed towards the bearer of the news. The disbelief in the handicap is made worse by any uncertainty about likely future outcomes. In the majority of cases it is impossible to give an unambiguous answer to parents' questions about the child's future such as whether the child will survive and how competent it will be. Yet parents need certainty and so they frequently seek second and third opinions. During this period they may deceive themselves and deny that their child is handicapped. Such denial postpones the start of parental adjustments that must be made and so is maladaptive. Following on quickly from the shock of learning of the handicap comes a sense of guilt. The child that parents have produced is handicapped, therefore parents argue they must in some way be to blame. Unrealistically, parents review possible occasions when their actions might have led to the problem. Mothers blame themselves for not taking better care during pregnancy and their sense of guilt may focus on sexual intercourse, in extreme cases resulting in the abandonment of all sexual activities, partly through fear of giving birth to another handicapped child (Carr, 1988). Marital relations tend to be more unhappy and there are more open antagonism, arguments and nagging, and less show of affection between the partners. However, there are large individual differences and a critical factor is the quality of the parents' relationship before the birth. Handicapped children put a strain on relationships and so the relationship has to be good to cope. If the prior relationship is good, then having a handicapped child gives the couple a shared responsibility and may even improve their already good relationship. Prior relationships that are only moderate or poor are likely to decline and are associated with unhappiness, hostility and arguments. In these cases mothers frequently complain that fathers fail to give them the sympathy and support that they need (Bristol and Gallagher, 1986; Carr, 1988; Gath, 1978). The changes occur early during a period when the handicapped child is no more demanding than a non-handicapped child. It is not the strains of looking after a difficult child that create difficulties for marriages, therefore, but the worries about the handicap. Later on the characteristics of the child do become important and marital quality is related to behaviour problems displayed by handicapped children (Gath and Gumley, 1986).

Another sign of the strain of looking after and living with the knowledge of a child's handicaps is illness and depression amongst parents. Mothers of handicapped children report themselves tired, having difficulty sleeping, with variable moods and feelings of depression. For their part, fathers report tiredness and irritability, and more fathers of handicapped children need treatment for psychiatric problems than do fathers of non-handicapped children (Gath, 1978). Families on low incomes are more likely to have mood disturbances, anxiety and depressive problems than their more affluent counterparts. They have to cope with the problems of material disadvantage as well as those associated more directly with the handicapped child. Better-off families, in contrast, have only to cope with the demands of the handicapped child. The effect of this can be seen in the success of intervention programmes. Families from a low socio-economic background benefit less from interventions than families from higher socio-economic backgrounds (Gallagher *et al.*, 1983). Psychiatric and mood disturbances are not associated with the severity of the child's handicap or the demandingness of the child. It is not only the reality of looking after a handicapped child that causes depression and moodiness, the idea of having a handicapped child in the family adds to the problem.

Handicapped children are more demanding of parents' resources, including financial resources and their time and energy, than non-handicapped children. Because of their handicaps children need to attend clinics and centres for assessment, monitoring and training. These trips involve transport costs and the investment of considerable time. Because of their slow rate of development, handicapped children are dependent on parents to carry out a variety of caretaking tasks long after other children have become self-sufficient. There is more soiling and dirtying of clothes and also more wear and tear on the home and its contents. Looking after a handicapped child is frequently hard unrelenting work. Moreover, because of the child's condition it is harder to find alternative care to allow parents a break. Consequently parents often feel overworked, tired and locked into a child-centred world. Following the birth, parents' social life changes; they lose touch with some former friends, have fewer breaks from home and have difficulty maintaining outside interests. Their identity becomes more and more bound to their role as provider for their child.

Handicapped children are demanding of financial resources, but their presence in the family can make it hard for the family to maintain or increase previous income levels to meet the extra costs of a highly dependent child. Mothers of handicapped children are less likely to be in paid employment than mothers of non-handicapped children. In her longitudinal study of families, Carr (1988) reports that even twenty or more years after the birth of a child mothers of non-handicapped children are nearly twice as likely to be in paid employment as mothers of handicapped children. If mothers of Down's children do work it is nearly always part-time work undertaken while the child attends a day centre. Without this source of income families with a handicapped member frequently suffer financial hardship. Because fathers are overloaded at home their working potential may be reduced. Consequently they may be less likely to seek overtime, promotion or a career change. Men claim that their work and careers do not suffer as a result of the handicapped child, although it must be remembered that parents may be unwilling to be seen to be blaming the handicapped child for things that are not running smoothly in their lives (Carr, 1988).

Parents who have conceived a handicapped child have to adjust to the child that has been born rather than to the idealized child that they may have hoped for; moreover, they have to adjust to the hard work involved in looking after a demanding child, and any stigma they believe attaches to parenting a handicapped child. Each parent tends to work through the various stages of adjustment that have been described. However, the process of adjustment is not a permanent one: parents never completely stabilize, and this is especially so for mothers (Damrosch and Perry, 1989). All sorts of events reactivate worries, guilts and preoccupations, including such things as the child starting at school. Mothers' and fathers' patterns of coping and adjustments vary. While sorrow, self-blame and depression recur for fathers to some extent, they see themselves as becoming steadily better with the passage of time. In contrast, mothers show no such recovery; they describe their adjustments as going through regular peaks and troughs, with no overall improvement (Damrosch and Perry, 1989). Because each parent has to work through their own sequence of adjustments at their own pace, it will frequently occur that one parent is preoccupied with different problems, feelings and emotions than the other (Parke and Beitel, 1988). This in itself can be a source of strain for the family and can lead to increased tensions, so that instead of supporting one another the parents are undermining each other's attempts to resolve their feelings about the child and its handicaps.

Family Reorganization

When the family includes a mentally handicapped child there are greater demands to be met that require some reorganization of normal family functioning. Frequently this means that mothers devote more of their time to the handicapped child and spend less time with remaining children. Fathers then devote more of their time to the non-handicapped children and are relatively uninvolved with the handicapped child (McConachie, 1982). For their part the brothers and sisters of the handicapped child are expected to become more independent and less demanding and to do more for themselves than they might otherwise do. Additionally, non-handicapped children, and especially girls, are expected to undertake more household chores such as cleaning and washing up and also more caretaking duties, helping to look after the handicapped child (Gath, 1978). By taking on slightly different roles all the family contribute to the task of bringing up a child with a handicap.

Mothers usually take principal responsibility for looking after handicapped children. This involves a great deal of hard work. Although these mothers are more prone to mental health problems than are mothers of normally developing children they are in general well adjusted given the task that confronts them (Gath and Gumley, 1986). Most do not suffer from feelings of guilt for very long and do not become depressed. It seems that when mothers devote themselves to their child they feel that they repay any debt they owe to the child. By devoting themselves to the child they can work through their guilt. However, a further reason for mothers coping relatively well is that the more time they spend with their child the better they get to know it, the more they appreciate their child's individuality and skills and the more they enjoy spending time with their child. These mothers can see that their efforts and sacrifices are worthwhile and that their child is developing into an interesting and competent person. For about 20 per cent of mothers, devoting so much of their time to the handicapped child results in them losing outside contacts and they become isolated and lonely (Carr, 1988).

How much time fathers spend with their handicapped children depends in part on the severity of the handicaps; the more severe the handicaps the less time fathers spend with the handicapped child. In part this reflects fathers' beliefs that the more handicapped the child the more it needs the specialist care they believe mothers provide. Fathers remain less involved because they believe that their partner can cope better with the child. However this is not the whole story. Fathers are also less involved in all household activities and mothers are more burdened. Fathers' sense of guilt at producing a non-perfect child and their embarassment at having to acknowledge a less than perfect child are probably involved in their decision to distance themselves from the child and the rest of the family. This is borne out by observations that fathers are less likely to take more severely handicapped children out of the house on outings (Cooke and Lawton, 1984).

Since fathers have little direct contact with handicapped children, and especially severely handicapped children, they have little direct influence on them. This does not mean they have no influence, because fathers can influence their handicapped children indirectly by the impact that they have on other family members and on family cohesion and atmosphere. Indeed Bristol and Gallagher (1986) suggest that this is fathers' most powerful influence and that they operate through mothers, influencing mothers' ability to cope with their children as well as influencing their attitudes to childcare.

Fathers spend relatively little time with their handicapped children and so, unlike mothers, their sense of guilt about the child's handicaps persists. Distancing themselves from the handicapped child is probably counter-productive. These men do not allow themselves the opportunity of reducing their guilt by helping the child to overcome its handicaps (Cummings, 1976). Indeed, men who spend more time with their handicapped children report less guilt and anxiety and seem better adjusted. Moreover, interventions that encourage men to be more involved with their handicapped children also result in a lowering of guilt and of depression and an increase in satisfaction (Price-Bonham and Addison, 1978; Vadasy *et al.*, 1985). The success of these interventions shows the importance of all the family accepting children and getting to know about their competences. The more that the child is known the more aware they are of the gains being made and the more pleasure they can take in the child's achievements.

Brothers and sisters of handicapped children grow up seeing their sibling receiving more attention than themselves and being expected to give the handicapped child attention and support. Additionally, more maturity demands are made of sisters and brothers of handicapped children and they are expected to grow up more quickly. Furthermore, siblings often report feeling a need to excel because they believe that their parents want them to make up for the handicapped child's limitations (Lobato, 1983). There is ample room for resentments to develop as children may feel robbed of their childhood and their parents' attention. When they are asked about this aspect of bringing up a handicapped child, parents deny that their other children have suffered (Carr, 1988). They claim that the brothers and sisters of handicapped children love them and are devoted to them. The siblings themselves view things differently. As children and young adolescents they see the handicapped child as a nuisance, interrupting their activities, their sleep and their social lives. However in this respect young handicapped children are viewed very similarly to younger non-handicapped siblings (McConachie, 1982; and see Chapter 6). Later, as young adults, siblings are much more positive about their experiences. The majority report that they have become more mature, sensitive and caring and better at taking the perspective of others. A sizeable group believe that there are both costs and benefits and that the two balance each other. Only a very small minority (about 5 per cent) believe that they had suffered (Carr, 1988).

Another way of looking at the impact of a mentally handicapped sibling on children is to look at records of their behaviour problems. Sisters and brothers of handicapped children reveal fewer behaviour problems at home and at school than do the siblings of non-handicapped children (Carr, 1988). However, there is variability and this seems to relate in part to the presence of problem behaviours in the handicapped child. According to Gath and Gumley (1986; 1987) psychiatric disorders in siblings are associated with behaviour disorders and troublesomeness in the handicapped child.

Positive Features of Life with a Handicapped Child

There is a tendency to dwell on the negative consequences of living in a family with a handicapped member. As Gath and Gumley (1984) point out, many families cope well and enjoy life. The challenges presented by the handicapped child can provide a growth point for family members. In retrospect, siblings report personal growth. For their part, mothers are thrust into a demanding role, but it is role that is clearly defined and pivotal within the family. Mothers become the expert, carrying out tasks that appear beyond the abilities of others. They can take pride in their capabilities and this provides an important boost to their self-esteem. Another positive outcome in the longer term is that parents frequently form new and deep friendships. In the short term the demands of looking after a handicapped child leave too little time to cultivate friendships and some social contacts are lost. However many report that they form close friendships with other parents of handicapped children and that these friendships provide important supports (Carr, 1988). A further and very important positive outcome is that the handicapped child can become a source of joy for the family. The handicapped child is an individual who is constantly developing new skills and in whom the family can take pleasure. The first tooth or the first dry night are events to be celebrated whether or not the child happens to have a handicap.

Being a Handicapped Child

Little consideration is given to how handicapped children experience and cope with their handicap. As they get older handicapped children become self-conscious, they realise that they are different and they frequently become unhappy about it. Kazak and Clark (1986) have shown that the self-concept of spina bifida children is lower than that of non-handicapped children from similar backgrounds. The comparable question has not been asked of children with Down's syndrome but it has been observed that they respond to success in similar ways to children who are not handicapped. Children with Down's syndrome can achieve greater academic success than their apparent general level of competence would suggest and their success can be a source of great pride and pleasure (Carr, 1988). Conversely, inappropriate teaching approaches can result in rather poor progress and a corresponding decline in self-regard (Gibson, 1978).

Nature of the Handicap

Some adjustments have commonly to be made whatever the specific handicap, including adjusting to the realization that the child's potential is limited. However there are also specific demands that each handicapping condition imposes which are reflected in differences in the reporting of stress by parents. Parents of physically handicapped children are more likely to report experiencing stress than any other group; they are followed by parents of deaf and blind children, parents of emotionally disturbed children, then by parents of mentally handicapped children. Each of these groups was more likely to report stress than parents of children with learning and speech difficulties (Palfrey *et al.*, 1989). In part different handicaps lead to different levels of stress as each disability makes different demands and imposes different restrictions on family life. For instance neuromuscular disease is associated with the steady deterioration of muscular control starting when the child is 3 to 5 years old which steadily worsens until the muscles controlling breathing and heartbeat fail. Children rarely survive into early adulthood. The disease does not show remissions, and as a result it calls for continuous adjustments as the child's capabilities decline. Parents of these children report very high levels of stress in nearly all areas of their functioning and their physical and emotional health is likely to be adversely affected compared to parents of children with diseases that are not so debilitating (Holroyd and Guthrie, 1986).

It is not only the impact on family life that makes one handicap more stressful than another. How the family and others perceive a disability is

important too. There is less stigma attached to 'medical' than to 'p
conditions (Holroyd and McArthur, 1976). Parents of children wi
syndrome have an explanation for the disability, they understan
disability has developed. This means they can come to terms wit
and present it to others more rationally. If there is a clear explanation this
lessens, although it does not eradicate, the opportunity for self-blame. Parents
of mentally retarded children where the cause of the retardation has not been
identified are more highly stressed than parents of Down's syndrome children
(Goldberg *et al.*, 1986). An important aspect of a handicapping condition is at
what stage in the life cycle it is diagnosed. Down's syndrome is typically
diagnosed at birth. Information can be given, support groups can be mobil-
ized and the family can start to come to terms with their situation. Other
handicapping conditions often are not recognized until the child is near
school age, e.g. developmental delay. The sooner that parents are aware of
their child's condition the sooner they can anticipate the demands that will be
made on them and begin to adjust to the child with their handicap (Gath and
Gumley, 1986; Parke and Beitel, 1988).

Individual Differences in Adjustments

Whatever the adverse event the family has experienced there are differences in
adjustments the family makes. There are a number of common themes that
appear to be associated with optimum adjustments. Byrne and Cunningham
(1985) list the health and energy of individual family members, their problem-
solving skills, their perceptions of the child and of their situation, relationships within the family and their access to and utilization of support
networks. They also point to the value of having two parents together to cope
with the handicapped child and the family; there is considerably more strain
on mothers when they are lone parents.

Social Support

Parents of handicapped or seriously ill children are generally stressed. They
often have a limited knowledge of the likely development of their children
and they do not know how best to look after them. These problems can be
alleviated by seeking help from others either within the family or from
outside. Some problems can be discussed with other family members, but
sometimes it is beneficial to talk to people beyond the family. Parents' own
parents or their parents-in-law are major sources of outside support (Pederson
et al., 1985). Mothers use informal support networks more than do fathers
and they use them largely to gain information and as sources of relaxation and
enjoyment (Parke and Tinsley, 1984). Woods *et al.* (1984) have shown that
women who have outside supports or a confidant are at lower risk of
psychiatric problems and are more accepting of their child. However, access
to outside support is not enough; family members need to know how to

utilize that support. If need be they can be trained to express their needs and to make use of available help (Kirkham *et al.*, 1986). Suelze and Keenan (1981) have pointed out that access to social support networks is not constant throughout the lifespan. Parents of teenagers and young adults are offered less support than parents of younger children, even though they perceive their need of support to be unchanged. The parents of Down's syndrome children tend to be older than parents of other handicapped groups and consequently their own parents are older and so may be less able to offer help.

Spousal Support and Family Cohesion

Anxieties and disappointments about a handicapped child can put strains on marital relationships. Among new parents marital quality is a good predictor of parental adjustment to the child whether handicapped or not (Friedrich, 1979). Marital quality may operate at a number of levels. If the relationship between the couple is poor then preoccupations with that relationship may interfere with the sensitive treatment of the child. Secondly, poor relationships can undermine the self-confidence and self-esteem of parents, affecting how the child is treated. Thirdly, poor relationships are associated with greater conflict and poorer conflict resolution and hence affect the ability to adjust well to a handicapped child (Nihira *et al.*, 1980). A final route is that marital quality affects spousal support. When parents are in harmony they are more likely to discuss issues about childrearing, they seek joint solutions to problems and are less likely to engage in contradictory childcare strategies. If they agree about their aims they reinforce each other's endeavours and provide each other with feedback about their effectiveness as parents. Lamb *et al.* (1985) argue that fathers' most important role is to reassure mothers that they are effective parents. Mothers are influenced by spousal support, they are more satisfied with parenting, are more responsive to children and have fewer adjustment problems when they are supported sensitively by their partners (Crnic *et al.*, 1983; Trause and Kramer, 1983). Fathers' parenting behaviour, too, is strongly influenced by support from their partners, and indeed they are worse than mothers at maintaining their parenting role in its absence (Dickie and Matheson, 1984). Harmony in other relationships within the family is also important and, in turn, handicapped children make greater strides in acquiring new skills when they come from cohesive and harmonious families (Frey *et al.*, 1989).

Characteristics and Personality of the Child

Various characteristics of the child influence how the family copes, including the severity of the handicap, its sex, temperament, self-esteem and age. Several studies have shown that the less severe the handicap or disability of a child the better the adjustments of all family members (Frey *et al.*, 1989; Holroyd and Guthrie, 1986; Nihira *et al.*, 1980). Siblings too are more likely to be disturbed the greater the level of handicap. Younger brothers and older sisters of severely handicapped children are most adversely affected, especially when the family is disadvantaged (Lobato, 1983).

The temperament of handicapped children has an impact on how parents respond to them: for instance, if they are easy, good-tempered and adaptable, parents tend to respond more appropriately and sensitively than if their temperament is difficult (Huntington *et al.*, 1987). Temperamentally difficult children who are not handicapped place greater demands on parents and others, but parents generally can cope. But when the child is handicapped as well this can overstretch parents' coping abilities, increasing parents' experience of stress and reducing their ability to relate sensitively to their child (Beckman, 1983). Other child characteristics which influence parents' reactions are the child's social responsiveness (the less responsive the greater the stress); how repetitive are the child's patterns of behaviour (the less variability the greater the stress); and how demanding is the child of unusual caretaking requirements. The self-esteem and happiness of the child may also influence the level of parental stress. The happier the child, the easier it is to look after the child and the easier it is for mothers to see that their sacrifices have been worthwhile. If the child is happy, parents can see that they have done a successful job in rearing a contented child despite the handicap.

The experiences of families are not static, but vary across time. Periods when the handicapped child experiences change are times when the family has to readjust too. Starting school, reaching adolescence and developing sexually, and becoming an adult are all turning points for the child and for the family (Carr, 1988; Winkler, 1986). An additional problem that has to be faced as the handicapped person gets older is that parents are aging and may be less able to provide support. This is a source of anxiety for parents who worry about who will care for the child when they no longer can (Carr, 1988).

How family members cope with the challenge of living with a handicapped child is determined largely by how they perceive the child and their situation. This can be seen in a study by Affleck and others (Affleck *et al.*, 1982; Tennen *et al.*, 1986) who examined the attributions that mothers made of the reasons for their newborn's perinatal problem. Some mothers blamed the infant's problem on something that they did themselves, others blamed other people, particularly medical personnel, and yet others put it down to chance. Those who blamed the child's problem on something that they had done were more convinced that they could also aid their infant's recovery. In contrast those who blamed others for the child's problem were less likely to believe that they could significantly help their infant overcome their disability. Mothers of chronically ill children display more depression than mothers of well children (Breslau *et al.*, 1982), but it is not the degree of disability that determines mothers' psychiatric health so much as their perceptions of the child's impairment. Regardless of the child's actual level of disability, mothers who believe their child deviates most from normal functioning in such areas as communication, mobility, sleeping and feeding show most depression.

However, the impact of perceived handicap on maternal well-being is moderated by the social supports available, mothers' physical health and experiences of other stressors (Jessop *et al.*, 1988). Help and support for families with ill or handicapped children is most effective when it helps family members develop a positive perception of the children and their abilities.

In Conclusion

The nature and severity of children's illness or disability and family variables influence how well family members cope. Individuals experience greater stress when the problem is perceived as severe, when it is unexpected, is long-lasting and does not respond to the efforts of the family to alleviate it. The less cohesive the family and the more isolated from social supports, the greater the demands made on family members. However, families can and do cope and having a child who is handicapped or disabled can be a growth point for family members.

Further Reading

BYRNE, E.A. and CUNNINGHAM C.C. (1985) 'The effects of mentally handicapped children on families: a conceptual review', *Journal of Child Psychology and Psychiatry*, **26**, pp. 847–64.

Reviews research examining the effect mentally handicapped children can have on the family. Consideration is given to which families are most vulnerable to stress and how coping strategies can be developed.

EISER, C. (1990) 'Psychological effects of chronic disease', *Journal of Child Psychology and Psychiatry*, **31**, pp. 85–98.

This review is not the easiest to follow, but it does cover some illnesses not covered in this chapter such as cancer and diabetes. It also gives consideration to the strain that the treatment of illness and disability places on children and on their families. The emphasis of the article is that the study of illness and the family is part of mainstream psychology examining ordinary people in exceptional circumstances.

PALFREY, J.S., WALKER, D.K., BUTLER, J.A. and SINGER, J.D. (1989) 'Patterns of response in families of chronically disabled children: an assessment in five metropolitan school districts', *American Journal of Orthopsychiatry*, **59**, pp. 94–104.

A very large number of parents were interviewed about their experiences of bringing up children who were disabled in some way. The disabilities varied from relatively minor speech difficulties to major physical and mental disorders. While many parents had found ways of coping with their child's disability, large numbers reported a direct stressful impact on the families' daily lives in terms of jobs, housing, friendships and marital harmony. The more severe the disability and the higher the parents' educational attainment the more reported stress. Various interpretations of the results are discussed and their implication for family-based intervention programmes considered.

Parke, R.D. and Beitel, A. (1988) 'Disappointment: when things go wrong in the transition to parenthood', *Marriage and the Family Review*, 12, pp. 221–65.

Focuses particularly on the impacts of prematurity and mental handicap on the family. They produce a useful model of the factors that determine the degree of stress associated with parenting children with different forms and levels of disability.

Chapter 10

Stress in the Family and Coping: Vulnerability and Resilience

In the previous three chapters we considered three types of events that can prove problematic for families. From the material reviewed so far it is clear that how individuals adapt depends on their coping strategies and inner resources, together with the amount of support available. In this chapter we explore further some of the events that seem problematic for children and their families and ask to what extent distress can be reduced and families helped to cope. Firstly, we identify the life circumstances that seem to be most strongly associated with the emergence of problems in development.

Problematic Adverse Events

We have already seen that family discord and breakup, poor relationships and abuse by parents and other family members and the presence of a handicapped person in the family are all life circumstances which family members can find problematic. The importance of these life circumstances is confirmed by longitudinal studies (e.g. Cohen and Work, 1988; Werner, 1989). Studies such as these collect detailed information about the life circumstances of large numbers of individuals over a number of years. Most of those individuals grow up psychologically and socially well adjusted, but some are less fortunate and develop emotional or behavioural problems. The life experiences of the well adjusted and less well adjusted are examined to see whether there are common features amongst those who develop problems that distinguish them from the population at large. In this way the emergence of problems is related to the experience of adverse life events, singly or in combination. One such study looked at children growing up on the Isle of Wight (Rutter *et al.*, 1976). At age 10 to 11 years a small subgroup was identified who exhibited many of the following characteristics: having poor concentration; being unpopular, restless and fidgety, disobedient, deceitful, aggressive, irritable, fearful, and dishonest. These children were classified as psychiatrically disturbed. They differed from their Isle of Wight age mates in that they were more likely to come from materially poorer homes, to be living in overcrowded conditions, to have a mother with a history of psychiatric illness, to have a father with a criminal record, to have spent some time in the care of the local authority, and to come from a discordant home. Children with problems had not experienced all of these adverse events, but they had experienced some of them. Each of these events seemed to have equal weight and have a similar sort of impact on the child. A similar study examined people growing up on a Hawaiian island over a thirty-two-year period from shortly before birth until those individuals were adults in their thirties (Werner, 1989). This group was studied to determine the characteristics of individuals who developed psychiatric problems, or who committed criminal offences, or who had problems at school. The group as a whole was brought up in disadvantaged circumstances, many experienced extreme poverty and/or a highly unstable family life, and some were exposed to major perinatal problems that interfered with normal development. Not surprisingly as a group they showed high levels of problem behaviours. One-third of them had behavioural or learning problems in their first ten years of life, and roughly 20 per cent had records for serious delinquency or had mental health problems by age 18 years. The events found to be most damaging to their emotional development were: perinatal obstetric complications; born into poverty; reared by mothers with little formal education; late birth order; prolonged separation from the mother in the first year of life; parental discord in the first two years of life; repeated childhood illness; father absent from home a good deal; family breakup; a mentally ill parent; an alcoholic parent; the presence of a handicapped brother or sister; death of a sibling or parent.

The events that can prove problematic for developing individuals identified in these and similar studies are those that interfere with normal family life. The adverse life events identified stem from problems occurring within the family that lead to unpredictability and uncertainty for the individual concerned. The uncertainty may arise when life circumstances change in a dramatic way or when individuals live in surroundings that represent persistent chronic uncertainty. These adverse circumstances create conditions in which children cannot readily predict what will happen to them. Some general themes can be seen in the list of adverse life circumstances. Several of the items relate to socio-economic status (poverty, overcrowding, poorly educated mother, criminal father). When children are brought up in families with inadequate material resources, including poor housing and insufficient money to meet basic living requirements, it may be hard for parents and siblings to attend to children sensitively. This is not to say that parents who are poor are necessarily insensitive and unresponsive to their children, nor that affluent parents are necessarily sensitive, but it may be easier to provide a harmonious and stable environment for children when there are fewer worries about money, housing, neighbours, police and so on. Other items are associated with non-optimum parenting (family discord, absent father, criminal father, alcoholic parent, mother with a psychiatric problem). In these families children are more likely to experience unpredictable and unstable family life where rules are not clearly laid down and enforced. The child may not have a clear idea about what to expect from others nor what others expect from them. A further feature of many of the events is that they relate to the experience of loss (death in family, family breakup, prolonged separation from mother, absent father). The loss experienced is often twofold: the individual loses the support of another close family member and frequently they lose familiar surroundings such as the family home and familiar belongings.

Cumulative Experience of Adversity and Steeling

Most individuals can cope easily with one area of uncertainty in their lives. However, when adverse events multiply and come together they are much more disruptive. When individuals have to adjust to uncertainty in two or more areas of their lives they run an increased risk of developing problems. Werner has shown in her study that two-thirds of those children who experience four or more risk factors before the age of 2 years develop serious learning difficulties or behavioural problems by the age of 10 years, or have delinquency records, mental health problems by the age of 18 years, or a criminal record or a broken marriage by age 30 years. In contrast only 15 per cent of the children with fewer than four risk factors develop any of these later problems. In a similar way Rutter (1978) found that children who experience just one adverse life event are no more at risk than children who experience none. However if a child experiences two there is a fourfold increase in risk and if they experience three a tenfold risk for later psychiatric problems and for later criminal convictions. In earlier chapters we have seen some specific examples of the cumulative effects of adversity.

In apparent contradiction to the above findings there is evidence that the experience of stress can make individuals better able to cope. Take two simple examples. Young children can find being taken into hospital for an extended period upsetting, particularly when no family member can stay with them. The experience presents them with a great deal of uncertainty, they may not understand what is happening to them and there are new routines to be learnt. However, children who have experienced alternative care in the form of occasional baby-sitters or regular day care are much better at coping (Stacey *et al.*, 1970). These children have benefited from a situation that was mildly stressful and learned from that experience, making them better able to adjust to a more stressful event later. The second example of building up resources by experiencing a challenging event is a young child experiencing the birth of a sister or brother. The birth of a second baby can be problematic for the first-born child. Initially, the new child may be resented, but for most children the experience of change leads to mastery of new skills and the child becomes more self-reliant and more confident in its own abilities (Dunn, 1984; Dunn and Kendrick, 1982). Once children have adjusted to the changes in their lives brought about by the birth of a sibling they have more resources to bring to bear when they are next presented with a challenge. The experience of mild stress has improved their skills and made them better able to cope with stressful events successfully. Experience of stress throughout life helps to build up adaptability, especially when individuals are exposed to a graduated series of challenges, allowing progressive development of coping strategies. It has been hypothesized that successfully overcoming minor problems 'steels' individuals, makes them tougher and enhances resilience (Bleuler, 1978). There are a growing number of case histories that support this view. Experiencing stress can build up adaptability, but only if the individual is allowed the time and support to develop effective coping strategies. Experiencing another stressful adverse event before the lessons of the first event have been absorbed reduces the ability to cope and so the timing of the multiple stressful events determines whether stress toughens or weakens the individual. However, the individual who has never experienced challenges may be in a weak position to face up to adversity when they encounter it.

Individual Differences in Stress Resistance: Vulnerability or Resilience?

In previous chapters we drew attention to individual differences in reactions to adversity and this is reinforced by the Werner longitudinal study where over a third of the high-risk children showed no later problems. This indicates that although some individuals experience great difficulties when exposed to adversity and develop problems, others cope with adversity well. The factors offering protection which have been identified fall into three broad categories: intrapersonal qualities such as positive personality dispositions; a supportive family environment; and access to supportive social agencies. Many of the qualities that protect children provide strength and resilience at all points through the lifespan, although there may be a need for somewhat different qualities and support at different points in time. This view is supported by findings from a British longitudinal study (Kolvin *et al.*, 1988). Boys brought up in disadvantaged conditions are protected during the first 5 years of life by close parental care and by positive social experiences; from 5 to 10 years protection comes from good supervision of children and from their easy temperamental qualities; for the next five years up to the age of 15 years protection comes from good cognitive development and progress at school.

Intrapersonal Qualities

A quality that moderates individuals' reactions to adversity is their temperament. These characteristics are apparent from early in children's lives. Werner (1989) demonstrates that individuals who as babies were 'easy' are less likely to respond to adversity later on with rebellion at school, delinquency or psychiatric illness than individuals who were difficult. The 'easy' babies were sociable and affectionate, were active in visual exploration of their environment, had good early coordination, had regular eating and sleeping habits and adjusted well to new experiences. These characteristics are relatively stable, for instance the sociable baby tends to have a good circle of friends when it is school-aged. These temperamental characteristics offer protection. One reason why temperament might be important is that when parents are under pressure they are more likely to be irritated by their children and to treat them insensitively. But some children are more irritating than others. Children who are more whiney, or more clumsy or more disobedient than others irritate stressed parents who then engage in more insensitive parenting because of their irritation. In turn, children exposed to more insensitive parenting are more likely to develop problems and consequently irritate their family even more. In contrast, the easier children of stressed parents do not exhibit negative behaviours, and because they do not add to the parents' burden they may elicit more sensitive parenting. Because they are easier to live with, these children continue to receive reasonably consistent and sensitive parenting and so are less affected by the deteriorating family circumstances.

We have seen in earlier chapters that life events can lead to different experiences for males and females. In general girls and women show greater resilience in the face of adversity than boys and men (see e.g. Werner, 1989). For instance, many girls become mothers at a young age and this places them at particular disadvantage financially and this disadvantage continues into their thirties. However, despite this, women in general cope better than men. The resilient men in Werner's study were less willing than the women to commit themselves to sustained intimate relationships. Women may be better adjusted because they are more willing to seek out and use social supports. Both men and women value and seek the support of a partner equally, but women are more willing to turn, in addition, to friends, older relatives, co-workers, professionals and mutual support groups.

A third protective quality is high self-esteem. Individuals with high self-esteem are less likely to develop behaviour problems, even in the face of extreme adversity (Garmezy, 1984; Rutter, 1978; Werner and Smith, 1982). Moreover they recover more quickly from the effects of adversity even if they do succumb (Garmezy, 1984). High self-esteem is associated with optimum adjustments in the face of adversity, partly because such individuals have confidence in their ability to cope and so persevere more in searching for effective coping strategies to solve problems in their lives. Werner (1989) also notes that high-resilience children are reported by both their teachers and parents as having a wide range of interests, hobbies and activities, which she suggests 'provided solace in adversity and a reason for pride'.

Supportive Family Environment

Throughout this book the value of sensitive, supportive care from others in the family has been stressed. Whether or not a family member has someone who remains sensitive to their needs has a bearing on their stress resistance. Often a good relationship allows children and adults to cope with difficulties. Thus children who have good relationships with their mothers are better able to cope with the adverse effects of a deterioration in their relationships with the father or the death of a close friend (Hetherington *et al.*, 1982). It is not only family members who can provide social support and protection; friends, neighbours and even schools can help too. Parents, friends and schools can offer protection by acting as confidants but also by providing much needed stability in children's lives. If parts of their lives are predictable and stable it is easier to cope with instability in other aspects of their lives. Schools that provide clearly defined and consistently enforced rules provide a child in turmoil some stability. When this is coupled with a supportive attitude from teachers and pupils, children are better able to resist the effects of adverse life events (Hetherington *et al.*, 1982; Rutter, 1978).

The studies reported so far identify events that are associated with the development of problems and those that offer protection for families. Each event identified is treated as if it were a uniform event, although in practice this is not the case. An event such as family discord is not a single consistent event. It varies from household to household and from time to time. Family discord varies in the frequency and ferocity with which it manifests itself; in some cases it takes the form of verbal attacks, in other cases physical attacks. Even when individuals within a family are exposed to identical events they do not all perceive them in the same way. For example the departure of a violent spouse may be viewed by the mother with relief and as a promising beginning, but by children or grandparents as a devastating, shameful failure. Events in practice are problematic when they are perceived as making demands that the individual is unable to meet. The ability of individuals to meet the demands made of them is determined by their coping strategies. Someone with high self-esteem experiences less distress than someone with lower self-esteem because they encounter fewer situations that they believe they cannot deal with effectively. Someone of low self-esteem may view even common situations as being too demanding, e.g. starting a new reading book at school. For them life is full of adversity, even though to an outside observer they are exposed to no more stressful events than other children.

Coping Strategies

All 'protective' factors operate in part by modifying the coping competences of individuals. The term coping is used to describe behaviours that involve efforts to change or alleviate a difficult situation, reduce the perceived threats and manage the symptoms created by the stress (Pearlin and Schooler, 1978). How effectively any coping strategy is pursued depends on the coping resources available. New demands require new ways of coping and different coping strategies may be required at different points through a stressful episode. For instance if an irate parent is threatening to hit a young child it would be counter-productive for the child to spend time trying to analyze what has led up to the problem: the immediate need is to avoid a beating, e.g. by running away. Having run away it would then be a good idea to try and work out what had led to the problem so that the child could avert future problems or deal with them more effectively when they do recur. In addition different things offer protection at different points in the course of an event. For instance Hobfoll and Leiberman (1987) found that women who had miscarried or given birth to a small vulnerable baby were more likely to avoid becoming depressed when the spouse was supportive at the time of the event but that such support was less help three months later. High self-esteem, however, offered protection at this later time point as well as at the time of the event. The implication for designing intervention programmes is that the resources offered must meet the situational demands of the moment, and that these vary across time. A helpful intervention at the onset of the event may be less effective if offered six months later.

It is important in coping with adversity to be able to analyze the situation and look for various ways of lessening its impact. This means being good at problem solving. Many of the adverse events that can occur are problems with relationships and so interpersonal problem-solving skills are likely to be particularly relevant. In Chapter 5 an account was given of aspects of parental interactive behaviour that help promote problem-solving skills. The rudiments of these skills are learned at home from parents. An important way in which they are further developed is through interacting with peers who provide different contexts and demand different skills and strategies. Experience with peers is very varied and consequently children have to think up a wide range of strategies to try out on them, they have to evaluate those strategies, to decide whether they are working or not and whether a new strategy needs to be introduced (Hartup, 1979). Such skills can be developed in individuals who lack them. This is particularly so if interventions are introduced while children are still young, before their old behavioural style has become too engrained. One such programme trains young children to generate large numbers of possible solutions to problems, to evaluate each of them by thinking forward to anticipate the likely outcome of an offered solution and to choose the best one. The intervention encourages children to be more reflective and to think through the consequences of their own actions and also reduces the likelihood of children developing problems at school (Shure and Spivak, 1982). In teaching problem-solving skills, home-based interventions are the most effective. In these, parents are trained in problem-solving skills and then attempt to train their children. The children who benefit most from this training have mothers who are best at mastering the skills and using them regularly in their lives. This reinforces the view that families provide one of the main contexts for the development of social problem-solving skills.

Social Supports

A coping stragegy that can be highly effective is the seeking out and use of social supports. The value of social supports has been reported in several chapters here. For example adults who cope best with the adjustments to be made as they become parents, parents who cope best with an ill or handicapped child, and parents and children who cope best with family breakup are those who have access to social supports. Social support can be offered informally by members of the immediate or extended family, by friends and by social groups or formally by support agencies such as social services or self-help groups. A large number of studies have demonstrated that parents and children who face adversity but have family and friends to whom they can turn are much less likely to succumb to that adversity than individuals who are socially isolated (e.g. Rubenstein *et al.*, 1989). Despite the large number of studies demonstrating the virtues of social support the term is poorly defined and it is usually unclear which dimensions of contact with others offer protection. Barrera and Ainlay (1983) have suggested six important needs that social support may satisfy. These are: (1) material aid (giving or lending money or goods), (2) behavioural assistance (helping with tasks), (3) problem-relevant intimate interaction (listening, giving reasurance), (4) guidance (offering advice, information), (5) feedback (about thoughts, feelings and behaviours), and (6) positive social interaction (providing fun and relaxation). Social contacts may or may not offer some of the above; to qualify as social support they must offer one of the above that the individual can use to reduce their sense of being overburdened.

Different problems require different solutions. To a woman who is overwhelmed by looking after triplet toddlers, being offered feedback that she is doing a valuable job well may offer no help at all, but being offered a session of baby-sitting (behavioural assistance) may make the difference between coping and not. On the other hand a first-time mother who is worried that her 10-month-old child cannot yet crawl will be helped by feedback and guidance in the forms of being told that she is doing the right things to encourage physical development and that her child is not at all unusual. To such a mother the offer of a session of baby-sitting would not offer any solution to her worries about her child's physical development.

Different aspects of social support offer benefits at different points in time. Some aspects of social support are beneficial to the recipient only when they are experiencing adversity and offer little benefit at other times. The term buffering is used to describe the protection that certain experiences offer to individuals only when they are under stress. Those same experiences have no, or weaker, benefits to offer the individual when they are not under stress. The buffering qualities of social support have been widely discussed and evaluated. In a review of the literature Cohen and Wills (1985) argue that some aspects of social support do have buffering qualities and are only of benefit when the individual is stressed. At these times contact with other people allows the individual to reappraise their situation and see it as less threatening, or to find effective solutions to their problem. For example the information transmission function of social support is most valuable when the need for that information is immediate and the advice can be put into immediate effect. Advice and information offered at other times are frequently forgotten before the need to apply them occurs. Additionally, formal and informal supports may operate when the individual is stressed to bolster their self-esteem and to help them to analyze their situation and to come to terms with it, to manage their physiological reaction to stress and to avoid harmful reactions to stress. In this, social support acts as a buffer between the stress experienced and the potential harmful outcomes of that stress. In addition, informal social support networks have a more generalized effect of increasing the psychological well-being of individuals whether or not they are stressed. They do this by providing feedback to the individual that they are a person to be esteemed and valued. For example the provision of positive social interaction benefits the individual at all times whether they are experiencing adversity or not. This kind of support relates to overall well-being and to a recognition of self-worth and can be effective even when it is provided by only a very small network of people. Just as different problems require different solutions it is possible that different individuals would benefit from different kinds of social support (Schradle and Dougher, 1985). Social support thus has a dual role to play; the socially isolated individual does not have access to the buffering qualities provided by social support and they suffer the stress of social isolation, whereas the socially supported individual does not suffer the stress of social isolation and they have access to buffering qualities.

In Conclusion

Instability in people's lives can lead them to develop problems of various sorts. Instability associated with the loss of or weakening of close family relationships has the most disruptive effects. Having a close and enduring relationship is probably the best protection available. Another important contribution to stress resistance is a life with graduated challenges that enhance the development of mastery skills, flexible coping strategies and adaptive personality attributes (steeling). The study of people who are invulnerable or resilient can be highly informative and help us to understand the combination of circumstances that can lead some individuals to become overburdened. It may also suggest strategies for increasing the stress resistance of individuals who are at risk. The study of invunerability hopefully will lead to the development of effective intervention packages.

Further Reading

COHEN, S. and WILLS, T.A. (1985) 'Stress, social support, and the buffering hypothesis', *Psychological Bulletin*, **98**, pp. 310–57.

This review is very specific: it explores the issue of buffering in great detail. It is long and dense and is directed at those readers with a good grasp of psychological concepts.

GOODYER, I.M. (1990) 'Family relationships, life events and childhood psychopathology', *Journal of Child Psychology and Psychiatry*, **31**, pp. 161–92.

A review of family events that can be problematic for developing individuals including the types of developmental problems associated with different family events.

HOBFOLL, S.E. and LEIBERMAN, J.R. (1987) 'Personality and social resources in immediate and continued stress resistance among women', *Journal of Personality and Social Psychology*, **52**, pp. 18–26.

This study considers the role of social support in moderating the effects of stressful events effecting the family and points to the need for congruence between the demands of the situation and the nature of the support offered.

MASTEN, A.S. and GARMEZY, N. (1985) 'Risk, vulnerability and protective factors in developmental psychopathology', in LAHEY, B.B. and KAZDIN, E. (Eds) *Advances in Clinical Child Psychology, Vol. 8*, New York, Plenum.

Garmezy has been writing for twenty years about resilience and protecting children from the effects of adversity. In this review the concepts of risk, protective factors and vulnerability are clearly set out before research findings are presented.

PRICE, R.H., COWEN, E.L., LORION, R.P. and McKAY, J.R. (1989) 'The search for effective intervention programs: what we learned along the way', *American Journal of Orthopsychiatry*, **59**, pp. 49–58.

An American Psychological Association task force was given the task of identifying prevention programmes which would serve as a model for those setting up programmes to assist individuals from high-risk groups. They identified fifteen programmes which were seen as particularly good and these are described. About half were family-based interventions.

RUTTER, M. (1985) 'Resilience in the face of adversity: protective factors and resistance to psychiatric disorder', *British Journal of Psychiatry*, **147**, pp. 598–611.

Rutter has been a very influential figure in the study of resilience. In this review he considers some specific adverse life events including early parental loss, being reared by a parent with a mental disorder, and being reared in an institution, and explores the development of resilience within those contexts, before considering issues more generally.

WERNER, E.E. and SMITH, R.S. (1982) *Vulnerable but Invincible: A Longitudinal Study of Resilient Children and Youth*, New York, McGraw-Hill.

Presents the findings of a large-scale multidisciplinary study of 698 infants born in 1955 on the island of Kauai, Hawaii, and reports on their progress up to the age of 18 years. About a third of the sample had unstable or difficult family lives. While many children were adversely affected by these experiences a large minority were resilient and adapted successfully. The book explores the roots of this resilience.

WERNER, E.E. (1989) 'High-risk children in young adulthood: a longitudinal study from birth to 32 years', *American Journal of Orthopsychiatry*, **59**, pp. 72–81.

This report provides a very useful summary of the findings from the Kauai longitudinal study including information about how the sample is coping in their adult lives. The relative impact of risk and protective factors changed at different points in the life cycle.

Chapter 11

Cultural and Ethnic Issues

In previous chapters we discussed the variety of family forms and the different ways in which parents bring up children. Parents all engage in similar tasks of caring for their children and preparing them to grow up and take their place in the wider community. But how they do this and the skills and characteristics they see as necessary or valuable vary from culture to culture and between communities in the same culture. Information about such variations extends our constructions of children and helps to ensure that theories of development are based on the realities of children's lives.

Cross-Cultural Approaches to Children and Parenting

Values and attitudes to children and family life have been explored through anthropologically-based research which considers parenting in different cultures. This points to some ways in which our ideas about childhood and parenting are specific to our culture. Parenting is at once a universal and a highly variable aspect of human behaviour. In all societies the family protects, nurtures and educates the young. How this is done is shaped by cultural values which become established in the attitudes and personal preferences of individuals who seek to re-establish them in the next generation. Different cultures have somewhat different ideas about children, how they want them to grow up and the activities in which it is considered that children should engage. These form the ideological context in which children are brought up, and influence how people relate to children, who is involved in childcare, and what kinds of emotions and behaviours are encouraged. Each culture has an adaptive formula for parenthood, a set of customs which relate to physical and geographical setting and economic activities of the group (Ingleby, 1986; Kessel and Siegel, 1981; LeVine, 1980; LeVine *et al.*, 1988; Ogbu, 1981).

For example, LeVine (1980) discusses childrearing patterns in sub-Saharan Africa. In these cultures, values for children are concerned with getting children to fit into the adult world and minimizing their disturbance of mothers' work in the field or market. As a result, obedience and passivity are encouraged and babies and children are quiet by European and US standards (LeVine *et al.*, 1988). Children are encouraged to be dependent upon the wider family and are taught the importance of obedience and respect for elders which prepares them to perform useful tasks at home and in the fields. Mothers tend not to respond to children's demands for attention and children are less likely to experience such attention as rewarding. Children are talked to less and parents engage in less one-to-one interaction than is the case for US or European parents. The strong emphasis on obedience is mitigated by children's playful, relaxed and emotionally nurturing interactions with other children and with other adults, many of whom are involved in childcare.

Such interdependence can be seen in many rural agricultural economies where mothers work in the fields and so have less time for childcare than women who live in more urban environments. This group orientation is maintained in some urban communities, e.g. in Italy where family solidarity is considered important and children are encouraged to remain reliant and dependent on the family (New, 1988). Mothers are not the only people involved in childcare; the wider family takes responsibility for children. Fathers, grandparents, and siblings are regularly involved. Patterns vary considerably from culture to culture. Fathers, for example, appear to be less involved in childcare activities in Sweden and Morocco than in the USA and UK (Birns and Hay, 1988; Lamb *et al.*, 1982). Children are often (but not always) encouraged to take responsibility for housework and for younger siblings, and siblings sometimes talk more to infants than mothers. These activities accustom children to taking care of and interacting well with others (Lamb and Sutton-Smith, 1982; LeVine *et al.*, 1988; Whiting and Whiting, 1975).

In many respects childrearing in the USA and in many western countries has different goals and values from those reported in studies in third world agricultural communities. In many western cultures parents invest considerable material and human resources (including maternal attention and sensitivity) on a small number of children. Their goal is a person who is confident, independent and able to cope with a changing environment. The family is not the unit of production, as is the case currently in many rural agricultural societies, and children do not contribute to family income. Instead children are costly, in part because mothers are frequently full-time caregivers who provide children with attention and support and are not active in the labour market (Kessel and Siegel, 1981). Economic considerations are often viewed as inimical or contradictory to the ethos of the family, as can be seen in the disapproval and antagonism often expressed over buying babies through adoption or surrogacy. Instead the benefits of children are conceptualized in terms of the emotional and moral satisfactions parents derive from parenting and their relationships with children (Michaels and Goldberg, 1988).

Major themes in the ideology of childrearing in the USA are independence, separateness, autonomy and high achievement. These are encouraged in a variety of ways (Kessel and Siegel, 1981). Children are expected to tolerate separation from an early age as they tend to sleep alone. In many other societies children are rarely alone but spend a great deal of time in the presence of adults, usually as non-participants in the interactions between adults (LeVine, 1980). In her study of Italian families, New (1988) found that the constant presence of other people is not necessarily translated into attention to or one-to-one interaction with children. Mothers played only occasionally with children and when they did, mothers were not particularly sensitive, but tended to do most of the initiating and terminating of interactions. This contrasts with the position in many families in the USA and the UK where children spend more time on their own. When they are with adults, however, children receive considerable attention. They tend to be held less than children in some cultures, but when they are held it is to facilitate interaction rather than to restrict their activity. In urban communities in the USA and in Sweden parents believe that even very young children can communicate and so talk to them extensively. Mothers value their children's language acquisition and enjoy their conversations with their children. US children are allowed, and often encouraged, to seek and demand attention, which they find more rewarding than do children in many other cultures (LeVine *et al.*, 1988).

Closely associated with separateness in children in the USA are self-sufficiency and self-confidence (LeVine *et al.*, 1988). In the early months, because they sleep on their own, children learn to pacify themselves. In other cultures children sleep with others and are pacified by the warmth of another person or they are rocked to sleep. In the USA children are treated as individuals capable of engaging in one-to-one dialogues from an early age and they are praised for their competence and autonomy. This happens less in other cultures, even though the demands for mature behaviour may be as great. Such praise increases children's self-confidence, and encourages them to be curious, responsive and competitive and relatively uninhibited in the presence of adults. These factors are thought to enhance children's capacity to cope with unfamiliar situations. This emphasis on independence in the early years is also seen in German children whose mothers are less responsive and spend less time interacting with children than do mothers in the USA (Grossman *et al.*, 1985). In contrast, Japanese children, like Italian children, tend to have experience only with familiar people and have little contact with strangers. These variations mean that German and Japanese children respond in different ways to US children especially when they find themselves in unfamiliar situations or with unfamiliar people. Because of this these children are rated as less securely attached in the 'strange situation' (McKaye *et al.*, 1985).

Cross-cultural studies can give the impression that cultural and parental values work together in the service of similar goals, but this is not always the case. There can be clashes between societal and family values. Evidence of this can be seen in some of the rituals and ceremonies which remove children from the influence of mothers to ensure that they are brought up to absorb the customs and values of the men of the community (Korbin, 1981). In western societies a clash can be seen sometimes between highly child-centred approaches to children which support children's emotional development and their expression of feelings and the wider society's competitiveness and emphasis on people's status or position rather than on personal qualities.

Differences within Cultures: Social Class and Ethnicity

Cross-cultural studies indicate a number of ways in which societies differ in their values for children and the ways in which children are brought up. It is useful to make comparisons because they point to the ways in which much of what is viewed as normal or natural is highly dependent on cultural values and traditions. But comparing cultures can obscure differences within cultures. Variability within cultures is associated with a multitude of factors, such as town or village dwelling, religion, family size, social class, ethnicity, the value system, personalities and styles of coping of parents, the number of people involved in childcare and the sex of the child (e.g. Boulton, 1983; Newson and Newson, 1968; Westwood and Bhachu, 1988).

Social Class

One factor which has been extensively studied is social class or socio-economic status. Social class is used as a shorthand for a large cluster of factors but focuses especially on the occupation of fathers (and sometimes mothers), with professional, managerial and white-collar workers (middle-class) often compared with manual workers (working-class). Differences in occupations are a useful, but a crude way of distinguishing between people's identities, attitudes and life styles. Occupation is linked to other aspects of family life; for example, working-class families tend to be larger, and their incomes and standards of housing are lower (Butler and Golding, 1986). Fathers occupations may influence childrearing practices through the values associated with the kinds of jobs they do. Fathers with professional and white-collar occupations are more likely to be required to manipulate ideas and interpersonal relations and to be self-directed in their work than are men in manual and unskilled occupations for whom standardization and conformity are emphasized more. These qualities are thought to carry over into their family relations and to be translated into values for children. As a result, middle-class families are considered to place greater stress on self-direction (e.g. imagination, curiosity and self-control) and working-class families on conformity (obedience, neatness, being well-mannered) (Boulton, 1983; Ogbu, 1981).

Parents' attitudes and their childrearing practices are linked in other ways to their occupational status, such as fathers' working hours, the regularity of their work, the division of labour within the family and the neighbourhood in which they live. Economic factors may encourage one kind of childrearing approach. For example, mothers may feel they can afford to be relaxed about children's curiosity and whether it leads children into situations where they get dirty, when they have a change of clothes and a washing machine so that cleaning clothes is relatively straightforward. Mothers may also be more willing to let children have friends home to play when children have a separate playroom and do not have to share the only living space with others who may not want to join in their games.

Social class differences have been found in a number of aspects of parents' childrearing practices and in children's development and achievement in school (Boulton, 1983; Ogbu, 1981). One study which points to some social class differences in childrearing patterns is that of Newson and Newson. They found a number of differences in specific behaviours but were more interested in the values and attitudes which underlie such differences. The accounts of mothers bringing up 4 and 7 year olds point to two major themes. These are how mothers control their children and ensure their compliance, and their child-centredness. Parents, of whatever class, want children to behave well. They are concerned with their children's compliance and with the long-term as well as the short-term effects of discipline. But their ways of obtaining compliance vary considerably. Newson and Newson (1968) found that middle-class mothers tended to adopt a style of control which emphasized reasoning, adjudication of quarrels, fairness in the sense of 'do as you would be done by' and general good manners. They were more likely than working-class mothers to set out general rules and principles and were less likely to use physical methods of punishment such as smacking. In contrast, working-class mothers tended to emphasize authority, children's self-reliance in quarrels, fairness in the sense of 'be done by as you did' and respect for adults. These differences reflect more general attitudes to childrearing which encourage independence and the use of verbal strategies in other situations. Middle-class mothers see themselves as influencing children's development more than working-class mothers and as helping children to make their own decisions and establish their own identity. Middle-class mothers supervise their children's play and encourage them to play close by, thereby increasing the opportunities for conversation and verbal interaction. This is particularly the case for mothers of girls (Newson and Newson, 1986). Middle-class mothers were also more willing to engage in fantasy play with children and told them stories as part of regular bedtime routines (LeVine *et al.*, 1988; Newson and Newson, 1968).

Tizard and Hughes (1984) report somewhat similar results from a study which combined interviews with mothers of 4-year-old girls with observations of their conversations. Middle-class mothers engaged in more imaginative play than working-class mothers, they employed a larger vocabulary and used language for complex purposes including conveying general information. They said they enjoyed answering children's questions and gave somewhat fuller answers. There was also more discussion of topics beyond the here and now. Control seemed to be more of an issue in working-class homes with a considerable number of disputes in some families. In over half the disputes recorded, mothers justified their position using explanations, with middle-class mothers doing this slightly more frequently. Although there were social class differences, they were not great. Within each social class group there was a wide range of language use: *all* mothers made some use of language for complex purposes, and at times became very explicit and gave full explanations, and *all* children asked questions on at least one occasion and used language for complex purposes (Tizard and Hughes, 1984).

Another central theme reported by Newson and Newson was child-centredness. One of the most child-centred of the mothers interviewed by Newson and Newson (1968) talked about her approach as follows:

> I do it for him at once, believe it or not. I mean, you may think it's nothing much and he can wait, but in a kiddy's mind it's important, just as much as your things are to you.... We don't get on each other's nerves — I don't get on his nerves, and he doesn't get on mine.... You've got to take some notice of their likes and dislikes — if he doesn't want to do something I can usually persuade him, but then I usually start off by making it sound a nice thing to do, I don't just tell him. (Newson and Newson, 1968: 530)

When children were aged 7 years, middle-class mothers were more child-centred than working-class mothers. Newson and Newson (1976) rated about half of their middle-class and a quarter of their working-class mothers as very child-centred. Working-class mothers were less child-centred with boys than with girls, but this was not found with middle-class mothers. Child-centredness seems to be a more central aspect of motherhood for middle-class than for working-class mothers and is reflected in the ways in which they talked about combining childcare and domestic work. Working-class mothers often view domestic work and childcare as separate and contradictory activities and regulate children in ways which make clear the distinctions between the two and the priority of domestic work. This sometimes leads to disputes and conflicts between mothers and children, although it would seem to be less of an issue between mothers and sons (Tizard and Hughes, 1984; Walkerdine and Lucey, 1989). The following example (extracted from McGuire, in Phoenix *et al.*, in press) demonstrates the pressures which mothers can experience:

> Julie's mother is trying to do the ironing but experiences a barrage of non-stop fussing and demands for her attention from Julie. At one point the mother stops ironing, spends some time with Julie and starts her on a jigsaw puzzle, saying:
>
> M: I'll come and do the jigsaws in a minute. I've got to finish ironing that pair of trousers.
> C: Nooo.
> M: Then I'll come back.
> C: No. Mummy's going to read.
> M: You can finish the puzzle then I'll come back. I've just got to finish this pair of trousers.
> C: No Mummy's going to read, Mummy's going to read.
> M: Yes, in a minute.

Middle-class mothers are more likely to combine domestic work and childcare by involving children in housework. In this way domestic work provides mothers with opportunities for verbal interactions and explanations. The relationship between middle-class mothers and children appears to to be based on democratic principles, with children as willing and equal partners. This may arise out of and encourage middle-class mothers in their use of reasons and rationality. Walkerdine and Lucey (1989) suggest that one result of this may be to teach children that with reason anything is possible and that being able engage in rational debate makes people powerful. However, as they point out, this ignores the strong feelings and emotions mothers and children have about one another, the clashes of wills and interests which are integral to their interactions and the power mothers have. Dealing with children rationally and as if they are equal partners may reduce children's opportunities to express and handle resistance, anger or aggression. Children are not entirely without power; they can challenge mothers and refuse to deal with issues in purely rational terms. Working-class mothers may give their daughters greater space to express negative emotions and may be more willing to recognize and respond to their feelings, even when they are not prepared to accede to them, as this example from Walkerdine and Lucey (1989) indicates:

> Sally wants her mother to do something for her.
> M: I will in a minute. I'll do the pastry first.
> C: Now.
> M: Sally! Don't tell me what to do.
> C: I want to beat you.
> M: You're getting too cheeky and you're going to get a
>   smack.
> (Walkerdine and Lucey, 1989: 130).

Finding a balance between domestic work and childcare is an issue for mothers and has an impact on their satisfactions with mothering (Boulton, 1983). At first glimpse the experiences of mothers of young children are similar regardless of their social class. Their lives are centred on their children for whom they have major responsibility. Boulton (1983) reports that many women found a sense of meaning and purpose in motherhood but at the same time about half found childcare a predominantly frustrating experience and their children difficult and demanding over extended periods of time (Boulton, 1983). Boulton did find social class differences in women's experience of motherhood. Working-class women were more likely to say that their children were good company, to enjoy the community of other mothers and to find satisfaction in childcare. There were also differences in where they located their frustrations with being mothers. When they did not find pleasure in looking after their children, working-class women tended to emphasize the practical difficulties and hoped that material changes such as more help or a washing machine would improve things. Middle-class women stressed more the sense of purpose and meaning that motherhood gave them and gave less priority to domestic activities. They were less likely to expect rewards from childcare itself and emphasized the frustrations of childcare in this society. They were more likely to describe themselves as monopolized or taken over by their children and as having lost their individuality in motherhood.

This approach suggests that how women view themselves as mothers and evaluate their experiences of motherhood does not develop in isolation but is related to other aspects of their lives. How they feel about and interact with their children is likely to be affected by factors such as social class, employment opportunities and social support availability (Phoenix *et al.*, in press). Also important are women's attitudes and expectations of motherhood and how the realities match their expectations. Middle-class mothers appear to have a greater commitment to sensitivity and facilitating their children's development. But when this involves putting aside their own interests and activities it increases the likelihood of frustration and their sense of loss of identity (Boulton, 1983).

Ethnicity

Ethnicity is another major factor which influences how parents bring up children. Like social class, ethnicity is complex and many-faceted. Moving to a different culture has been the experience of many families and in this society families come from a wide variety of ethnic communities. Ethnic groups differ in terms of their religion, language, skin colour, and the social standing and prestige of the community. But ethnic groups are also very heterogeneous. The country or part of the country they come from, social class, caste, occupation and income all vary widely as well as how much communities hold onto their customs and beliefs, how long people have lived in this country, where they were born and educated and hence how aware they are of the institutions and practices of the host society, the amount of contact they have with other members of their community, and the kinds of neighbourhoods in which they live. Being a member of an ethnic community is often associated with poverty and low status, but this is not always the case.

Their motivation for migration and the ties people maintain with their country of origin may also influence their experiences and their ideas about how to bring up their children. Some families move predominantly for economic reasons. They may be wealthy and well qualified and move looking for better opportunities, but others move because of hunger and poverty and others are political or religious refugees. People's motives for living in another country and whether they expect to return to their countries of origin influence their commitment to the habits of the host society, including the childrearing practices of the country. For many communities (such as black families in the USA) the country in which they are living is the only one they know and some communities, such as Native Americans, Maoris and Aborigines, are ethnic minorities in their own countries (Field and Widmayer, 1981).

The experiences of parents from different ethnic communities are mediated by a variety of factors. Butler and Golding (1986) for example, indicate some of the factors associated with ethnicity for Asian children born in the UK. Asian parents were more likely than other parents to have unskilled jobs and to live in a poor urban area. Mothers were less likely to smoke, children were more likely to be of low birthweight, to be living with both parents at the age of 5 years, and to have two or more siblings. Ethnicity is often associated with low status and low-paid work, as a result of poor English and lack of training as well as racism and discrimination. Because their families are poor, women from the ethnic communities frequently participate in paid employment, often in businesses run by people from their own community. For many women paid employment outside the home is a new experience (Sharpe, 1976; Westwood and Bhachu, 1988). The problems associated with combining work and parenting are similar for most mothers regardless of their ethnic origins. They are concerned about childcare and they have to combine work with domestic tasks, leaving little time to spend with their children. Employment may help women overcome the isolation of their lives especially when their traditional support network is unavailable because grandparents live far away. Participation in the labour force provides women with sources of information, companionship and support beyond their families. This may be especially important in a new country and when families are not well informed (Westwood and Bhachu, 1988).

In psychological studies ethnic communities are used largely as a testing ground for ideas derived from or having significance in the host society or to identify sources of poor achievement in minority groups (Ogbu, 1981). Take for example language acquisition. English is not the first or the main language spoken in some families, with the result that many children from ethnic communities grow up speaking two, three or even more languages. Rather than being seen as a benefit, children's fluency in several languages is often seen as a problem. For example, where there is a lack of educational success, children's use of several languages is often used to explain their lack of achievement in preference, say, to explanations based on their relative poverty or the racism they encounter. Nor are their experiences used to advance theory. There is little discussion, for example, of the questions raised by learning two or more languages and the insights it provides into the general process of language development (Ogbu, 1981).

Most ethnic communities adopt an approach to childrearing which reflects their own values and attitudes and aims to help children cope with their position in their own and the wider society. The form this takes varies according to the culture and contemporary events and attitudes. Studies of ethnic communities in the USA, the UK and Australia provide evidence for the importance of family life, the perceived value of a close-knit family and expectations of obedience and conformity to family norms and respect for elders (Anwar, 1978; Guttierrez *et al.*, 1988). For some communities this seems to be associated with high achievement (e.g. Chinese families in the USA) but family pressure for obedience and conformity may also militate against children doing well in education and employment where the emphasis is on individual achievement and competitiveness.

Parenting provides a powerful source of identity, meaning and achievement, especially for those for whom there are few other acceptable outlets, although the day to day activities of childcare may be largely influenced by a family's economic situation. Black women are more likely than women from some other ethnic communities to be bringing up children on their own and hence combining parenting with active participation in the labour force. The impact of such experiences on childrearing may be to discourage mother-infant play and encourage obedience and self-reliance. It is considered that this probably promotes resourcefulness, the ability to manipulate people and fight back, and mistrust of people in authority. As children grow up and recognize their mothers' powerlessness, they resist mothers' demands for obedience and look instead for support and identity from their peers and the street culture from which they discover different ways of acquiring status or fighting racism (Field and Widmayer, 1981; Ogbu, 1981; Birns and Hay, 1988).

The impact of ethnicity also depends on other factors such as accultura-tion or their familiarity with and commitment to the host culture and social class. In a study of Mexican-American and Anglo-American mothers, Gut-tierrez *et al.* (1988) found that Mexican-American mothers were more con-trolling and demanded more compliance than Anglo-American mothers and that their children showed more deference. But middle-class women and those with greater contact with the host culture had more complex ideas about their children's development. This suggests that being exposed to two sets of childrearing values and expectations had made them reflect carefully on their own attitudes and what they were doing as mothers.

It is often assumed that as they get older, children growing up in multi-ethnic societies will experience an identity crisis and feel themselves split between the culture of their parents and that of the host community (Kitwood, 1983). This may begin when children go to school. When parents do not have much contact with the wider community, children may act as interpreters, of the language and also of the customs of the host culture. Parents, and especially mothers, may rely on children to bring home informa-tion about education, food, clothes, health etc. This may increase children's awareness of family affairs and give them considerable experience of operating in the adult world. The assertiveness and curiosity this encourages may conflict with parents' expectations of appropriate behaviour for children. As they get older, young people explore the world of their contemporaries. This may result in conflicts between young people and their parents, as parents find young people's ideas alien and they disapprove of their children's activ-ities. But in many cases, young people remain firmly integrated in their own community and their close peer relations are generally with other young people in a similar position. They seem to use their new experiences to reassess aspects of their culture, but the impact is not always in the direction of greater westernization. Many Asian young people in the UK now positive-ly assert Islamic or Asian values and adopt Asian customs (Anwar, 1978; Kitwood, 1983; Stopes-Roe and Cochrane, 1988; Westwood and Bhachu, 1988). Close relations with parents may also result from their experience of racism. Even if they have lived in the host culture all their lives and are competent members of that society, they are often viewed as outsiders and such experiences may draw them closer to others in a similar position.

A number of studies have examined this concept of culture conflict and the problems for young people of being 'between two cultures'. Rosenthal

(1984) found evidence of greater conflict between young Australian people and their parents when parents came from Italy and Greece than when parents were of English origins. For some young people there did seem to be a clash between the Australian culture of their peers and the Italian or Greek culture of their parents. However the nature of the conflicts suggested that in many families problems resulted not so much from a clash of cultures but from the control techniques parents employed. Parents of Italian and Greek origins were more authoritarian and demanded conformity. As we have seen in Chapter 6, conflict between young people and parents is more likely when parents are authoritarian and are unwilling to concede autonomy to their children. Rosenthal *et al.* (1989) view the resistance of young people to their parents' demands (seen in struggles over dating and social behaviour for girls and for boys in study habits and how they spend their time at home) as part of an adolescent struggle for autonomy and a separate identity rather than as clashes between cultures. In addition they felt that in Italian-Australian and Greek-Australian families the expression of emotions, including conflict, is more readily acceptable than in Anglo-Australian families. Differences in the extent of conflicts may reflect, therefore, differences in the acceptability of emotional expression rather than level of conflict. The conflicts observed were rarely disruptive of good family relations, perhaps because parents and young people remained committed to one another, whatever their current difficulties (Rosenthal *et al.*, 1989).

Similar findings are reported in studies of the relations between Asian young people and their parents in the UK. Asian families in the UK have come from a number of areas on the Indian subcontinent, they differ in terms of religion (being mainly Hindus, Sikhs and Muslims), language and caste, wealth and experience of urban living (whatever their previous experiences, most now live in large urban communities). But there are a number a common features of family life and of their ideas about parenting and childrearing. Asian families are fairly stable, with family breakup less common than among many other groups in the UK. Family size tends to be somewhat greater (Butler and Golding, 1986). Family relations can be highly structured in terms of age and sex and governed by clearly articulated rules. The close family network and clear patterns of relations provide a close-knit and intelligible social order and sense of belonging for Asian children and young people (Anwar, 1978; Stopes-Roe and Cochrane, 1988).

Young people are expected to conform to family and community customs and to respect parents. Self-regulation and self-reliance are less highly esteemed than in non-Asian families. Conformity is valued by both young people and parents, although more so by parents, and more by working-class than middle-class Asian parents (Anwar, 1978; Sharpe, 1976; Stopes-Roe and Cochrane, 1990). Girls and young people from working-class families are more likely to say that they would like more freedom than boys or young people from middle-class homes. Anwar (1978) suggests that this is because middle-class parents are less conservative in outlook and less restrictive. Quarrels would seem to be largely about issues which are problematic for other young people and their parents such as what to do in their spare time, friends, dating and clothes. In most Asian communities girls are seen as the upholders of family traditions and family honour. For this reason there is more concern about young girls' behaviour and they are more closely supervised.

The general consensus between Asian young people and their parents can be seen in their attitudes to arranged marriages. Arranged marriages are still common, young people feel they work well and trust their parents to make a good choice. The forms of arrangement have changed so that young people are now involved and often will meet and get to know their partners prior to marriage (Anwar, 1978; Sharpe, 1976; Stopes-Roe and Cochrane, 1988). But family patterns are changing and nuclear families are becoming more common. Many young people welcome the more egalitarian relations this brings, with greater contact and close relationships between husband and wife and greater involvement by fathers in childcare (Anwar, 1978; Woollett and Dosanjh-Matwala, 1990).

In Conclusion

Discussion of differences between and within cultures points to yet another source of variability in childrearing practices and the value of considering the various goals for childrearing. These emphasize the importance of the wider cultural context in which families are embedded. Families which do not subscribe to the dominant values around parenting and childrearing find ways to adjust and help children to cope with these discrepancies. In particular they demonstrate some of the ways which families find for living between the different and sometimes contradictory approaches to parenting and childrearing.

Further Reading

INGLEBY, D. (1986) 'Development in social context', in RICHARDS, M. and LIGHT, P. (Eds) *Children of Social Worlds*, Cambridge, Polity Press.

This and other chapters in this collection look critically at the ways in which developmental psychology has considered children's development. It points usefully to the dangers of merely considering the social context as extra variables to consider in designing studies and points to the need to see children and childhood as socially constructed. Interesting, but not an easy read.

KESSEL, F.S. and SIEGEL, A.W. (Eds) (1981) *The Child and Other Cultural Inventions*, New York, Praeger Scientific.

Different historical and cultural ideas about children are examined. It is suggested that many of the themes of developmental psychology reflect those current within US society, including the notion of an individual and self-contained child who is independent and separate from others.

LeVine, R.A., Miller, P.M. and West, M.M. (1988) *Parental Behavior in Diverse Societies*, San Francisco, Jossey-Bass.

A series of studies of childrearing in different societies are reported. These include Africa, South America, Italy and the USA. Comparisons are made between the societies in terms of parental practices and how these relate to social and economic factors (such as mothers' work outside the home and whether children are reared in extended family groups) and cultural expectations about how children should behave and express themselves.

Newson, J. and Newson, E. (1968) *Four Years Old in an Urban Community*, Harmondsworth, Penguin.

A report of part of a longitudinal study with mothers bringing up young children. Mothers of 4-year-olds were asked how they brought up their children, about their children's behaviour and about their feelings and reactions to what children did. Social class and gender differences are discussed.

Ogbu, J.V. (1981) 'Origins of human competence: a cultural-ecological perspective', *Child Development*, **52**, pp. 413–29.

This article takes as its theme that children develop in their families the competencies and skills considered appropriate or valuable for the context in which they live. Research tends to place value on the skills necessary for living in a white middle-class world and views less positively and is less concerned with the development of skills considered important for children reared in other settings and especially children from ethnic communities.

Walkerdine, V. and Lucey, H. (1989) *Democracy in the Kitchen: Regulating Mothers and Socialising Daughters*, London, Virago.

Uses data collected by Tizard and Hughes (1984) to examine some of the assumptions made in psychology about what constitutes 'good' mothering. This is done by arguing that many of our ideas about 'good' mothering are based on middle-class assumptions about what are useful skills and the appropriate ways to express power in mother-child relations.

References

ABRAMOVITCH, R., CORTER, C., PEPLER, D.J. and STANHOPE, L. (1986) 'Sibling and peer interaction: a final follow up and a comparison', *Child Development*, 57, pp. 217–29.

AFFLECK, G., ALLEN, D., McGRADE, B.J. and McQUEENEY, M. (1982) 'Maternal causal attributions at hospital discharge of high risk infants', *American Journal of Mental Deficiency*, 86, pp. 575–80.

AINSWORTH, M.D.S., BELL, S.M. and STAYTON, D.J. (1974) 'Infant-mother attachment and social development: "socialisation" as a product of reciprocal responsiveness to signals', in RICHARDS, M.P.M. (Ed.) *The Integration of the Child into a Social World*, London, Cambridge University Press.

ANTONIS, B. (1981) 'Motherhood and mothering', in Cambridge Women's Studies Group (Eds) *Women in Society: Interdisciplinary Essays*, London, Virago.

ANWAR, M. (1978) *Between Two Cultures: A Study of Relationships between Generations in the Asian Community in Britain*, London, Commission for Racial Equality.

ARMSDEN, G.C. and GREENBERG, M.T. (1987) 'The inventory of parent and peer attachment: individual differences and their relationship to psychological well-being in adolescence', *Journal of Youth and Adolescence*, 16, pp. 427–54.

ARNOT, M. and WEINER, G. (1987) *Gender and the Politics of Schooling*, Milton Keynes, Open University Press.

BACON, M.K. and ASHMORE, R.D. (1985) 'How mothers and fathers categorise descriptions of social behaviour attributed to daughters and sons', *Social Cognition*, 3, pp. 193–217.

BARRERA, M. and AINLAY, S.L. (1983) 'The structure of social support: a conceptual and empirical analysis', *Journal of Community Psychology*, 11, pp. 133–43.

BATES, E., BRETHERTON, I., BEEGHLY-SMITH, M. and McNEW, S. (1982) 'Social bases of language development', in REESE, H.W. and LIPSITT, L.P. (Eds) *Advances in Child Development and Behaviour*, Volume 16, New York, Academic Press.

BAUMRIND, D. (1967) 'Child care practices anteceding three patterns of preschool behaviour', *Genetic Psychology Monographs*, 75, pp. 43–88.

BAUMRIND, D. (1973) 'The development of intrumental competence through socialisation', in PICK, A.E. (Ed.) *Minnesota Symposium on Child Psychology*, Minneapolis, University of Minnesota Press.

BAUMRIND, D. (1982) 'Are androgynous individuals more effective persons and parents?', *Child Development*, 53, pp. 44–75.

References

BEAIL, N. and McGUIRE, J. (Eds) (1982) *Fathers: Psychological Perspectives*, London, Junction Books.

BECKER, W.C. (1964) 'Consequences of different kinds of parental discipline', in HOFFMAN, M.L. and HOFFMAN, L.W. (Eds) *Review of Child Development Research*, Volume 1, New York, Russell Sage Foundation.

BECKMAN, P.J. (1983) 'Influence of selected child characteristics on stress in families of handicapped infants', *American Journal of Mental Deficiency*, **88**, pp. 150–6.

BELL, R.Q. (1979) 'Parent, child, and reciprocal influences', *American Psychologist*, **34**, pp. 821–826.

BELSKY, J. (1981) 'Early human experience: a family perspective', *Developmental Psychology*, **17**, pp. 3–23.

BELSKY, J. (1984) 'The determinants of parenting: a process model', *Child Development*, **55**, pp. 83–96.

BELSKY, J., SPANIER, G.B. and ROVINE, M. (1983) 'Stability and change in marriage across the transition to parenthood', *Journal of Marriage and the Family*, **45**, 567–78.

BELSKY, J., GILSTRAP, B. and ROVINE, M. (1984a) 'Stability and change in mother-infant and father-infant interaction in a family setting: one-three-nine months', *Child Development*, **55**, pp. 706–17.

BELSKY, J., ROBINS, E. and GAMBLE, W. (1984b) 'The determinants of parental competence: towards a contextual theory', In LEWIS, M. (Ed.) *Beyond the Dyad*, New York, Plenum Press.

BELSKY, J., WARD, M.J. and ROVINE, M. (1986) 'Prenatal expectations, postnatal experiences, and the transition to parenthood', In ASHMORE, R.D. and BRODZINSKY, D.M. (Eds) *Thinking about the Family: Views of Parents and Children*, Hillsdale, NJ, Lawrence Erlbaum Associates.

BERNDT, T.J. and PERRY, T.B. (1986) 'Children's perceptions of friendships as supportive relationships', *Developmental Psychology*, **22**, pp. 640–8.

BIFULCO, A.T., BROWN, G.W. and HARRIS, T.O. (1987) 'Childhood loss of parents, lack of adequate parental care and adult depression: a replication', *Journal of Affective Disorders*, **12**, pp. 115–28.

BILLER, H.B. (1976) 'The father and personality development: paternal deprivation and sex-role development', in LAMB, M.E. (Ed.) *The Role of the Father in Child Development*, New York, Rawson, Wade.

BIRKSTED-BREEN, D. (1986) 'The experience of having a baby: a developmental view', *Free Associations*, **4**, pp. 22–35.

BIRNS, B. and HAY, D.F. (Eds) (1988) *The Different Faces of Motherhood*, New York, Plenum Press.

BLACK, D. (1984) 'Sundered families: the effect of loss of a parent', *Adoption and Fostering*, **8**, pp. 38–43.

BLEULER, M. (1978) *The Schizophrenic Disorders: Long-Term Patients and Family Studies*, New Haven, Yale University Press.

BLOCK, J.H., BLOCK, J. and GJERDE, P.F. (1986) 'The personality of children prior to divorce: a prospective study', *Child Development*, **57**, pp. 827–40.

BOHMAN, M. and SIGVARDSSON, S. (1985) 'A prospective longitudinal study of adoption', in NICOL. A.R. (Ed.) *Longitudinal Studies in Child Psychology and Psychiatry: Practical Lessons from Research Experience*, Chichester, Wiley.

BOOTH, C.L. and MELTZOFF, A.N. (1984) 'Expected and actual experience in labour and delivery and their relationship to maternal attachment', *Journal of Reproductive and Infant Psychology*, **2**, pp. 79–91.

BOTTING, B., MACFARLANE, A. and PRICE, F. (1990) *Three, four and More: A Study of Triplets and Higher Order Births*, London, HMSO.

BOULTON, M.G. (1983) *On Being a Mother: A Study of Women with Preschool Children*, London, Tavistock.

BOWLBY, J. (1969) *Attachment and Loss: Volume 1, Attachment*, London, Hogarth Press.

BRAND, E., CLINGEMPEEL, W.G. and BOWEN-WOODWARD, K. (1988) 'Family relationships and children's psychological adjustment in stepmother and stepfather families', in HETHERINGTON, E.M. and ARASTEH, J. (Eds) *The Impact of Divorce, Single Parenting and Step-Parenting on Children*, Hillsdale, NJ, Lawrence Erlbaum Associates.

BRANNEN, J. and MOSS, P. (1988) *New Mothers at Work: Employment and Childcare*, London, Unwin Paperbacks.

BRAY, J.H. (1988) 'Children's development during early remarriage', in HETHERINGTON, E.M. and ARASTEH, J. (Eds) *The Impact of Divorce, Single Parenting and Step-Parenting on Children*, Hillsdale, NJ, Lawrence Erlbaum Associates.

BRESLAU, N., STARUCH, K.S. and MORTIMER, E.A. (1982) 'Psychological distress in mothers of disabled children', *American Journal of Diseases in Children*, **136**, pp. 682–6.

BRETHERTON, I. and WATERS, E. (Eds) (1985) 'Growing points in attachment theory and research', *Monographs of the Society for Research in Child Development*, Vol. 50, No. 209.

BRISTOL, M. and GALLAGHER, J. (1986) 'Research on fathers of young handicapped children', In GALLAGHER, J. and VIETZE, P. (Eds) *Families of Handicapped Persons*, Baltimore, Paul H. Brookes.

BRODY, G.H. and FOREHAND, R. (1988) 'Multiple determinants of parenting: research findings and implications for the divorce process', in HETHERINGTON, E.M. and ARASTEH, J. (Eds) *The Impact of Divorce, Single Parenting and Step-Parenting on Children*, Hillsdale, NJ, Lawrence Erlbaum Associates.

BRODY, G.H., STONEMAN, Z. and MACKINNON, C. (1982) 'Role assymmetries in interactions among school-aged children, their younger siblings, and their friends', *Child Development*, **51**, pp. 529–44.

BRODY, G.H., PELLEGRINI, A.D. and SIGEL, I. (1986) 'Marital quality and mother child and father child interactions with school-aged children', *Developmental Psychology*, **22**, pp. 291–298.

BRONFENBRENNER, U. (1979) *The Ecology of Human Development: Experiments by Nature and Design*, Cambridge, Mass., Harvard University Press.

BRONFENBRENNER, U. (1986) 'Ecology of the family as a context for human development: research perspectives', *Developmental Psychology*, **22**, pp. 723–42.

BRONFENBRENNER, U., ALVAREX, W.F. and HENDERSON, C.R. (1984) 'Working and watching: maternal employment status and parents' perceptions of their three-year-old children', *Child Development*, **55**, pp. 1362–78.

BROOME, A. (1984) 'The termination of pregnancy', In BROOME, A. and WALLACE, L. (Eds) *Psychology and Gynaecological Problems*, London, Tavistock.

BROWN, G. and HARRIS, T. (1978) *The Social Origins of Depression*, London, Tavistock.

BROWNE, A. and FINKELHOR, D. (1986) 'Impact of child sexual abuse: a review of the research', *Psychological Bulletin*, **99**, pp. 66–77.

BROWNE, K., DAVIES, C. and STRATTON, P. (Eds) (1988) *Early Prediction and Prevention of Child Abuse*, Chichester, Wiley.

BRYANT, B.K. (1985) *The Neighbourhood Walk: Sources of Support in Middle Childhood*, Monograph of Society for Research in Child Development 50, 3 (serial number 210).

BRYANT, B.K. and CROCKENBERG, S. (1980) 'Correlates and dimensions of prosocial behaviour: a study of female siblings and their mothers', *Child Development*, **51**, pp. 529–44.

BUHRMESTER, D. and FURMAN, W. (1987) 'The development of companionship and intimacy', *Child Development*, **58**, pp. 1101–13.

BUMPASS, L. (1984) 'Children and marital disruption: a replication and update', *Demography*, **21**, pp. 71–82.

BUSFIELD, J. (1987) 'Parenting and parenthood', in COHEN, G. (Ed.) *Social Change and the Life Course*, London, Tavistock.

BUTLER, N.R. and GOLDING, J. (1986) *From Birth to Five: A Study of the Health and Behaviour of Britain's Five Year Olds*, Oxford, Pergamon.

BYRNE, E.A. and CUNNINGHAM, C.C. (1985) 'The effect of mentally handicapped children on families: a conceptual review', *Journal of Child Psychology and Psychiatry*, **26**, pp. 847–64.

CALDERA, Y.M., HUSTON, A.C. and O'BRIEN, M. (1989) 'Social interactions and play patterns of parents and toddlers with feminine, masculine and neutral toys', *Child Development*, **60**, pp. 70–6.

CAMERA, K.A. and RESNICK, G. (1988) 'Interparental conflict and cooperation: factors moderating children's post divorce adjustments', in HETHERINGTON, E.M. and ARASTEH, J. (Eds) *The Impact of Divorce, Single Parenting and Step-Parenting on Children*, Hillsdale, NJ, Lawrence Erlbaum Associates.

CARR, J. (1988) 'Six weeks to twenty-one years old: a longitudinal study of children with Down's syndrome and their families', *Journal of Child Psychology and Psychiatry*, **29**, pp. 407–31.

CHASSIN, L., PRESSON, C.C., SHERMAN, S.J., MONTELLO, D. and McGREW, J. (1986) 'Changes in peer and parent influence during adolescence: longitudinal versus cross-sectional perspectives on smoking initiation', *Developmental Psychology*, **22**, pp. 327–34.

CLARKE, A.M. and CLARKE, A.D.B. (1976) *Early Experience: Myth and Evidence*, London, Open Books.

CLARKE-STEWART, K.A. (1978) 'And daddy makes three: The father's impact on mother and young child', *Child Development*, **49**, pp. 466–78.

COHEN, E.L. and WORK, W.C. (1988) 'Resilient children, psychological wellness and primary prevention', *American Journal of Community Psychology*, **16**, pp. 591–607.

COHEN, S. and WILLS, T.A. (1985) 'Stress, social support, and the buffering hypothesis', *Psychological Bulletin*, **98**, pp. 310–57.

COLEMAN, J.C. and HENDRY, L. (1990) *The Nature of Adolescence*, 2nd ed., London, Routledge.

CONDON, J.T. (1987) 'Psychological and physical symptoms during pregnancy: A comparison of male and female expectant parents', *Journal of Reproductive and Infant Psychology*, **5**, pp. 207–220.

COOKE, K. and LAWTON, D. (1984) 'Informal support for carers of disabled children', *Child: Care, Health and Development*, **10**, pp. 67–80.

CORDELL, A.S., PARKE, R.D. and SAWIN, D.B. (1980) 'Fathers' views on fatherhood with special reference to infancy', *Family Relations*, **29**, pp. 331–338.

CORTER, C., ABRAMOVITCH, R. and PEPLER, D.J. (1983) 'The role of the mother in sibling interaction', *Child Development*, **54**, pp. 1599–1605.

COWAN, C.P. and COWAN, P.A. (1985) 'A preventive intervention for couples becoming parents', in BOUKYDIS, C.F.Z. (Ed.) *Research on Support for Parents and Infants in the Postnatal Period*, New York, Ablex.

CRNIC, K.A., FRIEDRICH, W.N. and GREENBERG, M.T. (1983) 'Adaptation of families with mentally retarded children: a model of stress, coping, and family ecology', *American Journal of Mental Deficiency*, **88**, pp. 125–38.

CROUTER, A.C., MACDERMID, S.M., MCHALE, S.M. and PERRY-JENKINS, M. (1990) 'Parental monitoring and perceptions of children's school performance and conduct in dual- and single-earner families', *Developmental Psychology*, **26**, pp. 649–57.

CROWE, C. (1987) 'Women want it: in vitro fertilization and women's motivations for participation', in SPALLONE, P. and STEINBERG, D.L. (Eds) *Made to Order: The Myth of Reproductive and Genetic Progress*, Oxford, Pergamon Press.

CUMMINGS, E.M., ZAHN-WAXLER, C. and RADKE-YARROW, M. (1981) 'Young children's responses to expressions of anger and affection by others in the family', *Child Development*, **52**, pp. 1274–82.

CUMMINGS, E.M., ZAHN-WAXLER, C. and RADKE-YARROW, M. (1984) 'Developmental changes in children's reactions to anger in the home', *Journal of Child Psychology and Psychiatry*, **25**, pp. 63–74.

CUMMINGS, E.M., IANNOTTI, R.J. and ZAHN-WAXLER, C. (1985) 'Influence of conflict between adults on the emotions and aggression of young children', *Developmental Psychology*, **21**, pp. 495–507.

CUMMINGS, S.T. (1976) 'The impact of the child's deficiency on the father: a study of fathers of mentally retarded and of chronically ill children', *American Journal of Orthopsychiatry*, **46**, pp. 246–55.

CUNNINGHAM, C.E., REULER, E., BLACKWELL, J. and DECK, J. (1981) 'Behavioural and linguistic development in the interactions of normal and retarded children with their mothers', *Child Development*, **52**, pp. 62–70.

DAMON, W. (1983) *Social and Personality Development: Infancy through Adolescence*, New York, W.W. Norton.

DAMROSCH, S.P. and PERRY, L.A. (1989) 'Self reported adjustments, chronic sorrow, and coping of parents of children with Down's syndrome', *Nursing Research*, **38**, pp. 25–30.

DICKIE, J. and MATHESON, P. (1984) 'Mother-father-infant: who needs support?', paper presented at the Annual Meeting of the American Psychological Association, Toronto.

DIX, T., RUBLE, D.N., GRUSEC, J.E. and NIXON, S. (1986) 'Social cognition in parents: inferential and affective reactions to children at three age levels', *Child Development*, **57**, pp. 879–94.

DIX, T., RUBLE, D.N. and ZAMBARANO, R.J. (1989) 'Mothers' implicit theories of discipline: child effects, parent effects, and the attribution process', *Child Development*, **60**, pp. 1373–91.

DONALDSON, M. (1978) *Children's Minds*, Glasgow, Fontana.

DUNN, J. (1984) *Sisters and Brothers*, London, Fontana.

DUNN, J. (1988) *The Beginnings of Social Understanding*, Oxford, Basil Blackwell.

DUNN, J. and KENDRICK, C. (1982) *Siblings: Love, Envy and Understanding*, London, Grant McIntyre.

DUNN, J. and MUNN, P. (1985) 'Becoming a family member: family conflict and the development of social understanding in the second year', *Child Development*, **56**, pp. 480–92.

DUNN, J. and MUNN, P. (1986) 'Sibling quarrels and maternal intervention: individual differences in understanding and aggression', *Journal of Child Psychology and Psychiatry*, **27**, pp. 583–95.

References

DUNN, J. and SHATZ, M. (1989) 'Becoming a conversationalist despite (or because of) having an older sibling', *Child Development*, 60, pp. 399–410.

DUNN, J. and STOCKER, C. (1989) 'The significance of differences in siblings' experiences within the family', in KREPPNER, K. and LERNER, R.M. (Eds) *Family Systems and Life Span Development*, Hillsdale, NJ, Lawrence Erlbaum Associates.

EASTERBROOKS, M.A. and GOLDBERG, W.A. (1984) 'Toddler development in the family: impact of father involvement and parenting characteristics', *Child Development*, 55, pp. 740–52.

EMERY, R.E. (1989) 'Family violence', *American Psychologist*, 44, pp. 321–8.

FARRANT, W. (1985) 'Who's for amniocentesis? The politics of prenatal screening', in HOMANS, H. (Ed.) *The Sexual Politics of Reproduction*, Aldershot, Gower.

FEIN, R. (1976) 'Men's entry into parenthood', *Family Co-ordinator*, 25, pp. 341–8.

FEIRING, C. and LEWIS, M. (1984) 'Changing characteristics of the US family: implications for family networks, relationships, and child development', in LEWIS, M. (Ed.) *Beyond the Dyad*, New York, Plenum.

FELDMAN, S.S., NASH, S.C. and ASCHENBRENNER, B.G. (1983) 'Antecedents of fathering', *Child Development*, 54, pp. 1628–36.

FERGUSON, D.M., HARWOOD, L.J. and SHANNON, F.T. (1984) 'A proportional hazards model of family breakdown', *Journal of Marriage and the Family*, 46, pp. 539–49.

FIELD, T. (1978) 'Interaction patterns of primary versus secondary caretaking fathers', *Developmental Psychology*, 14, pp. 183–5.

FIELD, T. (1987) 'Affective and interactive disturbances in infants', in OSOFSKY, J. (Ed.) *The Handbook of Infant Development*, 2nd ed., New York, Wiley.

FIELD, T.M. and WIDMAYER, S.M. (1981) 'Mother-infant interactions among lower SES black, Cuban, Puerto Ricans and South American immigrants', in FIELD, T.M., SOSTEK, A.M., VIETZE, P. and LEIDERMAN, P.H. (Eds) *Culture and Early Interactions*, Hillsdale, NJ, Lawrence Erlbaum Associates.

FINKELHOR, D. (1984) *Child Sexual Abuse: New Theory and Research*, New York, Free Press.

FLEMING, A.S., STEINER, M. and ANDERSON, V. (1987) 'Hormonal and attitudinal correlates of maternal behaviours during the early postpartum period in first time mothers', *Journal of Reproductive and Infant Psychology*, 5, pp. 193–205.

FOGELMAN, K. (1976) *Britain's 16-Year-Olds*, London, National Children's Bureau.

FORGATCH, M.S., PATERSON, G.R. and SKINNER, M.L. (1988) 'A mediational model for the effect of divorce on antisocial behaviour in boys', in HETHERINGTON, E.M. and ARASTEH, J. (Eds) *The Impact of Divorce, Single Parenting and Step-Parenting on Children*, Hillsdale, NJ, Lawrence Erlbaum Associates.

FREY, K.S., FEWELL, R.R. and VADASY, P.F. (1989) 'Parental adjustment and changes in child outcome among families of young handicapped children', *Topics in Early Childhood Special Education*, 8, pp. 38–57.

FRIEDRICH, W.N. (1979) 'Predictions of the coping behavior of mothers of handicapped children', *Journal of Consulting and Clinical Psychology*, 47, pp. 1140–1.

FRIEDRICH, W.N. and BORISKIN, J.A. (1980) 'The role of the child in abuse: a review of the literature', *American Journal of Orthopsychiatry*, 46, pp. 580–90.

FRODI, A.M., LAMB, M.E., LEAVITT, L.A., DONOVAN, W.L., NEFF, C. and SHERRY, D. (1978) 'Fathers' and mothers' responses to the faces and cries of normal and premature infants', *Developmental Psychology*, 14, pp. 490–8.

FRUDE, N. and GOSS, A. (1980) 'Maternal anger and the young child', in FRUDE, N. (Ed.) *Psychological Approaches to Child Abuse*, London, Batsford.

FURSTENBERG, F.F. (1988) 'Child care after divorce and remarriage', in HETHERINGTON, E.M. and ARASTEH, J. (Eds) *The Impact of Divorce, Single Parenting and Step-Parenting on Children*, Hillsdale, NJ, Lawrence Erlbaum Associates.

FURSTENBERG, F.F. and SELTZER, J.A. (1986) 'Divorce and child development', in ADLER, P.A. and ADLER, P. (Eds) *Sociological Studies of Child Development*, vol. 1, London, JAI Press.

GALLAGHER, J.J., BECKMAN, P. and CROSS, A.H. (1983) 'Families and handicapped children: sources of stress and its amelioration', *Exceptional Children*, 50, pp. 10–19.

GANONG, L.H. and COLEMAN, M.M. (1987) 'Step children's perception of their parents', *Journal of Genetic Psychology*, 148, pp. 5–17.

GARMEZY, N. (1984) 'Risk and protective factors in children vulnerable to major mental disorders', In GRINSPOON, L. (Ed.) *Psychiatry 1983 (Vol. III)*, Washington, DC, American Psychiatric Press.

GATH, A. (1978) *Down's Syndrome and the Family*, New York, Academic Press.

GATH, A. and GUMLEY, D. (1984) 'Down's syndrome and the family: follow up of children first seen in infancy', *Developmental Medicine and Child Neurology*, 26, pp. 500–8.

GATH, A. and GUMLEY, D. (1986) 'Family background of children with Down's syndrome and of children with a similar degree of mental retardation', *British Journal of Psychiatry*, 149, pp. 161–71.

GATH, A. and GUMLEY, D. (1987) 'Retarded children and their siblings', *Journal of Child Psychology and Psychiatry*, 28, pp. 15–30.

GERSON, M-J., ALPERT, J.L. and RICHARDSON, M.S. (1984) 'Mothering: the view from psychological research', *Signs: Journal of Women in Culture and Society*, 9, pp. 434–53.

GIBSON, D. (1978) *Down's Syndrome: The Psychology of Mongolism*, London, Cambridge University Press.

GILL, O. and JACKSON, B. (1983) *Adoption and Race: Black, Asian and Mixed Race Children in White Families*, London, Batsford.

GOLD, D. and ANDRES, D. (1978) 'Developmental comparisons between 10-year-old children with employed and non employed mothers', *Child Development*, 49, pp. 75–84.

GOLDBERG, S., MARCVITCH, S., MacGREGOR, D. and LOJKASEK, M. (1986) 'Family response to developmentally delayed preschoolers: Etiology and the father's role', *American Journal of Mental Deficiency*, 90, pp. 610–17.

GOLDSMITH, H.H., BUSS, A.H., PLOMIN, R., ROTHBART, M.K., THOMAS, A., CHESS, S., HINDE, R.A. and McCALL, R.B. (1987) 'Round table: what is temperament? Four approaches', *Child Development*, 58, pp. 505–29.

GOLINKOFF, R.M. and AMES, G.J. (1979) 'A comparison of fathers' and mothers' speech to their young children', *Child Development*, 50, pp. 28–32.

GOODNOW, J.J. (1988) 'Parents' ideas, actions, and feelings: Models and methods from developmental and social psychology', *Child Development*, 59, pp. 286–320.

GOODSITT, J., RAITAN, J.G. and PERLMUTTER, M. (1988) 'Interactions between mothers and preschool children when reading a novel and familiar book', *International Journal of Behavioural Development*, 11, pp. 489–505.

GORDON, L. (1986) 'Feminism and social control: the case of child abuse and neglect', In MITCHELL, J. and OAKLEY, A. (Eds) *What is Feminism?*, Oxford, Basil Blackwell.

GORDON, T. (1990) *Feminist Mothers*, London, Macmillan.

GRAHAM, H. (1980) 'Mothers' accounts of anger and aggression towards their babies', In FRUDE, N. (Ed.) *Psychological Approaches to Child Abuse*, London, Batsford.

GREENBERGER, E. and GOLDBERG, W.A. (1989) 'Work, parenting, and the socialisation of children', *Developmental Psychology*, 25, pp. 22–35.

GROSSMAN, F., EICHLER, L. and WINICKOFF, S. (1980) *Pregnancy, Birth and Parenthood*, San Francisco, Josey Press.

GROSSMAN, F.K., POLLACK, W.S. and GOLDING, E. (1988) 'Fathers and children: predicting the quality and quantity of fathering', *Developmental Psychology*, 24, pp. 82–91.

GROSSMAN, K., GROSSMAN, K., SPANGLER, G., SUERS, G. and UNZER, L. (1985) 'Maternal sensitivity and newborns' orientation responses as related to quality of attachment in Northern Germany', *Monographs of the Society for Research in Child Development*, 50, 209.

GRUNDY, E. (1985) 'Divorce, widowhood, remarriage and geographical mobility among women', *Journal of Biosocial Science*, 17, pp. 415–35.

GUIDUBALDI, J. and PERRY, J.D. (1984) 'Divorce, socioeconomic status, and children's cognitive-social competence at school entry', *American Journal of Orthopsychiatry*, 54, pp. 459–68.

GUTTIERREZ, J., SAMEROFF, A.J. and KARRER, B.M. (1988) 'Acculturation and SES effects on Mexican-American parents' concepts of development', *Child Development*, 59, pp. 250–5.

HAIMES, E. (1989) 'Recreating the family: policy considerations relating to "new" reproductive technologies', In McNEIL, M., VARCOE, I. and YEARLEY, S. (Eds) *The New Reproductive Technologies*, London, Macmillan.

HAIMES, E. and TIMMS, N. (1985) *Adoption, Identity and Social Policy: The Search for Distant Relatives*, Aldershot, Gower.

HALLETT, C. (1988) 'Research in child abuse: some observations on the knowledge base', *Journal of Reproductive and Infant Psychology*, 6, pp. 119–24.

HARGREAVES, D.J. and COLLEY, A.M. (Eds) (1986) *The Psychology of Sex Roles*, London, Harper and Row.

HARTUP, W.W. (1979) 'The social worlds of childhood', *American Psychologist*, 34, pp. 944–50.

HARTUP, W.W. (1983) 'Peer relations', in HETHERINGTON, E.M. (Ed.) *Handbook of Child Psychology. Volume 4: Socialization, Personality and Social Development*, 4th ed., New York, Wiley.

HASKEY, J.C. (1987) 'Divorce in the early years of marriage in England and Wales: results from a prospective study using linked records', *Journal of Biosocial Sciences*, 19, pp. 255–71.

HEINECKE, C.M., DISKIN, S.D., RAMSEY-KLEE, D.M. and GIVEN, K. (1983) 'Pre-birth parent characteristics and family development in the first year of life', *Child Development*, 54, pp. 194–208.

HERNANDEZ, D.J. (1988) 'Demographic trends and the living arrangements of children', In HETHERINGTON, E.M. and ARASTEH, J. (Eds) *The Impact of Divorce, Single Parenting and Step-Parenting on Children*, Hillsdale, NJ, Lawrence Erlbaum Associates.

HERZBERGER, S.D. and TENNEN, H. (1986) 'Coping with abuse: children's perspectives on their abusive treatment', in ASHMORE, R.D. and BRODZINSKY, D.M. (Eds) *Thinking about the Family: Views of Parents and Children*, Hillsdale, NJ, Lawrence Erlbaum Associates.

HETHERINGTON, E.M. (1972) 'Effects of father absence on personality development in adolescent daughters', *Developmental Psychology*, 7, pp. 313–26.

HETHERINGTON, E.M. (1979) 'Family interaction and the social, emotional and cognitive development of children after divorce', in BRAZELTON, T.B. and VAUGHN, V.C. (Eds) *The Family: Setting Priorities*, New York, Science and Medicine Publishing.

HETHERINGTON, E.M. (1988) 'Parents, children and siblings: six years after divorce', In HINDE, R.A. and STEVENSON-HINDE, J. (Eds) *Relationships with Families*, Oxford, Clarendon Press.

HETHERINGTON, E.M. and PARKE, R.D. (1986) *Child Psychology: A Contemporary Viewpoint*, 3rd ed., New York, McGraw-Hill.

HETHERINGTON, E.M., COX, M. and COX, R. (1982) 'Effects of divorce on parents and children', in LAMB, M. (Ed.) *Non-Traditional Families: Parenting and Child Development*, Hillsdale, NJ, Lawrence Erlbaum Associates.

HINDE, R.A. and STEVENSON-HINDE, J. (1988) *Relationships within Families: Mutual Influences*, Oxford, Clarendon Press.

HOBFOLL, S.E. and LEIBERMAN, J.R. (1987) 'Personality and social resources in immediate and continued stress resistance among women', *Journal of Personality and Social Psychology*, 52, pp. 18–26.

HODGES, J. and TIZARD, B. (1989a) 'IQ and behavioural adjustment of ex-institutional adolescents', *Journal of Child Psychology and Psychiatry*, 30, pp. 53–76.

HODGES, J. and TIZARD, B. (1989b) 'Social and family relationships of ex-institutional adolescents', *Journal of Child Psychology and Psychiatry*, 30, pp. 77–8.

HOFFERTH, S.L. (1985) 'Updating children's life course', *Journal of Marriage and the Family*, 47, pp. 93–115.

HOLROYD, J. and GUTHRIE, D. (1986) 'Family stress with chronic childhood illness: cystic fibrosis, neuromuscular disease, and renal disease', *Journal of Clinical Psychology*, 42, pp. 552–61.

HOLROYD, J. and McARTHUR, D. (1976) 'Mental retardation and stress on the parents: a contrast between Down's syndrome and childhood autism', *American Journal of Mental Deficiency*, 80, pp. 431–6.

HOOSHYAR, N.T. (1987) 'Relationship between maternal language parameters and the child's language competency and developmental condition', *International Journal of Rehabilitation Research*, 10, pp. 321–4.

HUMPHREY, M. and HUMPHREY, H. (1988) *Families with a Difference: Varieties of Surrogate Parenthood*, London, Routledge.

HUNTER, F.T. (1985) 'Adolescent perceptions of discussions with parents and friends', *Developmental Psychology*, 21, pp. 433–40.

HUNTINGTON, G.S. and SIMEONSSON, R.J. (1987) 'Down's syndrome and toddler temperament', *Child: Care, Health and Development*, 13, pp. 11–17.

HUNTINGTON, G.S., SIMEONSSON, R.J., BAILEY, D.B. and COMFORT, M. (1987) 'Handicapped child characteristics and maternal involvement', *Journal of Reproductive and Infant Psychology*, 5, pp. 105–18.

HWANG, C.P., LAMB, M.E. and BRÖBERG, A. (1989) 'The development of social and intellectual competence in Swedish preschoolers raised at home and in out-of-home care facilities', in KREPPNER, K. and LERNER, R.M. (Eds) *Family Systems and Lifespan Development*, Hillsdale, NJ, LEA.

INGLEBY, D. (1986) 'Development in social context', in RICHARDS, M. and LIGHT, P. (Eds) *Children of Social Worlds*, Cambridge, Polity Press.

JESSOP, D.J., RIESSMAN, C.K. and STEIN, R.E.K. (1988) 'Chronic childhood illness and maternal mental health', *Developmental and Behavioural Paediatrics*, **9**, pp. 147–56.

JOHNSON, J.E. and McGILLICUDDY-DELISI, A.V. (1983) 'Family environment factors and children's knowledge of rules and conventions', *Child Development*, **54**, pp. 218–26.

JONES, O.H.M. (1977) 'Mother-child communication with prelinguistic Down's syndrome and normal infants', in SCHAFFER, H.R. (Ed.) *Studies in Mother-Infant Interaction*, New York, Academic Press.

JONES, O.H.M. (1980) 'Prelinguistic communication skills in Down's syndrome and normal infants', in FIELD, T.M. (Ed.) *High Risk Infants and Children: Adult and Peer Interactions*, New York, Academic Press.

KAYE, K. (1982) *The Mental and Social Life of Babies: How Parents Create Persons*, London, Methuen.

KAZAK, A.E. and CLARK, M.W. (1986) 'Stress in families of children with myelomeningocele', *Developmental Medicine and Child Neurology*, **28**, pp. 220–8.

KEMPE, R.S. and KEMPE, C.H. (1978) *Child Abuse*, Glasgow, Fontana.

KESSEL, F.S. and SIEGEL, A.W. (Eds) (1981) *The Child and Other Cultural Inventions*, New York, Praeger Scientific.

KIER, C.A. and FOUTS, G.T. (1989) 'Sibling play in divorced and married parent families', *Journal of Reproductive and Infant Psychology*, **7**, pp. 139–46.

KIRKHAM, M.A., SCHILLING, R.F., NORELUIS, K. and SCHINKE, S.P. (1986) 'Developing coping styles and social support networks: An intervention outcome study with mothers of handicapped children', *Child: Care, Health and Development*, **12**, pp. 313–23.

KITWOOD, T. (1983) 'Self-conception among young British-Asian Muslims: confutation of a stereotype', in BREAKWELL, G. (Ed.) *Threatened Identities*, Chichester, John Wiley.

KITZINGER, J. (1989) 'Child sexual abuse and the role of the teacher', in HOLLY, L. (Ed.) *Girls and Sexuality: Teaching and Learning*, Milton Keynes, Open University Press.

KITZINGER, S. (1978) *Women as Mothers*, London, Fontana.

KLAUS, M.H. and KENNEL, J.H. (1982) *Maternal-Infant Bonding*, 2nd ed., New York, Wiley.

KOCH, H.L. (1960) 'The relation of certain formal attributes of siblings to attitudes held toward each other and toward their parents', *Monographs of the Society for Research in Child Development*, Vol. 25, No. 4.

KOLVIN, I., MILLER, F.J.W., FLEETING, M. and KOLVIN, P.A. (1988) 'Risk/protective factor for offending with particular reference to deprivation', in RUTTER, M. (Ed.) *Studies of Psychosocial Risk: The Power of Longitudinal Data*, Cambridge, Cambridge University Press.

KOPP, C.B. and KRAKOW, J.B. (1983) 'The developmentalist and the study of biological risk: a view of the past with an eye towards the future', *Child Development*, **54**, pp. 1086–1108.

KORBIN, J.E. (1981) *Child Abuse and Neglect: Cross-Cultural Perspectives*, Berkeley, University of California Press.

KREPPNER, K., PAULSEN, S. and SCHUETZE, Y. (1982) 'Infant and family development: from triads to tetrads', *Human Development*, **25**, pp. 373–91.

KRUPER, J.C. and UZGIRIS, I.C. (1987) 'Fathers' and mothers' speech to young infants', *Journal of Psycholinguistic Research*, **16**, pp. 597–614.

KUCHNER, J.F. and PORCINO, J. (1988) 'Delayed motherhood', in BIRNS, B. and HAY, D.F. (Eds) *The Different Faces of Motherhood*, New York, Plenum Press.

KUCZYNSKI, L., KOCHANSKSA, G., RADKE-YARROW, M. and GIRNIUS-BROWN, O.

(1987) 'A developmental interpretation of young children's noncompliance', *Developmental Psychology*, **23**, pp. 799–806.

KURDEK, L.A. (1981) 'An integrative perspective on children's divorce adjustment', *American Psychologist*, **36**, pp. 856–66.

KURDEK, L.A. (1986) 'Children's reasoning about parental divorce,' in ASHMORE, R.D. and BRODZINSKY, D.M. (Eds) *Thinking about the Family: Views of Parents and Children*, Hillsdale, New Jersey, Lawrence Erlbaum Associates.

KURDEK, L.A. (1988) 'A 1-year follow up study of children's divorce adjustment, custodial mothers' divorce adjustment, and postdivorce parenting', *Journal of Applied Developmental Psychology*, **9**, pp. 315–328.

LA FONTAINE, J. (1990) *Child Sexual Abuse*, Cambridge, Polity Press.

LAMB, M.E. (1982) 'Maternal employment and child development: a review', in LAMB, M.E. (Ed.) *Non-Traditional Families: Parenting and Child Development*, Hillsdale, New Jersey, Lawrence Erlbaum Associates.

LAMB, M.E. and SUTTON-SMITH, B. (Eds) (1982) *Sibling Relationships: Their Nature and Significance across the Lifespan*, Hillsdale, NJ, Lawrence Erlbaum Associates.

LAMB, M.E., FRODI, A.M., HWANG, C.P., FRODI, M. and STEINBERG, J. (1982) 'Mother- and father-infant interaction involving play and holding in traditional and non-traditional Swedish families', *Developmental Psychology*, **18**, pp. 215–21.

LAMB, M.E., PLECK, J.H. and LEVINE, J.A. (1985) 'The role of the father in child development: the effects of increased paternal involvement', in LAHEY, B.B. and KAZDIN, E. (Eds) *Advances in Clinical Child Psychology*, Vol. 8, New York, Plenum.

LAMB, M.E., PLECK, J.P., CHARNOV, E.L. and LEVINE, J.A. (1987) 'A biosocial perspective on paternal behaviour and involvement', in LANCASTER, J.B., ALTMANN, J., ROSSI, A. and SHERROD, L.R. (Eds) *Parenting Across the Lifespan: Biosocial Perspectives*, Hawthorne, NY, Aldine.

LAMB, M.E., HWANG, C-P., BROBERG, A., BOOKSTEIN, F.L., HULT, G. and FRODI, M. (1988) 'The determinants of paternal involvement in primiparous Swedish families', *International Journal of Behavioural Development*, **11**, pp. 433–49.

LAMBERT, L. and STREATHER, J. (1980) *Children in Changing Families: A Study of Adoption and Illegitimacy*, London, Macmillan.

LAOSA, L.M. (1988) 'Ethnicity and single parenting in the United States', in HETHERINGTON, E.M. and ARASTEH, J. (Eds) *The Impact of Divorce, Single Parenting and Step-Parenting on Children*, Hillsdale, NJ, Lawrence Erlbaum Associates.

LA ROSSA, R. and LA ROSSA, M.M. (1981) *Transition to Parenthood: How Infants Change Families*, London, Sage.

LAY, K-L., WATERS, E. and PARK, K.A. (1989) 'Maternal responsiveness and child compliance: the role of mood as mediator', *Child Development*, **60**, pp. 1405–11.

LEES, S. (1986) *Losing Out: Sexuality and Adolescent Girls*, London, Hutchinson.

LEIFER, A.D., LEIDERMAN, P.H., BARNETT, C.R. and WILLIAMS, J.A. (1972) 'Effects of mother infant separation on maternal attachment behaviour', *Child Development*, **43**, pp. 1203–18.

LERNER, R.M. and SPANIER, G.B. (1978) *Child influences on marital and family interaction: a life-span perspective*, New York, Academic Press.

LEVINE, R.A. (1980) 'A cross-cultural perspective on parenting', in FANTINI, M.D. and CARDENAS, R. (Eds) *Parenting in a Multicultural Society*, New York, Longman.

LEVINE, R.A., MILLER, P.M. and WEST, M.M. (1988) *Parental Behavior in Diverse Societies*, San Francisco, Jossey-Bass.

LEVY-SHIFF, R. (1986) 'Mother – father – child interactions in families with a mentally retarded young child', *American Journal of Mental Deficiency*, **91**, pp. 141–9.

References

LEVY-SHIFF, R. and ISRAELASHVILI, R. (1988) 'Antecedents of fathering: some further exploration', *Developmental Psychology*, **24**, pp. 434–40.

LEWIS, C., NEWSON, E. and NEWSON, J. (1982) 'Father participation through childhood and its relation to career aspirations and delinquency', in BEAIL, N. and McGUIRE, J. (Eds) *Fathers: Psychological Perspectives*, London, Junction Books.

LEWIS, M. and FEIRING, C. (1984) 'Some American families at dinner', in LAOSA, L.M. and SIGEL, I.E. (Eds) *Families as Learning Environments for Children*, New York, Plenum Press.

LLEWELYN, S. and OSBORNE, K. (1990) *Women's Lives*, London, Routledge.

LOBATO, D. (1983) 'Siblings of handicapped children: a review', *Journal of Autism and Developmental Disorders*, **13**, pp. 347–64.

LYTTON, H. (1980) *Parent-Child Interaction: The Socialisation Process Observed in Twin and Singleton Families*, New York, Plenum.

MACCOBY, E.E. (1988) 'Gender as a social category', *Developmental Psychology*, **24**, pp. 755–65.

MACCOBY, E.E. and JACKLIN, C.N. (1987) 'Gender segregation in childhood', in REESE, E.H. (Ed.) *Advances in Child Development and Behaviour: Volume 20*, New York, Academic Press.

MACCOBY, E.E. and MARTIN, J.A. (1983) 'Socialisation in the context of the family', in HETHERINGTON, E.M. (Ed.) *Handbook of Child Psychology: Volume 4: Socialisation, Personality and Social Development*, 4th ed., New York, Wiley.

MACCOBY, E.E., DEPNER, C.E. and MNOOKIN, R.H. (1988) 'Custody of children following divorce', in HETHERINGTON, E.M. and ARASTEH, J. (Eds) *The Impact of Divorce, Single Parenting and Step-Parenting on Children*, Hillsdale, NJ, Lawrence Erlbaum Associates.

McCONACHIE, H. (1982) 'Fathers of mentally handicapped children', in BEAIL, N. and McGUIRE, J. (Eds) *Fathers: Psychological Perspectives*, London, Junction Books.

MACFARLANE, A. (1977) *The Psychology of Childbirth*, London, Fontana.

MACK, J. and LANSLEY, S. (1985) *Poor Britain*, London, George Allen and Unwin.

MACKINNON, C.E. (1989) 'An observational investigation of sibling interactions in married and divorced families', *Developmental Psychology*, **25**, pp. 36–44.

MAHONEY, G. (1988) 'Maternal communication style with mentally retarded children', *American Journal on Mental Retardation*, **92**, 352–9.

MAIN, M. (1980) 'Abusive and rejecting infants', in FRUDE, N. (Ed.) *Psychological Approaches to Child Abuse*, London, Batsford.

MAIN, M. and WESTON, D. (1981) 'The quality of the toddler's relationship to mother and father: related to conflict behaviour and readiness to establish new relationships', *Child Development*, **52**, pp. 932–40.

McKAYE, K., CHEN, S. and CAMPOS, J. (1985) 'Infant temperament, mothers' mode of interaction and attachment in Japan', in BRETHERTON, I. and WATERS, E. (Eds) *Growing Points in Attachment Theory and Research*, Monographs of Society for Research in Child Development, 50, 209.

MANNARINO, A.P. (1978) 'Friendship patterns and self concept development in preadolescent males', *Journal of Genetic Psychology*, **133**, pp. 105–10.

MARTIN, H.P. (1976) *The Abused Child: Multi-Disciplinary Approach to Development Issues and Treatment*, Cambridge, Mass., Ballinger.

MICHAELS, G.Y. and GOLDBERG, W.A. (Eds) (1988) *Transition to Parenthood: Theory and Research*, Cambridge, Cambridge University Press.

MONTEMAYOR, R. (1983) 'Parents and adolescents in conflict: all families some of the time and some families most of the time', *Journal of Early Adolescence*, **3**, pp. 83–103.

MORGAN, D.H.J. (1985) *The Family: Politics and Social Theory*, London, Routledge and Kegan Paul.

MORGAN, M. and GRUBE, J.W. (1989) 'Adolescent cigarette smoking: a developmental analysis of influences', *British Journal of Developmental Psychology*, 7, pp. 179–89.

MOSS, P., BOLLAND, G., FOXMAN, R. and OWEN, C. (1986) 'Marital relations during the transition to parenthood', *Journal of Reproductive and Infant Psychology*, 4, pp. 57–67.

MOSS, P., BOLLAND, G., FOXMAN, R. and OWEN, C. (1987a) 'The division of household work during the transition to parenthood', *Journal of Reproductive and Infant Psychology*, 5, pp. 71–86.

MOSS, P., BOLLAND, G., FOXMAN, R. and OWEN, C. (1987b) 'The hospital inpatient stay: the experience of first time parents', *Child: Care, Health and Development*, 13, pp. 153–67.

MUNDY, P., SIGMAN, M., KASARI, C. and YIRMIYA, N. (1988) 'Nonverbal communication skills in Down's syndrome children', *Child Development*, 59, pp. 235–49.

NEW, C. and DAVID, M. (1985) *For the Children's Sake: Making Childcare More Than Women's Work*, Harmondsworth, Penguin.

NEW, R.S. (1988) 'Parental goals and Italian infant care', in LEVINE, R.A., MILLER, P.M. and WEST, M.M. (Eds) *Parental Behaviour in Diverse Societies*, San Francisco, Jossey-Bass.

NEWSON, J. and NEWSON, E. (1968) *Four Years Old in an Urban Community*, Harmondsworth, Penguin.

NEWSON, J. and NEWSON, E. (1976) *Seven Years Old in the Home Environment*, Harmondsworth, Penguin.

NEWSON, J. and NEWSON, E. (1980) 'Parental punishment strategies with eleven-year-old children', in FRUDE, N. (Ed.) *Psychological Approaches to Child Abuse*, London, Batsford.

NEWSON, J. and NEWSON, E. (1986) 'Family and sex roles in middle childhood', in HARGREAVES, D.J. and COLLEY, A.M. (Eds) *The Psychology of Sex Roles*, London, Harper and Row.

NICHOLSON, J., GIST, J.F., KLEIN, R.D. and STANDLEY, K. (1983) 'Outcomes of father involvement in pregnancy and birth', *Birth*, 10, pp. 5–9.

NICOLSON, P. (1986) 'Developing a feminist approach to depression following childbirth', in WILKINSON, S. (Ed.) *Feminist Social Psychology*, Milton Keynes, Open University Press.

NIHIRA, K., MEYERS, C.E. and MINK, I.T. (1980) 'Home environment, family adjustment and the development of mentally retarded children', *Applied Research in Mental Retardation*, 1, pp. 5–24.

OAKLEY, A. (1981) *From Here to Maternity: Becoming a Mother*, Harmondsworth, Penguin.

OFFICE OF POPULATION AND CENSUS STATISTICS (1989) London, HMSO.

OGBU, J.V. (1981) 'Origins of human competence: a cultural-ecological perspective', *Child Development*, 52, pp. 413–29.

O'TOOLE, R., TURBETT, P. and NALEPKA, C. (1983) 'Theories, professional knowledge and diagnosis of child abuse', in FINKELHOR, D., GELLES, R.J., HOTALING, G.T. and STRAUS, M.A. (Eds) *The Dark Side of Families*, Beverley Hills, Sage.

PALFREY, J.S., WALKER, D.K., BUTLER, J.A. and SINGER, J.D. (1989) 'Patterns of response in families of chronically disabled children: an assessment in five metropolitan school districts', *American Journal of Orthopsychiatry*, 59, pp. 94–104.

References

PALKOVITZ, R. (1985) 'Fathers' birth attendance, early contact, and extended contact with their newborns: a critical review', *Child Development*, **56**, pp. 392–406.

PARKE, R.D. (1981) *Fathering*, London, Fontana.

PARKE, R.D. (1988) 'Families in life span perspective: a multilevel developmental approach', in HETHERINGTON, E.M., LERNER, R.M. and PERLMUTTER, M. (Eds) *Child Development in Life Span Perspective*, Hillsdale, NJ, Lawrence Erlbaum Associates.

PARKE, R.D. and BEITEL, A. (1988) 'Disappointment: when things go wrong in the transition to parenthood', *Marriage and the Family Review*, **12**, pp. 221–65.

PARKE, R.D. and TINSLEY, B.R. (1984) 'Fatherhood: historical and contemporary perspectives', in McCLUSKEY, K. and REESE, H. (Eds) *Life Span Development: Historical and Generational Effects*, New York, Academic Press.

PARKE, R.D., MacDONALD, K.B., BURKS, V.M., BHAVNAGRI, N., BARTH, J.M. and BEITEL, A. (1989) 'Family and peer systems: in search of the linkages', in KREPPNER, K. and LERNER, R.M. (Eds) *Family Systems and Lifespan Development*, Hillsdale, NJ, LEA.

PEARLIN, L.I. and SCHOOLER, C. (1978) 'The structure of coping', *Journal of Health and Social Behaviour*, **19**, pp. 112–21.

PEDERSON, D.R., JENKINS, S., EVANS, B., CHANGE, G.W. and FOX, A.M. (1985) 'Maternal responses to the birth of a preterm infant', paper presented at the biennial meeting of the Society of Research in Child Development, Toronto, April.

PEDERSON, F.A., CAIN, R. and ZASLOW, M. (1982) 'Variations in infant experience associated with alternative family roles', in LAOSA, L. and SIGEL, I. (Eds) *The Family as a Learning Environment*, New York, Plenum.

PEPLER, D., CORTER, C. and ARAMOVITCH, R. (1982) 'Social relations among children: siblings and peers', in RUBIN, K. and ROSS, H. (Eds) *Peer Relationships and Social Skills in Childhood*, New York, Springer-Verlag.

PETERSEN, J.L. and ZILL, N. (1986) 'Marital disruption, parent-child relationships, and behaviour problems in children', *Journal of Marriage and the Family*, **48**, pp. 295–307.

PETTIT, A.J. and BLOOM, B.L. (1984) 'Whose decision was it? The effects of initiator status on adjustments to marital disruption', *Journal of Marriage and the Family*, **46**, p. 587.

PETTIT, G.S., DODGE, K.A. and BROWN, M.M. (1988) 'Early family experience, social problem solving patterns, and children's social competence', *Child Development*, pp. 107–20.

PFEFFER, N. and WOOLLETT, A. (1983) *The Experience of Infertility*, London, Virago.

PHOENIX, A. (1991) *Young Mothers?*, Cambridge, Polity Press.

PHOENIX, A., WOOLLETT, A. and LLOYD, E. (in press) *Motherhood: Meanings, Practices and Ideologies*, London, Sage.

PIANTA, R.C., SROUFE, L.A. and EGELAND, B. (1989) 'Continuity and discontinuity in maternal sensitivity at 6, 24, and 42 months in a high risk sample', *Child Development*, **60**, pp. 481–7.

POWER, T.G. and PARKE, R.D. (1982) 'Play as a context for early learning: lab and home analysis', in LAOSA, L.M. and SIGEL, I.E. (Eds) *Families as a Learning Environment for Children*, New York, Plenum.

POWER, T.G. and PARKE, R.D. (1986) 'Patterns of early socialization: mother- and father-infant interaction in the home', *International Journal of Behavioural Development*, **9**, pp. 331–41.

POWER, T.G. and SHANKS, J.A. (1989) 'Parents as socializers: maternal and paternal views', *Journal of Youth and Adolescence*, **18**, pp. 203–20.

PRATT, M.W., KERIG, P., COWAN, P.A. and COWAN, C.P. (1988) 'Mothers and fathers teaching 3-year-olds: authoritative parenting and adult scaffolding of young children's learning', *Developmental Psychology*, 24, pp. 832–9.

PRICE-BONHAM, S. and ADDISON, S. (1978) 'Families and mentally retarded children: emphasis on the father', *The Family Coordinator*, 27, pp. 221–30.

PUCKERING, C. (1989) 'Maternal depression', *Journal of Child Psychology and Psychiatry*, 30, pp. 807–18.

PUTALLAZ, M. and GOTTMAN, J.M. (1981) 'An interactional model of children's entry into peer groups', *Child Development*, 52, pp. 986–94.

RADIN, N. (1982) 'Primary caregiving and role-sharing fathers', in LAMB, M.E. (Ed.) *Nontraditional Families: Parenting and Child Development*, Hillsdale, NJ, Erlbaum.

RADIN, N. and GOLDSMITH, R. (1985) 'Caregiving fathers of preschoolers: four years later', *Merrill-Palmer Quarterly*, 31, pp. 375–84.

RAPOPORT, R., RAPOPORT, R.N. and STRELITZ (1977) *Fathers, Mothers and Others*, London, Routledge and Kegan Paul.

RAYNOR, L. (1980) *The Adopted Child Comes of Age*, London, George Allen and Unwin.

ROBERTS, W. and STRAYER, J. (1987) 'Parents' responses to the emotional distress of their children: relations with children's competence', *Developmental Psychology*, 23, pp. 415–22.

ROSENTHAL, D.A. (1984) 'Intergenerational conflict and culture: a study of immigrant and non-immigrant adolescents and their parents', *Genetic Psychology Monographs*, 109, pp. 53–75.

ROSENTHAL, D.A., DEMETRIOU, A. and EFKLIDES, A. (1989) 'A cross-national study of the influence of culture on conflict between parents and adolescents', *International Journal of Behavioural Development*, 12, pp. 207–19.

ROSS, J.M. (1982) 'Mentorship in middle childhood', in CATH, S.H., GURWITT, A.R. and ROSS, J.M. (Eds) *Developmental and Clinical Perspectives*, Boston, Little, Brown.

ROSSI, A.S. (1987) 'Parenthood in transition: from lineage to child to self-orientation', in LANCASTER, J.B., ALTMANN, J., ROSSI, A.S. and SHERROD, L.R. (Eds) *Parenting Across the Life Span: Biosocial Dimensions*, New York, Aldine De Gruyter.

ROWLAND, R. (1985) 'The social and psychological consequences of secrecy in artificial insemination by donor (AID) programmes', *Social Science and Medicine*, 21, pp. 391–6.

RUBENSTEIN, J.L., HEEREN, T., HOUSMAN, D., RUBIN, C. and STECHLER, G. (1989) 'Suicidal behaviour in "normal" adolescents: risk and protective factors', *American Journal of Orthopsychiatry*, 59, pp. 59–71.

RUBIN, Z. (1980) *Children's Friendships*, London, Fontana.

RUBLE, D., FLEMING, A.S., HACKEL, L.S. and STANGOR, C. (1988) 'Changes in the marital relationship during the transition to first time motherhood: effects of violated expectations concerning the division of household labour', *Journal of Personality and Social Psychology*, 55, pp. 78–87.

RUSSELL, G. (1983) *The Changing Role of Fathers*, Milton Keynes, Open University Press.

RUTTER, M. (1970) 'Sex differences in children's responses to family stress', in ANTHONY, E.J. and KOUPERNIK, C. (Eds) *The Child in his Family*, New York, Wiley.

RUTTER, M. (1978) 'Early sources of security and competence', in BRUNER, J.S. and GARTON, A. (Eds) *Human Growth and Development*, London, Oxford University Press.

References

RUTTER, M. (1980) *Changing Youth in a Changing Society*, Harvard, Harvard University Press.

RUTTER, M. (1981) *Maternal Deprivation Reassessed*, Harmondsworth, Penguin.

RUTTER, M., TIZARD, J., YULE, M., GRAHAM, P. and WHITMORE, K. (1976) 'Isle of Wight studies, 1964–1974', *Psychological Medicine*, 6, pp. 313–32.

SAGI, A., LAMB, M.E., SHOHAM, R. and LEWKOWICZ, K.S. (1985) 'Parent infant interactions in families on Israeli kibbutzim', *International Journal of Behavioural Development*, 8, pp. 273–84.

SANTROCK, J.W., WARSHAK, R.A. and ELLIOTT, G.L. (1982) 'Social development and parent-child interaction in father custody and stepmother families', in LAMB, M.E. (Ed.) *Non-Traditional Families: Parenting and Child Development*, Hillsdale, NJ, Lawrence Erlbaum Associates.

SAVIN-WILLIAMS, R.C. and SMALL, S.A. (1986) 'The timing of puberty and its relationship to adolescent and parent perceptions of family interactions', *Developmental Psychology*, 22, pp. 342–7.

SCARR, S. and DUNN, J. (1987) *Mother Care/Other Care: The Child-Care Dilemma for Women and Children*, Harmondsworth, Penguin.

SCHAFFER, H.R. (1986) 'Child psychology: the future', *Journal of Child Psychology and Psychiatry*, 27, pp. 761–79.

SCHAFFER, H.R. and CROOK, C.K. (1978) 'The role of the mother in early social development', in McGURK, H. (Ed.) *Issues in Childhood Social Development*, London, Methuen.

SCHAFFER, H.R. and EMERSON, P.E. (1964) 'The development of social attachments in infancy', *Monographs of Society for Research in Child Development*, Vol. 29, No. 94.

SCHRADLE, S.B. and DOUGHER, M.J. (1985) 'Social support as a mediator of stress: theoretical and empirical issues', *Clinical Psychology Review*, 5, pp. 641–61.

SCOTT-HEYES, G. (1983) 'Marital adaptation during pregnancy and after childbirth', *Journal of Reproductive and Infant Psychology*, 1, pp. 18–28.

SEARS, R.R., MACCOBY, E.E. and LEVIN, H. (1957) *Patterns of Child-Rearing*, Evanston, Ill., Row, Peterson.

SHAPIRO, E.R. (1979) *Transition to Parenthood in Adult and Family Development*, Unpublished PhD dissertation, Amherst, University of Massachusetts. Reported by Rossi (1987).

SHARPE, S. (1976) *Just like a Girl: How Girls Learn to be Women*, Harmondsworth, Penguin.

SHARPE, S. (1984) *Double Identity: The Lives of Working Mothers*, Harmondsworth, Penguin.

SHURE, M.B. and SPIVAK, G. (1982) 'Interpersonal problem solving in young children: a cognitive approach to prevention', *American Journal of Community Psychology*, 10, pp. 341–56.

SILVERBERG, S.B. and STEINBERG, L. (1990) 'Psychological well-being of parents with early adolescent children', *Developmental Psychology*, 26, pp. 658–66.

SINGER, L.M., BRODZINSKY, D.M. and RAMSAY, D. (1985) 'Mother-infant attachment in adoptive families', *Child Development*, 56, pp. 1543–51.

SMITH, D. (1990) *Stepmothering*, Hemel Hempstead, Harvester Wheatsheaf.

SPOCK, B. (1955) *Baby and Child Care*, London, Bodley Head.

STACEY, M., DREARDEN, R., PILL, R. and ROBINSON, D. (1970) *Hospitals, Children and their Families: The Report of a Pilot Study*, London, Routledge and Kegan Paul.

STANWORTH, M. (Ed.) (1987) *Reproductive Technologies: Gender, Motherhood and Medicine*, Cambridge, Polity Press.

STARR, R.H. (1988) 'Pre- and perinatal risk and physical abuse', *Journal of Reproductive and Infant Psychology*, **6**, pp. 125–38.

STEINBERG, L., ELMEN, J.D. and MOUNTS, N.S. (1989) 'Authoritative parenting, psychosocial maturity, and academic success among adolescents', *Child Development*, **60**, pp. 1424–36.

STEINBERG, L.D. (1981) 'Transformations in family relations at puberty', *Developmental Psychology*, **17**, pp. 833–40.

STERN, D. (1977) *The First Relationship: Infant and Mother*, London, Fontana.

STEVENSON, M.B., LEAVITT, L.A., THOMPSON, R.H. and ROACH, M.A. (1988) 'A social relations model analysis of parent and child play', *Developmental Psychology*, **24**, pp. 101–8.

STEWART, R.B., MOBLEY, L.A., VAN TUYL, S.S. and SALVADOR, M.A. (1987) 'The first born's adjustment to the birth of a sibling: a longitudinal study', *Child Development*, **58**, pp. 341–55.

STONEMAN, Z., BRODY, G.H. and BURKE, M. (1989) 'Marital quality, depression, and inconsistent parenting: relationship with observed mother-child conflict', *American Journal of Orthopsychiatry*, **59**, pp. 105–17.

STOPES-ROE, M. and COCHRANE, R. (1988) 'Marriage in two cultures', *British Journal of Social Psychology*, **27**, pp. 159–69.

STOPES-ROE, M. and COCHRANE, R. (1990) 'The child-rearing values of Asian and British parents and young people: an inter-ethnic and inter-generational comparison in the evaluation of Kohn's 13 qualities', *British Journal of Social Psychology*, **29**, pp. 149–60.

STRATTON, P. and SWAFFER, R. (1988) 'Maternal causal beliefs for abused and handicapped children', *Journal of Reproductive and Infant Psychology*, **6**, pp. 201–16.

SUELZE, M. and KEENAN, V. (1981) 'Changes in family support networks over the life cycle of mentally retarded persons', *American Journal of Mental Deficiency*, **86**, pp. 267–74.

SVEDJA, M.J., CAMPOS, J.J. and EMDE, R.R. (1980) 'Mother-infant bonding: a failure to generalise', *Child Development*, **51**, pp. 775–9.

TENNEN, H., AFFLECK, G. and MERSHMAN, K. (1986) 'Self-blame among parents of infants with perinatal complications: the role of self-protective motives', *Journal of Personality and Social Psychology*, **50**, pp. 690–6.

TETI, D.M., BOND, L.A. and GIBBS, E.D. (1988) 'Mothers, fathers, and siblings: a comparison of play styles and their influence upon infant cognitive level', *International Journal of Behavioural Development*, **11**, pp. 415–32.

TINSLEY, B.R. and PARKE, R.D. (1984) 'Grandparents as support and socialization agents', in LEWIS, M. (Ed.) *Beyond the Dyad*, New York, Plenum.

TIZARD, B. (1977) *Adoption: A Second Chance*, London, Open Books.

TIZARD, B. and HUGHES, M. (1984) *Young Children Learning: Talking and Thinking at Home and at School*, London, Fontana.

TRAUSE, M.A. and KRAMER, L.L. (1983) 'The effect of premature birth on parents and their relationship', *Developmental Medicine and Child Neurology*, **24**, pp. 459–65.

URWIN, C. (1985) 'Constructing motherhood: the persuasion of normal development', in STEEDMAN, C., URWIN, C. and WALKERDINE, V. (Eds) *Language, Gender and Childhood*, London, Routledge and Kegan Paul.

VADASY, P.F., FEWELL, R.R. MEYER, D.J. and GREENBERG, M.T. (1985) 'Supporting fathers of handicapped young children: preliminary findings of program effects', *Analysis and Intervention in Developmental Disabilities*, **5** (Special Issue: Early intervention), pp. 151–63.

VANDELL, D.L. (1979) 'A microanalysis of toddlers' social interaction with mothers and fathers', *Journal of Genetic Psychology*, **134**, pp. 299–312.

References

VETERE, A. and GALE, A. (1981) *Ecological Studies of Family Life*, Chichester, Wiley.

WACHS, T.D. and GRUEN, G.E. (1982) *Early Experience and Human Development*, New York, Plenum.

WADSWORTH, M.E. (1985) 'Parenting skills and their transmission through generations', *Adoption and Fostering*, 9, pp. 28–32.

WADSWORTH, M.E. and MACLEAN, M. (1986) 'Parents' divorce and children's life chances', *Children and Youth Services Review*, 8, pp. 145–59.

WALKERDINE, V. and LUCEY, H. (1989) *Democracy in the Kitchen: Regulating Mothers and Socialising Daughters*, London, Virago.

WALLERSTEIN, J.S., CORBIN, S.B. and LEWIS, J.M. (1988) 'Children of divorce: a ten year study', in HETHERINGTON, E.M. and ARASTEH, J. (Eds) *The Impact of Divorce, Single Parenting and Step-Parenting on Children*, Hillsdale, NJ, Lawrence Erlbaum Associates.

WEINRAUB, M. and WOLF, B.M. (1983) 'Effects of stress and social supports on mother-child interactions in single- and two-parent families', *Child Development*, 54, pp. 1297–1311.

WEISS, R.S. (1984) 'The impact of marital dissolution on income and consumption in single-parent households', *Journal of Marriage and the Family*, 46, pp. 115–27.

WERNER, E.E. (1989) 'High-risk children in young adulthood: a longitudinal study from birth to 32 years', *American Journal of Orthopsychiatry*, 59, 72–81.

WERNER, E.E. and SMITH, R.S. (1982) *Vulnerable but Invincible: A Longitudinal Study of Resilient Children and Youth*, New York, McGraw Hill.

WESTWOOD, S. and BHACHU, P. (1988) *Enterprising Women: Ethnicity, Economy and Gender Relations*, London, Routledge.

WHITE, D.G., PHILLIPS, K.C., CLIFFORD, B.R., DAVIES, M.M., ELLIOTT, J.R. and PITTS, M.K. (1989) 'AIDS and intimate relationships: Adolescents' knowledge and attitudes', *Current Psychology: Research and Reviews*, 8, pp. 130–143.

WHITE, D.G. and WOOLLETT, A. (1987) 'The father's role in the neonatal period', in HARVEY, D. (Ed.) *Parent-Infant Relationships*, New York, Wiley.

WHITING, B.B. and WHITING, J.W.M. (1975) *Children of Six Cultures: A Psychocultural Analysis*, Cambridge, Mass., Harvard University Press.

WICKS, M. and KEIRNAN, K. (1990) *Family Change and Future Policy*, Joseph Rowntree Memorial Trust.

WILLIAMSON, N.E. (1976) *Sons or Daughters: A Cross-Cultural Survey of Parental Preferences*, London, Sage Publications.

WILSON, M.N. and TOLSON, T.F.J. (1988) 'Single parenting in the context of three-generational black families', in HETHERINGTON, E.M. and ARASTEH, J. (Eds) *The Impact of Divorce, Single Parenting and Step-Parenting on Children*, Hillsdale, NJ, Lawrence Erlbaum Associates.

WINKLER, L.M. (1986) 'Periodic stresses of families of older mentally retarded children: an exploratory study', *American Journal of Mental Deficiency*, 90, pp. 703–6.

WOLFE, D.A. (1985) 'Child-abusive parents: an empirical review and analysis', *Psychological Bulletin*, 97, pp. 462–82.

WOLKIND, S. and ZAJICEK, E. (1981) *Pregnancy: A Psychological and Social Study*, London, Academic Press.

WOODS, P.A., CORNEY, M.J. and PRYCE, G.J. (1984) 'Developmental progress of Down's syndrome children receiving a home-advisory service: an interim report', *Child: Care, Health and Development*, 10, pp. 287–300.

WOOLLETT, A. (1986) 'The influence of older siblings on the language environment of young children', *British Journal of Developmental Psychology*, 4, pp. 235–45.

WOOLLETT, A. and DOSANJH-MATWALA, N. (1990) 'Asian women's experiences of childbirth in the East End: the support of fathers and female relatives', *Journal of Reproductive and Infant Psychology*, **8**, pp. 11–22.

WOOLLETT, A., LYON, L. and WHITE, D. (1983) 'The reactions of East London women to medical intervention in childbirth', *Journal of Reproductive and Infant Psychology*, **1**, pp. 37–46.

YOGMAN, M.W. (1985) 'The father's role with preterm and fullterm infants', in CALL, J., GALENSON, E. and TYSON, R. (Eds) *Frontiers in Infant Psychiatry*, New York, Basic Books.

YOUNNIS, J. (1980) *Parents and Peers in Social Development: A Sullivan-Piaget Perspective*, Chicago, University of Chicago Press.

ZASLOW, M.J. (1989) 'Sex differences in children's response to parental divorce: 2. Samples, Variables, Ages, and Sources', *American Journal of Orthopsychiatry*, **59**, pp. 118–41.

ZILL, N. (1988) 'Behaviour, achievement, and health problems among children in stepfamilies: findings from a national survey of child health', in HETHERINGTON, E.M. and ARASTEH, J. (Eds) *The Impact of Divorce, Single Parenting and Step-Parenting on Children*, Hillsdale, NJ, Lawrence Erlbaum Associates.

Notes on the Authors

David White lectures in Developmental Psychology at the Polytechnic of East London and is also Head of its AIDS Research Unit. His current research interests are in the areas of family functioning, particularly the role of fathers in child development and health psychology, including occupational stress, the control of hypertension through behavioural intervention, and the primary prevention of HIV/AIDS. Currently he is engaged upon studies of the attitudes, experiences and behaviours of injecting drug users in relation to HIV/AIDS, including evaluations of harm minimization programmes. This work is funded by the North West Thames Regional Health Authority. He is also engaged upon a study of health and occupational stress supported by the London Borough of Newham.

Anne Woollett lectures in Developmental Psychology at the Polytechnic of East London where she is also Deputy Head of the Psychology Department. Her research interests are centred around families and family building. With Naomi Pfeffer she wrote *The Experience of Infertility* (Virago, 1983) which examines the adjustments of men and women to infertility investigations and reproductive problems. She is also interested in the experience of parenting and family life for mothers and young children. With Ann Phoenix and Eva Lloyd she has edited a collection entitled *Motherhood: Meanings, Practices and Ideologies* to be published in 1991 by Sage. Currently she is engaged in a study of the attitudes and experiences of Asian young people and parents living in East London to family size and fertility control, childbirth and childcare which is funded by the ESRC.

Author Index

Subject Index